RECOVERING THE SCANDAL OF THE CROSS

Atonement in New Testament & Contemporary Contexts

JOEL B. GREEN &
MARK D. BAKER

InterVarsity Press
Downers Grove, Illinois

InterVarsity Press
P.O. Box 1400, Downers Grove, IL 60515
World Wide Web: www.ivpress.com
E-mail: mail@ivpress.com

InterVarsity Press® is the book-publishing division of InterVarsity Christian Fellowship/USA®, a student movement active on campus at hundreds of universities, colleges and schools of nursing in the United States of America, and a member movement of the International Fellowship of Evangelical Students. For information about local and regional activities, write Public Relations Dept., InterVarsity Christian Fellowship/USA, 6400 Schroeder Rd., P.O. Box 7895, Madison, WI 53707-7895.

All Scripture quotations, unless otherwise indicated, are the authors' translation.

Cover illustration: Roberta Polfus

ISBN 0-8308-1571-6

Printed in the United States of America ∞

Library of Congress Cataloging-in-Publication Data

Baker, Mark D. (Mark David), 1957-
  Recovering the scandal of the cross : the atonement in New Testament & contemporary
contexts / Mark D. Baker & Joel B. Green.
    p. cm.
  Includes bibliographical references and index.
  ISBN 0-8308-1571-6 (pbk. : alk. paper)
    1. Atonement. 2. Jesus Christ—Crucifixion. I. Green, Joel B., 1956- II. Title.

BT265.2 .B35 2000
232'.3—dc21

                                                                                        00-033508

20 19 18 17 16 15 14 13 12 11   10 9 8 7 6 5
16 15 14 13 12 11 10 09 08 07

To
H. Allison Green
& Lynn M. Baker

They ask the hard questions.

Contents

Abbreviations

ca.	*circa*, approximately
cf.	confer
ch(s).	chapter(s)
cp.	compare
ed.	edited by; or edition
e.g.	*exempli gratia*, for example
esp.	especially
ET	English translation
i.e.	*id est*, that is
KJV	King James Version
LXX	Septuagint
NASB	New American Standard Bible
NCV	New Century Version
n.d.	no date given
n(n).	note(s)
NIV	New International Version
NRSV	New Revised Standard Version
vol.	volume
v(v).	verse(s)

Dead Sea Scrolls and Related Texts

1QS	*Serek hayyaad* or *Rule of the Community* or *Manual of Discipline* from Qumran Cave 1
4QpNah	*Pesher on Nahum* from Qumran Cave 4
5Q15	*New Community* from Qumran Cave 5
11QTS	*Temple Scroll* from Qumran Cave 11 (= 11Q19)

Targumim

Tg. Onq.	*Targum Onqelos*
Tg. Ps-J.	*Targum of Pseudo-Jonathan*

Other Ancient Authors and Writings

Josephus
J.W.	*Jewish War*

Justin
1 Apol.	*First Apology*

Philo
Post. C.	*De Posteritate*

Somn.	*De Somni*
Spec. Leg.	*De Specialibus Legibus*

Modern Literature

ABD	*Anchor Bible Dictionary.* Edited by David Noel Freedman.
ABRL	Anchor Bible Reference Library
AS	Advances in Semiotics
BJRL	*Bulletin of the John Rylands University Library of Manchester*
CurTM	*Currents in Theology and Mission*
DJG	*Dictionary of Jesus and the Gospels.* Edited by Joel B. Green and Scot McKnight.
DPL	*Dictionary of Paul and His Letters.* Edited by Gerald F. Hawthorne, Ralph P. Martin and Daniel G. Reid.
EDNT	*Exegetical Dictionary of the New Testament.* 3 vols. Edited by Horst Balz and Gerhard Schneider.
EvQ	*Evangelical Quarterly*
GP	Gospel Perspectives
HTS	Harvard Theological Studies
Int	*Interpretation*
JBL	*Journal of Biblical Literature*
JR	*Journal of Religion*
JSNT	*Journal for the Study of the New Testament*
JSNTSup	Journal for the Study of the New Testament Supplement Series
JPSSup	Journal of Pentecostal Studies Supplement Series
JTS	*Journal of Theological Studies*
LTPM	Louvain Theological and Pastoral Monographs
NICNT	New International Commentary on the New Testament
NovTSup	Supplements to Novum Testamentum
OBT	Overtures to Biblical Theology
RB	*Revue Biblique*
TDNT	*Theological Dictionary of the New Testament.* 10 vols. Edited by Gerhard Kittel and Gerhard Friedrich.
TDOT	*Theological Dictionary of the Old Testament*
TynB	*Tyndale Bulletin*
WBC	Word Biblical Commentary
WUNT	Wissenschaftliche Untersuchungen zum Neuen Testament
ZNW	*Zeitschrift für die neutestamentliche Wissenschaft*

1

THE CHURCH
& THE CROSS

A Case of Selective Memory

L uke records in the final chapter of his Gospel a scene that embodies our dilemma. Two traveling companions, Cleopas and his friend, saddened by the death of Jesus in Jerusalem, are met on the road by a third traveler, a stranger to them. When asked the topic of their conversation, Cleopas speaks of Jesus of Nazareth, "a prophet mighty in deed and word," now condemned to death and crucified. "But," Cleopas adds, "we had hoped that he was the one to redeem Israel."

For these two disciples, the death of Jesus on a Roman cross was an event that lacked within itself a self-evident, unambiguous interpretation. Their affect and their words together communicate the presumed incongruity between the nature of Jesus' ministry and the manner of his end. Though they go on to speak of the empty tomb, it remains for them an enigma, not unlike Jesus himself. Having understood Jesus' ministry in terms borrowed from expectation of a liberator like Moses,[1] these disciples have no interpretive tools for making sense of his execution at the hands of the Romans.

Their dilemma is ours, though we rarely experience it at this depth. The significance of the cross has become for many of us an obvious matter of theological affirmation. Indeed, subsequent Christian reflection has typically found in the cross less an enigma and more a slogan. Little more than two decades following Jesus' death, Paul himself would assert that, among the Corinthians, he had "purposed to know nothing while I was with you except Jesus Christ and him crucified" (1 Cor 2:2). Even this Pauline declaration raises an important question about our theological discourse on the cross, however. In this context Paul emphasizes not so much the idea that "Christ died for our sins" as much as the claim that in the cross God intervened so as to destroy the old eon and usher in the new. Christian reflection more recently has been less nuanced. The question, What is the importance of the death of Jesus? in local congregations typically attracts either no answer at all other than looks of puzzlement or endorsements of the atonement. And by "atonement" many churchgoers today have in mind a particular definition of Christ's saving work:

He paid the price,
And set me free.[2]

*   *   *

O perfect redemption, the purchase of blood,
to every believer the promise of God.[3]

*   *   *

---

[1]See the phrases "powerful in words and deeds" and "to redeem Israel" (Lk 24:19, 21; also used in Acts 7:22 in Stephen's description of Moses) as well as the phrase "before God and all the people," found in Moses' epitaph in Deuteronomy 34:10-12.
[2]From "I Will Sing of My Redeemer" (Philip P. Bliss).
[3]From "To God Be the Glory" (Fanny Crosby).

What can wash away my sin?
Nothing but the blood of Jesus.[4]

In other words, in many Christian circles today "the importance of the death of Jesus" is virtually equated with "the meaning of the atonement"—that is, the doctrinal affirmation that Christ died for our sins.

What is more, even though the pages of the New Testament and the landscape of historical theology are replete with many and diverse metaphors for rendering plain the meaning of the cross both in and outside Christian communities, the affirmation that "Christ died for our sins" has, in the last two centuries, increasingly been articulated in the form of the doctrine of "penal substitution" or "satisfaction": Jesus satisfies the wrath of God by enduring the punishment we deserved on account of our sin. In fact, for many American Christians "penal substitutionary atonement" interprets the significance of Jesus' death fully, completely, without remainder.

Having attributed such favorable value to the cross, we identify less easily with Cleopas and his companion. Jesus' execution under Pilate presents for us no riddles to be resolved. Why did he die? He died for us, to rescue us from our just deserts.

Yet it is surely consequential that within the Lukan narrative, when Jesus upbraids the Emmaus travelers, it is not for failing to sketch the meaning of the cross in penal substitutionary categories. Having chided his companions on the road, "Oh, how foolish you are, how slow of heart to believe all that the prophets declared!" (Lk 24:25), Jesus does not proceed to articulate any doctrine of the atonement at all. Rather, he builds on a pattern present both within Israel's Scriptures and within the Third Gospel. The cross was a scandal that provided an occasion for stumbling for these disciples because they failed to see in what way Jesus fulfilled the prophetic pattern: rejection, suffering and violent death. Jesus, by correlating the presumed destiny of the prophets with messiahship, contended

---

[4]From "Nothing but the Blood" (Robert Lowry).

that the Scriptures portend the figure of an eschatological king who must suffer before entering into his glory.[5] From a human point of view, the ignominy of the cross was an incontrovertible refutation of divine status; from the point of view of God—a view lodged in the Scriptures—no such equation could be drawn. It was precisely in his humiliation and exaltation that Jesus exemplified the nature of salvation and made salvation available for those of "humble circumstances"—the hungry, the powerless, the lost, the marginal. Jesus' death thus occupied the central ground in the divine-human struggle over how life was to be lived, whether in humility or self-glorification.[6]

Similarly, Paul himself provides evidence that we have too easily made sense of the scandal of the death of God's Messiah. In 1 Corinthians 1:18-25, Paul outlines a perspective on the cross many of us have learned to overlook. Here he testifies to the lunacy of the cross for the first-century Roman, matched by its ignominious character among the Jewish people.[7] The Christian proclamation of a crucified malefactor was moronic to persons weaned on a love of learning, virtuousness and aesthetic pleasure. The Messiah, like Moses before him, should evidence the power of God in ways that legitimate his status and augur deliverance from the tyranny and oppressiveness of imperial subjugation. In Paul's argument with the Corinthians, the cross does not have the appearance of "good news" but of absurdity. The message of the cross calls for a worldview shift of colossal proportions because it subverts conventional, taken-for-granted ways of thinking and knowing.

As becomes transparent elsewhere in Paul's Corinthian correspon-

---

[5]See Mark L. Strauss, *The Davidic Messiah in Luke-Acts: The Promise and Its Fulfillment in Lukan Christology*, JSNTSup 110 (Sheffield: Sheffield Academic Press, 1995), pp. 255-58.

[6]Joel B. Green, "'Salvation to the End of the Earth': God as the Saviour in the Acts of the Apostles," in *Witness to the Gospel: The Theology of Acts*, ed. I. Howard Marshall and David Peterson (Grand Rapids, Mich.: Eerdmans, 1998), pp. 83-106.

[7]The usual translation of μωρία as "folly" is probably too weak. See Martin Hengel, *Crucifixion in the Ancient World and the Folly of the Message of the Cross* (Philadelphia: Fortress, 1977), p. 1. Justin writes: "They say that our madness (μανία) consists in the fact that we put a crucified man in second place after the unchangeable and eternal God, the Creator of the world" (*1 Apol.* 13.4).

dence, the believers in Corinth are slow to embrace the perspective on the cross he sketches. Conversion of the imagination is slow in coming. What seems always to have been second nature is not easily reassessed, much less discarded. Thus, Paul himself becomes the target of Corinthian ire on account of his suffering. How can an authentic messenger from God, a divinely commissioned apostle, so often end up on the losing side of history? The opposition Paul attracts dislegitimizes his apostleship in the eyes of some, with the result that Paul must engage in self-defense. Given the formative shift in his own way of seeing the world, a way of seeing that is no longer indebted to "fleshly" values (2 Cor 5:16-17), it is not surprising that Paul commends himself as a divine servant, a minister of Christ, by enumerating instances of rejection, misunderstanding and suffering (e.g., 6:3-10; 11:21-33). His best endorsement resides in the degree to which he has shared in the suffering of Christ, becoming like Christ in his death (see Phil 3:10).[8]

In short, in the early decades of the Christian movement, the scandal of the cross was far more self-evident than was its meaning. What quickly becomes clear from a survey of the New Testament material, though, is (1) the crucifixion of the one to whom Jesus' followers referred as God's Messiah could not be accidentally overlooked, purposefully ignored, nor strategically swept aside. The historical moment of Jesus' death under Pontius Pilate was and is written too large to be bypassed in reflection on the meaning of his life or on the faith and experience of his followers. Additionally, (2) the portrait of Jesus' execution could not be painted with a single color. Against the horizons of God's purpose, the Scriptures of Israel, and Jesus' life and ministry, and in relation to the life worlds of those for whom its significance was being explored, the death of Jesus proved capable of multiple interpretations. Scandal thus seems to have been tilled into soil fertile with interpretive possibilities. With the aging of

---

[8]See John S. Pobee, *Persecution and Martyrdom in the Theology of Paul*, JSNTSup 6 (Sheffield: JSOT, 1985), pp. 93-106.

the Christian faith, though, the many-hued mural interpreting Jesus' death has lost its luster, the theological soil becomes almost barren, capable of supporting only one or two affirmations concerning the cross.

Early Reflection on the Cross

For early disciples, the cross was a puzzle to be contemplated, a paradox to be explored, a question on which to reflect. It is highly significant, for example, that our Gospels devote an inordinate amount of space to deliberation on the death of Jesus. John's Gospel, which provides a three-year chronology of Jesus' ministry, nevertheless devotes nine of its twenty-one chapters to the brief time period (one long weekend!) extending from Jesus' last evening with his followers to his resurrection. By means of the central position they give the motif of conflict, growing hostility and assorted schemes against Jesus' life, together with Jesus' own predictions of his death and lengthy narratives of his suffering and death, all four Gospels sketch the significance of Jesus' death in ways that suggest not only its importance to his ministry and to the fledgling Christian faith but also the depth of early Christian contemplation on its meaning. Indeed, over a century ago, with some justification Martin Kähler could characterize the Gospels as "passion narratives with extended introductions."[9] This was Kähler's attempt to underscore the early church's concern with the nature of Jesus' work, and thus to indicate how the essential focus of the Gospels fell on the passion of Jesus.

Many scholars believe that when the Second Evangelist wrote the Gospel of Mark, he had available for use an account of Jesus' final days that had already been given both substantive shape and theological depth.[10] Some see the origins of this narrative reflection on the death of Jesus

---

[9]Martin Kähler, *The So-Called Historical Jesus and the Historic, Biblical Christ*, trans. Carl E. Braaten (Philadelphia: Fortress, 1964), p. 80 n. 11.

[10]See the surveys in Joel B. Green, *The Death of Jesus in Early Christianity: Tradition and Interpretation in the Passion Narrative*, WUNT 2:33 (Tübingen: J. C. B. Mohr [Paul Siebeck], 1988), pp. 9-14; John T. Carroll and Joel B. Green, *The Death of Jesus in Early Christianity* (Peabody, Mass.: Hendrickson, 1995), pp. 3-22.

in the worship and preaching life of early Christian communities, others more particularly in early attempts to articulate the nature of the Christian movement and its faith over against other forms of Judaism. In any case, a number of interpretive motifs surface from examination of this passion material, the most dominant of which is the location of the cross of Christ at the center of God's redemptive plan. Although the *instrumentality* of Jesus' death in God's plan receives little attention within the narratives of Jesus' passion, *that* the cross has this role never really leaves center stage. The early tradition is evidently more interested in the affirmation that Jesus' death, far from taking God by surprise, was actually the means by which Jesus' messiahship was most transparent, and is less concerned to tie down with precision *how* Jesus' death was effective in bringing about the salvation of the world.

One of the more prominent categories by which the centrality of Jesus' death to God's overarching purpose is communicated in the early passion material represented in the Gospels is the Old Testament figure of the "suffering righteous one." Borrowing especially from the Psalms, throughout the passion materials Jesus is portrayed in dress borrowed from the "suffering righteous"—who, for example:

☐ had enemies that plotted against him, abused him, accused him falsely, divided his clothes, offered him a drink and anticipated his rescue from death

☐ is betrayed by a table intimate

☐ is forsaken by friends—one of whom denies him and follows from a distance, so that he must suffer alone

☐ is innocent and maintains his silence

☐ anticipates his own vindication

☐ experiences anguish and abandonment by God

☐ is vindicated at his death and declared "Son of God"

Other motifs are present as well. Examining both the background and foreground of the passion accounts in our Gospels, we can discern interests in portraying Jesus as the Servant of the Lord, as the long-awaited

17

Messiah and as the prophet; his death is regarded as a cosmic event, the turning point in history and so on. Manifestly, early interpreters of Jesus' death were interested in showing how the cross was fully explicable in terms of the divine will, foreshadowed in the Scriptures, even anticipated within the overarching purpose of God. Jesus' death was central to God's redemptive will, but how it functioned in this way seems to have been less a compelling concern than certifying the presence of such a connection.

The development of the passion narrative is only one example of the pervasiveness of early Christian deliberation on the enigma of Jesus' death, the mystery provided by the cross of Christ. Others could be sketched as well, and, indeed, we will turn to additional New Testament materials in the chapters that follow in order to show how early Christians struggled to articulate meaningfully the significance of Jesus' suffering. Enough has been said thus far, though, to provide a basis for a pressing theological question—namely, to what degree have we learned from these New Testament witnesses the importance of and means by which to struggle with the message of the cross in our own contexts?

We want to suggest that many modes of theological reflection and declaration today, many but not all of which are shared popularly, have failed to take seriously the legacy of the New Testament. Many of us have been content merely to repeat the words of the New Testament itself, as though those words were themselves self-interpreting, requiring no translation. In a world where we tend to see personal suffering or social tragedy as a discredit to our faith, many of us have found the suffering of Christ an embarrassment, with the result that his death is rarely mentioned. Even those who have continued to locate the cross at the center of Christian faith have often done so by destigmatizing its significance for contemporary discipleship. The cross is thus often discussed either in positive terms, with an emphasis on its "cash value" for our salvation, or in negative terms, with an emphasis on how the ignominy of the cross was overturned in Jesus' resurrection on the third day. As a result, our Christian brothers and sisters, whether overseas in the Two-Thirds World or in our own inner cities, rightly complain that Western theology has stripped the faith of an important aspect of the New Testament portrayal of Jesus—the one who joins us in our suffering. "The crucified one is the living one," we want to say; but so also is "the living one" "the crucified one."

This is only half of the picture, however. The cross has been used (might we say abused?) in other ways as well. Especially among those who are the bearers of power and privilege in particular social contexts, the cross is sometimes deployed as a model for others. The least, the left out and the lost of society are thus urged to welcome the decay of their lives or communities, and those who suffer abuse, the harassed and the ill-used are encouraged to submit quietly, for in this way they can "be like Jesus." As David Batstone has observed, when the Spanish arrived on Latin-American shores, two images of the adult Christ were introduced: the suffering Jesus who remained passive in the midst of his passion as an expression of his submission to his destiny before God; and the royal, conquering Christ who reigns over his kingdom. This suffering Jesus was the image with which the native peoples were to identity, while the image of the conquering Christ was embodied by those conquistadors who brought Christian faith and Spanish rule to the Aztecs, Mayas and Incas.[11] "Your pain, your loss," this typology seems to urge, "is an opportunity for you to identify with the passion of Jesus." On the other hand, "our victories, our imperial dominion is nothing less than a reflection of the divine conquest over the forces of evil."

The cross of Christ continues to be corrupted similarly, whether in large, social and political movements such as the extension of the empire of Spain, or in small communities and families, where those in pain are urged to embrace their pain with passive acceptance, even to revel in their suffering, in order to be like Jesus. Jesus, as we will demonstrate in the following chapters, is portrayed in the New Testament neither as a forbear-

---

[11]David Batstone, *From Conquest to Struggle: Jesus of Nazareth in Latin America* (Albany: State University of New York Press, 1991), pp. 14-18.

ing, resigned victim nor as a masochist who, entangled in his own twisted motivations, welcomed the suffering and death of a Roman cross. The history of his demise allows no basis for masking over the injustice of those who manufactured the cross and placed him on it.[12] This is not to say that faithful discipleship is or will be devoid of pain. We cannot escape the words of Jesus directed to would-be disciples, "If any want to become my followers, let them deny themselves, take up the cross daily, and follow me" (Lk 9:23), nor the related words of Paul and Barnabas following their own experiences of violent persecution in Acts, "It is through many persecutions that we must enter the kingdom of God" (Acts 14:22). This, however, is not to say that the cross is a symbol of resignation. The suffering of Jesus, as well as that of Paul and Barnabas, was grounded in their active pursuit of the mission of God, their struggle against those who opposed God's purpose.

Developing Metaphors

If contemporary thinking about the significance of Jesus' death is out of step in important ways with the theological enterprise represented within the pages of the New Testament, this is not to say that the history of reflection on the cross is similarly problematic. A number of important efforts to articulate the meaning of Jesus' death for new times and places appear on the historical landscape. As is often the case in our use of the New Testament, our use of tradition often falters because we learn less *how* the theological task has been undertaken and exemplified, and attempt instead to carry over into our own lives and pronouncements models and metaphors that belong to another age and that are dead to us. Metaphors work within cultures where a shared encyclopedia can be assumed. Crossing cultures requires the creation of new metaphors, new ways of conceptualizing and communicating. Often to the detriment of

---

[12]See Leonardo Boff, *Passion of Christ, Passion of the World: The Facts, Their Interpretation, and Their Meaning Yesterday and Today* (Maryknoll, N.Y.: Orbis, 1987), pp. 1-4.

fidelity in understanding do we borrow metaphors from other cultures and use them as if they were our own.

Although we shall return to the atonement theology of Anselm of Canterbury (1033-1109) in chapter five, it will be helpful already at this early point to consider his model as an illustration of the process of enculturation we are describing. Arguing against an earlier "ransom theory" of the atonement—that is, the idea that Jesus' death served as a ransom paid to Satan in order that sinful humanity might be released from Satan's grip—he put forward his own "theory of satisfaction." What did Jesus' death "satisfy"? Borrowing from Anselm today, we often articulate Anselm's view with respect to God's anger: Jesus' death "satisfies" God's anger so that God's hostility toward us, now borne by Jesus, is turned away. Such an understanding not only gives rise to such bizarre views as the question, "So Jesus came to save us from God?"[13]—a view that has far more credence in popular views of the atonement than we might want to admit. It also constitutes a gross distortion of Anselm's work.

Anselm was convinced that the essential problem with salvation is not what is "due" the devil; the problem, rather, had to do with the wrong done to God. Humans had substituted sinful lives for their vocations of faithfulness and service. Working within a culture characterized fundamentally by the needs of honor and shame (and not, as in much of Western culture, by the concerns of guilt and innocence), Anselm saw that the human predicament was the consequence of the human assault on God's honor. That is, it was not that God's anger required appeasement but that his honor needed to be restored. On account of our own predilections for interpreting the cross, we may urge that, in sketching the human problem in this way, Anselm has not understood Paul very well. In fact, given that the Roman world was likewise oriented around the pivotal values of honor and shame, Anselm may be closer to Paul than we think. In any

---

[13]Reported by Stephen H. Travis, "The Doctrine of the Atonement: Popular Evangelicalism and the Bible," *Catalyst* 22, no. 1 (1995): 1-3.

case, Anselm never claimed to be narrowly Pauline in his thinking about the instrumentality of salvation. Anselm was trying to articulate the meaning of the atonement for persons in his world, not in the first century (nor for the twenty-first).

In his essay "Why Did God Become Human?" (*Cur Deus Homo*), Anselm observes that in order for honor to be restored, restitution must be initiated by those responsible for shaming the dishonored party. This means that reparations must be made from the human side—a virtual impossibility since the depth and reach of sin undercuts any such human efforts. Only God is competent to make amends. Why did God become human? Only Christ, divine and human, could accomplish the restoration of God's honor and thus repair the breach between God and humanity. Only he could fulfill the human vocation to live faithfully; only he could offer his life in death to restore God's honor.

It will not do for us simply to borrow Anselm's theory, as though it could be read into our lives with any significance resembling that of his own world. The social history of Anselm was characterized by feudalism, with the landowner, or "lord," living in peace with his vassals (or serfs) at the intersection of a carefully managed series of reciprocal obligations. The lord provided capital and protection; the serf provided honor, loyalty and tribute. The stability of this social world rested on slavish fidelity and allegiance. In this context, Anselm's understanding of the atonement reads as a kind of allegory, with the lord as the Lord and the serfs as the human family. "Satisfaction" for us, in our criminal-justice system, has to do with the apprehension and punishment of the guilty, while for Anselm and his contemporaries, satisfaction hinged on the fulfillment of certain obligations related to loyalty and honor.

In fact, reflecting on Anselm's theory of satisfaction, we might wonder whether our theologies of the cross might sometimes reflect too much of the cultures in which they are articulated. When viewed against the historical backdrop of Anselm's feudal society, his theology of the cross may too closely reflect a culture of patronage that holds certain members of society hostage to the debt-obligations at the heart of relationships characterized by honor and shame. By painting God in the guise of a feudal lord, Anselm may have (however inadvertently) provided divine sanction for the subjugation of those vassals, those human subjects on whose back the feudal system was built and depended. One might argue that the "word of the cross" as articulated in the New Testament actually speaks against feudalism, with the result that Anselm's theory of atonement was itself built on cultural concepts and practices that ought to have been challenged rather than vaunted in this way.

Contemporary Atonement Theology

To raise questions about Anselm's theory of satisfaction, however, is equally to raise questions about the forms of atonement theology popular among our contemporaries. By almost any accounting, the understanding of the atonement most evident in fashionable hymnody and other expressions of popular Christian faith is the theory of "penal substitution." This is the view that Jesus' death was a self-offering to God, whereby he bore the punishment God would otherwise have inflicted on us, thus turning God's hostility away from us. Why has this view become so widespread? What is its appeal? The easy answer, of course, would be, "This is the biblical view" or "This is the classical Christian view." As we will document in subsequent chapters, however, the idea that the Bible or the classical Christian tradition has "one" view of the atonement is unfounded. In the New Testament, the saving effect of Jesus' death is represented primarily through five constellations of images, each of which is borrowed from the public life of the ancient Mediterranean world: the court of law (e.g., justification), the world of commerce (e.g., redemption), personal relationships (e.g., reconciliation), worship (e.g., sacrifice) and the battleground (e.g., triumph over evil). Within these categories are clusters of terms, leading us to the conclusion that the significance of Jesus' death could not be represented without remainder by any one concept or theory of metaphor. Neither is it legitimate to argue that the Christian tradition has focused exclusively or even primarily on the theory of penal substitution. As we have already hinted, Anselm's theory of satisfaction cannot be equated with penal substitutionary atonement, and other views have been championed besides—for example, theories of ransom, of moral influence, of cosmic drama and more.[14] Why, then, are people of our day drawn to this particular theory?

One important reason for the ascendency of penal substitutionary atonement in the West has been our particular view of justice, with its orientation toward guilt and innocence on the one hand, and toward autobiography on the other. In the criminal-justice system, the question of guilt is paramount, together with the infliction of punishment upon the person or entity found guilty of having transgressed the law. The convictions, procedures and processes of "criminal justice" are not in our society limited to courts of law but pervade our lives. The assignation of blame has reached the status of a vocation for some in the media, and the twofold process of determining fault and meting out punishment occupies families, schools, businesses and more. A world where this system of justice has reached the stage of "the way the world works" or "the way the world really is," or even "the way the world was made by God," is naturally receptive of a theory of atonement like that provided in penal substitution. Indeed, to suggest that such a theory is limited, only a theory, or even inadequate in light of the biblical witness would be to call into question a central aspect of the world that most of us take for granted.

What is more, because the criminal justice system is fundamentally concerned with the determination of guilt and punishment of the guilty party, it is necessarily interested in what we might call "autobiographical justice." That is, the system has tended to work on the basis of the view that individuals perform acts of transgression, so that individuals (or individual entities) ought to be examined and punished for their complicity.

---

[14]For accessible surveys, see John Driver, *Understanding the Atonement for the Mission of the Church* (Scottdale, Penn.: Herald, 1986), pp. 37-67; Herman-Emiel Mertens, *Not the Cross, but the Crucified: An Essay in Soteriology*, LTPM 11 (Grand Rapids, Mich.: Eerdmans, 1992).

Who started this fight? Who called the first name? Whose idea was this? Until relatively recently, people were looked upon principally in an atomistic way—as individuals, not as persons embedded within social systems.

We have found this autobiographical notion of justice operative on a daily basis in our interactions with people about the hungry and homeless. Why is this woman living on the street? *She made a bad decision.* Why are these men not working? *They are lazy.* And so on. Theories of atonement like penal substitution preserve and support such thinking, since they locate responsibility (or fault or blame) primarily at the level of the individual.

It is not surprising, then, that this particular way of construing the significance of the cross also supports our treasured individualistic soteriology. "Soteriology" refers to our understanding of salvation, and our understanding of salvation has been dominated historically by the doctrine of justification by faith. Irrespective of the celebrated history and significance of the doctrine of "justification by faith,"[15] not least in the Protestant tradition, for many contemporary Christians, this doctrine has an individualistic orientation and bias that is not only comforting but instinctive, natural. Justification by faith, as traditionally understood, refers to a legal transaction: the manifestly guilty person stands before the divine judge for sentencing and hears the verdict, "Not guilty!" Penal substitutionary atonement provides a workable foundation for this soteriology, making this atonement theory all the more palatable or inviting.

Finally, we may be drawn to a penal substitutionary account of the significance of Jesus' death because this theory gives us permission to disregard the suffering of Jesus. Given the way Jesus' death on the cross is dramatized in many American churches during Holy Week, this may seem a strange assertion. Popular books on the last week of Christ often focus on Jesus' pain, and pulpiteers sometimes follow in their wake,

---

[15]See especially Alister E. McGrath, *Iustia Dei: A History of the Christian Doctrine of Justification*, 2 vols. (Cambridge: Cambridge University Press, 1986).

sketching the agony of Jesus' flogging, the raw penetration of the long, sturdy thorns encircling his head, the anguish of having a wooden beam placed across his lacerated shoulders, the torture of carrying the cross uphill to the place of execution, the excruciating placement of the nails on his hands and feet, the painful thud of the cross as it was dropped into its hole in the rocky hill and so on. Unfortunately for such portraits, our knowledge of the specifics of crucifixion in the ancient world is almost nil,[16] with the result that these reports are often little more than the products of active, dramatic imaginations. What is more, in the ancient world, crucifixion became the choice mode of execution not because it was particularly painful when compared, say, with torturing a boy with whips and thongs before scalping him, cutting out his tongue, cutting off his feet and hands, then placing him in a huge frying pan.[17] Crucifixion proved to be a deterrent against crimes against the Empire on account of its public, humiliating quality. As the Jewish historian Josephus noted, suspension on a Roman cross was "the most pitiable of deaths,"[18] a tragic misfortune, but this had to do with its status as a gruesome, despicable act, not its overwhelming physical distress. Historical accuracy is not at issue in the portraits of Jesus' death painted by these pulpiteers, however. What comes into focus, rather, is the dramatic, sentimentalizing of his pain *in the service of the theory of penal substitutionary atonement.* Dramatizing the cross of Christ has the rhetorical affect of demonstrating the depths of agony to which Jesus went on the cross. In this way, he took upon himself the punishment for which the whole world had been destined. He suffered so severely, according to popular readings of the cross, so that we would not have to.

According to the conventions of first-century Jewish and Roman society, the suffering Jesus experienced on the cross was less about physical pain and more about degradation, rejection and humiliation. Those

---

[16]See Joel B. Green, "Death of Jesus," in *DJG*, pp. 147-48.
[17]See 2 Maccabees 7.
[18]Josephus *J.W.* 7.6.4 §203.

whose lives are unreservedly oriented toward the purpose of God in a world that has set itself over against that purpose can expect little else. Jesus says as much when he turns from the prediction of his own demise to his delineation of the cost of discipleship: "If any want to become my followers, let them deny themselves, take up the cross, and follow me" (Mk 8:27-38). The dominance of the penal substitutionary theory of the atonement in our world, however, allows us to disregard this aspect of Jesus' suffering in our rush to construe the cross positively for its soteriological "cash value." Jesus' suffering is effective, not exemplary; it is "for us." Of course, we often also look to the resurrection for a similar interpretive move. To our way of thinking, the passion of Jesus is swallowed up in the resurrection. Jesus is raised from the dead "in spite of" his suffering—that is, in order to overturn the negative evaluation of him that would normally accrue to a victim of crucifixion. Rarely do we think of the resurrection as an affirmation of Jesus and his cross, with the consequence that we fail to see the profundity of the claim that the cross places on the faith and life of the church.

Pressing Questions

If it is true that penal substitutionary atonement is an attractive account of the saving significance of the death of Jesus for many in the West, need more be said? If it is true that how we understand the importance of the cross is and ought to be worked out in ways appropriate to peoples' lives, what more can be said? In fact, a number of pressing questions needs to be raised.

1. First and centrally we may ask whether the theory of penal substitutionary atonement is faithful to the teaching of Scripture. That is, most attempts to articulate a theological method give preeminence to the Bible, with the result that it is not enough to seek after "relevance." We must inquire more fully into relevance in relation to "biblical fidelity." The theological task is in some ways a balancing act, in which we are asked to go beyond the insights of Scripture in order to address ever-unfolding chal-

lenges, while at the same time ensuring that our extensions of the biblical witness are consonant with the central insights of Scripture.[19] To what degree is penal substitution grounded in Scripture? This is one of the questions to which we will devote ourselves in chapters two, three and four.

2. Our awareness must also be raised to the possibility, even probability, that our theological commitments with regard to atonement theology do not simply speak to our culture but actually grow out of it. In fact, in ways that we do not often recognize, all of our attempts at theological formulation are themselves "cultural products" in the sense that they arise in particular sociohistorical contexts, address matters pertinent to those contexts, serve the interests of those contexts, and, thus, in some sense, embody the values of those contexts. As Alister McGrath helpfully notes, our affirmations, including our affirmations about God, are historically rooted and thus are subject to sociohistorical processes. Hence, we face the pressing questions, Which of our affirmations are true? and, Who decides?[20] All statements, and therefore all theological statements, relate to, speak to and make themselves relevant to their own social environment. If they do not, then they are likely to be dismissed as hopelessly abstract, unrealistic, impertinent, meaningless, artificial. If their relationship with their social environment is too intimate, on the other hand, they are likely to be regarded as parochial, time bound, irrelevant to a wider audience. Moreover, they will lack the capacity to speak over against their social environment. They will be impotent to challenge the status quo. Robert Wuthnow refers to this as the "problem of articulation"—"the delicate balance between the products of culture and the social environments in which they are produced."[21]

---

[19]See Alister E. McGrath, *The Genesis of Doctrine: A Study in the Formation of Doctrinal Criticism* (Grand Rapids, Mich.: Eerdmans, 1990), p. 6.

[20]Ibid., pp. 81-102.

[21]Robert Wuthnow, *Communities of Discourse: Ideology and Social Structure in the Reformation, the Enlightenment, and European Socialism* (Cambridge, Mass.: Harvard University Press, 1989), p. 3.

In what ways is the theory of penal substitution shaped by the Western culture in which it has grown and gained its popularity? To what degree is this theory able to disengage from its social roots in the West so as to challenge the very culture in which it has taken root? Does it articulate so closely with our social environment that it is devoid of transcendent value—with the result that it will soon be irrelevant in our part of the globe and has always lacked relevance in other cultures?

In putting the question in this way, we have moved to the forefront two more questions about penal substitutionary atonement.

3. If this theory has been well-suited to modern culture in the West, what will be its fate with the ascendancy of postmodern culture? Here we have in mind postmodern challenges

☐ to individualism, in favor of a communal accounting of human nature;

☐ to autobiographical justice, in favor of systems theory, including the determinative role of genes and family experience in human behavior; and

☐ to the existence and progress of an autonomous humanity, in favor of a portrait of the human family that locates humanity within the cosmos, so that the human predicament and soteriology must account for creation as a whole.

We mention these three considerations not only because they are central tenets of postmodern ways of thinking but also because, at least in these respects, postmodernism is arguably more at home in the biblical tradition than modernism has been.

4. If, at least to a significant degree, penal substitutionary atonement has been a "cultural product" of life in the West, is it any surprise that proclamation of the gospel grounded in this theory has tended to fall on deaf ears in other social worlds? Christian missionaries from the West, armed with this central affirmation of the gospel—namely, the good news that Jesus has come to take away your guilt, that Jesus has been punished for you so that God can declare you not guilty—have often reported their surprise upon discovering the huge populations of our world for whom guilt is a nonissue. What are we to make of a theory of atonement that

many of us have come to regard as central to the Christian message and which popular Christianity practically equates with the work of Christ, yet which is unrelated to much of global Christian mission?

5. Finally, we must face the reality that, even when it is articulated by its most careful and sophisticated adherents, penal substitutionary atonement remains susceptible to misunderstanding and even bizarre caricature. Accordingly, the drama of the death of Jesus becomes a manifestation of God's anger—with God as the distant Father who punishes his own son in order to appease his own indignation. One of us has received a report from a friend leading a Sunday school class in which a boy observed, "Jesus I like, but the Father seems pretty mean!" "Why is God always so angry?" another friend asked. "A policeman with a billy club writing up a ticket for yet another of my transgressions; an official at a basketball game always blowing the whistle: 'Foul! Foul! Technical foul! You're out of here!'—these are the images of God I knew," our friend observed.

For others, atonement theology represents an even more startling drama in which God takes on the role of the sadist inflicting punishment, while Jesus, in his role as masochist, readily embraces suffering.[22] From this perspective, it is only a small step from the crucifixion of Jesus to the legitimation of unjust human suffering or the idealization of the victim. As bewildering as this view might seem, the fact remains that the popular model of penal substitution is represented in songs and sermons in ways that lend themselves to such a reading. Paul observed that the cross of Christ was scandalous, but those who reject the saving drama of the death

---

[22]For related views see, for example, Rita Nakashima Brock, "And a Little Child Will Lead Us: Christology and Child Abuse," in *Christianity, Patriarchy, and Abuse: A Feminist Critique*, ed. Joanne Carlson Brown and Carole R. Bohn (New York: Pilgrim, 1989), pp. 42-61; Rita Nakashima Brock, *Journeys by Heart: A Christology of Erotic Power* (New York: Crossroad, 1988); Beverly W. Harrison and Carter Heyward, "Pain and Pleasure: Avoiding the Confusions of Christian Tradition in Feminist Theory," in *Christianity, Patriarchy, and Abuse: A Feminist Critique*, ed. Joanne Carlson Brown and Carole R. Bohn (New York: Pilgrim, 1989), pp. 148-73; Joanne Carlson Brown and Rebecca Parker, "For God So Loved the World?", in *Christianity, Patriarchy, and Abuse: A Feminist Critique*, ed. Joanne Carlson Brown and Carole R. Bohn (New York: Pilgrim, 1989), pp. 1-30; Dorothee Sölle, *Thinking About God: An Introduction to Theology* (London: SCM Press, 1990).

of Jesus because it seems to reflect "divine child abuse" have located the scandal of the cross in the wrong place and encountered the scandal of the cross in the wrong way. Because of the prominence of this view of the atonement as "divine child abuse" in some quarters of the church today, we cannot afford to give it only passing mention but must discuss it more thoroughly in chapter four.

Less bizarre but likewise problematic is another phenomenon related to representations of the theory of penal substitutionary atonement. Proponents of this theory often leave little room for the importance of ethical comportment. If Jesus has deflected onto himself the anger of God, if on this basis we have been made the objects of a legal (penal) transaction whereby we are declared "not guilty," what basis for moral behavior remains? Apart from allowing my name to be moved to the correct side of God's legal ledger, what significance has the cross of Christ for faith and life, according to this view?

It is also true that this particular way of portraying the significance of Jesus' death has had little voice in how we relate to one another in and outside of the church or in larger, social-ethical issues. That a central tenet of our faith might have little or nothing to say about racial reconciliation, for example, or issues of wealth and poverty, or our relationship to the cosmos, is itself a startling reality. It is all the more discomforting, though, when it is remembered that the death of Jesus was the consequence of social and political factors as well as theological ones. Jesus was crucified as a threat to the Roman empire. His message, his words and deeds, served to bring him to the attention of the Jewish authorities in Jerusalem and the Roman ruler in Judea, who perceived in him a great enough threat that his death was requested and given. There is perhaps no greater affirmation and reminder that a faith grounded in the cross of Christ is a faith that has profound and far-reaching, this-worldly implications.

Someone may wish to argue that there is nothing intrinsic to the theory of penal substitutionary atonement that leads one necessarily in these problematic directions. This is not our point. We are simply observing that popularly interpreted and characterized, this brand of atonement theology has been understood in ways that have proven detrimental to the witness of the church.

Setting an Agenda

We find ourselves then at an important crossroads in our understanding of the saving work of the death of Jesus. If not the most pervasive metaphor, then certainly one of the most pervasive metaphors for making sense of the cross of Christ, penal substitution,

☐ has engendered forms of Christian faith and practice that are suspect;

☐ has been construed by persons within and outside the church as a form of "divine child abuse," and so at the very least invites more careful articulation;

☐ has not been heard as "good news" in contemporary cultures in and outside of the West which are not guilt based;

☐ may well have increasingly less relevance among twenty-first century Christians; and

☐ at the very least, constrains overmuch the richness of biblical thinking concerning the death of Jesus.

In the chapters that follow, we intend to address these issues more fully in three ways. First, we will examine some of the relevant biblical material (chapters two, three and four). In this section of the book, we want to accomplish two primary objectives: first, to orient ourselves to the profundity of atonement thought particularly in the New Testament, and to evaluate some of the key theological issues and terms in which our understanding of God's redemptive plan is based. What does Scripture intend in its references to important concepts such as "the wrath of God," for example? Is contemporary thinking about the nature of salvation and the importance of the death of Jesus consonant with how Scripture develops the notion of "God's wrath"? What range of metaphors are employed for making sense of the death of Jesus? From where do those metaphors derive? To what realities and needs do they best speak? What are we to make of the variety of atonement images used within the New Testament? In what ways does this variety speak to issues of the identity of the church and to the nature of Christian mission?

Second, we move from a concentration on biblical materials to reflection on historical and theological materials related to the atonement (chapter five). Within the history of the Christian church, how has thinking about the death of Jesus developed? What are the implications of the various views on the cross for the life of the church and the theological task?

Our investigations of biblical and historical material do not grow out of antiquarian interests alone. We hope to learn from Scripture and the historical witness of the church something of how to engage in the balancing act of which we spoke earlier—that is, how our understanding, teaching and proclamation of the saving significance of the death of Jesus might arise in and speak to our particular social contexts *and* evidence fidelity to the central insights of Scripture. In chapters six through nine, then, we hope to explore more fully how best to generate faithful and appropriate cross talk. This will not lead us to recommend or sanction any one image of the cross for contemporary culture, or any one set of such images. For us to engage in this sort of activity, we hope to show, would be to contradict the biblical witness and theological tradition. However, we will provide illustrative narratives of persons and communities situated in particular contexts, who are addressing in helpful ways the question, How is the message of the cross good news for these people, in this context, in this time? And, reflecting on the material of the book as a whole, we will outline a series of coordinates that will figure in our attempts to engage the New Testament faithfully within the integrity of its own discourse and world at the same time that we grapple with the needs, vocabulary and values of the worlds in which we live and serve.

From the standpoint of fidelity to the New Testament, we cannot overlook or downplay the importance of the death of Jesus for our faith and life as his disciples. At the turn of the third millennium, however, we must face the reality that our thinking about the cross has actually kept it from occupying a central place in our lives. Our chief images for interpreting the saving significance of Jesus' death have kept the word of the cross distant from issues that press in on us—such as questions related to faith and wealth, racial relations, environmental ethics and so on—with the result that the word through which we are to find the hope of salvation has lost the capacity to challenge us in the day-to-day realities of our lives. We need to hear again the word, the scandal of the cross.

2

THE CROSS &
THE NEW TESTAMENT

A Mélange of Voices
(Part One)

One of the obstacles facing any exploration of "the atonement in the New Testament" is the problem of language. In the New Revised Standard Version (NRSV), for example, the words *atonement* and *atoning* occur in the New Testament only twice each. Similarly, in the New International Version (NIV) of the New Testament, forms of the verb "to atone" appear only five times. Were we to limit our investigation to those usages, our study would be completed quickly, its results meager. Unlike much of our theological vocabulary, *atonement* and "to atone" have a relatively recent history, having been derived from the Middle English expression *make at one* or *at one-ment*. This etymology might lead us to assume that "atonement" has to do with "reconciliation";[1] although this is a valuable

---

[1]Thus, Joseph A. Fitzmyer, "Reconciliation in Pauline Theology," in *No Famine in the Land: Studies in Honor of John L. McKenzie*, ed. James W. Flanagan and Anita Weisbrod Robinson (Missoula, Mont.: Scholars, 1975), pp. 155-77.

observation, it provides little additional help, since, again using the NRSV, the verb and noun forms of "to reconcile" appear only twelve times in the New Testament with reference to the work of God in Christ. What is more, in the English of the King James Version (KJV, 1611), the language of atonement indicates connotations of a more judiciary sort rather than relational. Evidently, if we are to gain our bearings regarding the meaning of the atonement in the New Testament, we will be less interested in the appearance of particular *vocabulary*[2] and more concerned with the *concept* of atonement, which we will define broadly as "the saving significance of Jesus' death."

Any exploration of the death of Jesus in the New Testament will indicate immediately the great variety of ways in which the cross is regarded as meaningful for Christian faith and practice.[3] The narrow concerns of this chapter will not allow for a full-orbed discussion of the significance of the cross in the New Testament writings. How Paul develops his understanding of his own sufferings in light of the sufferings of Christ, how Luke presents the cross as an exposition of Christian life and mission— such perspectives as these will not be explored in detail. Instead, we will focus our discussion on several of the more prominent New Testament voices as they articulate the saving significance of the death of Jesus.

One of those voices will be that of Jesus himself, and this raises a complex set of issues that must be acknowledged. Since we have nothing actually written by Jesus, we have no direct access to his thoughts about his own death. During major periods of the last two centuries, this reality has been enough for some to exclude from discussion any notion of Jesus' self-understanding—including whether he anticipated his own death or

---

[2] See, however, the approach taken in Leon Morris, *The Apostolic Preaching of the Cross*, 3d ed. (Leicester, U.K.: Inter-Varsity Press, 1965); and, *The Atonement: Its Meaning and Significance* (Leicester, U.K.: Inter-Varsity Press; Downers Grove, Ill.: InterVarsity Press, 1983). In a third book, *The Cross in the New Testament* (Grand Rapids, Mich.: Eerdmans, 1965), Morris adopts an approach that is less tied to the appearance of particular vocabulary.

[3] See, for example, John T. Carroll and Joel B. Green, *The Death of Jesus in Early Christianity* (Peabody, Mass.: Hendrickson, 1995).

whether he reflected theologically on its importance. As a result, some will undoubtedly view our attempt to hear in the Gospels evidence of Jesus' creative interpretation of his impending death as a flight of fantasy. We will not attempt to defend this approach in this chapter for three reasons: (1) from a pragmatic point of view, to launch such an apology would require another book altogether; (2) because our approach will show how the nature of Jesus' death is so intimately tied to what we know of his life, we believe that our ruminations on how Jesus might have understood his death rest on a broadly defensible foundation;[4] and (3) those who refuse to grant the possibility that we can know something of Jesus' aims and understanding with regard to his execution can nonetheless construe our discussion as a representation of the saving significance of Jesus' death *insofar as this is represented in the New Testament Gospels*[5]—and, from the standpoint of our agenda in this chapter, this too would be a worthwhile exercise.

Following this literary and historical assessment of Jesus' understanding of the saving (or salvific) significance of his own death, we will devote a major section of our analysis to the interpretation of the cross in Paul's letters. This is due to the prominence the cross occupies in Paul's thought, as well as to the variety of ways in which Paul has formulated its salvific importance. In the next chapter we will turn to a more cursory consideration of the importance of the cross in the soteriology of Luke's writings, Luke-Acts. When juxtaposed with the Pauline material, Luke's two-part narrative is interesting primarily because of the contrasting nature of his witness. Luke provides a weighty New Testament voice with respect to the theology of salvation; yet his two volumes do little to ground the salva-

---

[4]Indeed, one of the primary criteria employed in current historical-Jesus research focuses on how our understanding of his life and mission makes sense of his death on a Roman cross. See, for example, John P. Meier, *A Marginal Jew: Rethinking the Historical Jesus*, vol. 1: *The Roots of the Problem and the Person*, ABRL (New York: Doubleday, 1991), p. 177.

[5]From a historical vantage point, this means that we exclude as a major, extracanonical source for the death of Jesus the Gospel of Peter—contra, e.g., John Dominic Crossan, *The Cross That Spoke: The Origins of the Passion Narrative* (San Francisco: Harper & Row, 1988). See Joel B. Green, "The *Gospel of Peter*: Source for a Pre-Canonical Passion Narrative?" *ZNW* 78 (1987): 293-301.

tion of God in the crucifixion of Jesus. Exploration of the salvific importance of the death of Jesus in the Johannine material (which we will define broadly to include the Fourth Gospel, the Johannine epistles and the book of Revelation), in Hebrews and in 1 Peter will complete our presentation of the mélange of ways in which the New Testament characterizes the death of Jesus as saving event.

Jesus and the Gospels: The Death of Jesus and the Restoration of God's People

The death of Jesus casts its shadow back from the crucifixion onto almost every page of the Gospels.[6] This is because of the opposition he attracted from early on in his ministry—opposition that leads to important scenes of conflict as well as plots against his life (e.g., Mk 3:1-6). The Gospels agree, too, that Jesus spoke of his impending demise (e.g., Mk 8:31; 9:31; 10:33-34), tying it into the overarching purpose of God. Only rarely does he speak of his death as in some sense salvific, however. Only rarely do we encounter the concept of the atoning death of Jesus in the Gospels.

According to the Synoptic Gospels—Matthew, Mark and Luke—Jesus speaks of his own death clearly in terms of atonement theology at only two points: (1) Mark 10:45 and its parallel in Matthew 20:28, and (2) Mark 14:22-25 and its parallels in Matthew 26:26-29 and Luke 22:19-20 (see also 1 Cor 11:23-25).[7] These are the so-called ransom sayings: "The Son of Man came not to be served but to serve, and to give his life

---

[6]This section is adapted from Joel B. Green, "The Death of Jesus and the Ways of God: Jesus and the Gospels on Messianic Status and Shameful Suffering," *Int* 52 (1998): 24-37.

[7]The authenticity of the ransom saying has been argued in, for example, Peter Stuhlmacher, "Vicariously Giving His Life for Many, Mark 10:45 (Mt 20:28)," in *Reconciliation, Law, and Righteousness: Essays in Biblical Theology* (Philadelphia: Fortress, 1986), pp. 116-29; Sydney T. Page, "The Authenticity of the Ransom Logion (Mark 10:45b)," in *Studies of History and Tradition in the Four Gospels*, GP 1, ed. R. T. France and David Wenham (Sheffield: JSOT, 1980), pp. 137-61. On the eucharistic sayings, see, for example, I. Howard Marshall, *Last Supper and Lord's Supper* (Grand Rapids, Mich.: Eerdmans, 1980); Markus Barth, *Das Mahl des Herrn: Gemeinschaft mit Israel, mit Christus und unter den Gasten* (Neukirchen-Vluyn: Neukirchener, 1987); Xavier Léon-Dufour, *Sharing the Eucharistic Bread: The Witness of the New Testament* (New York: Paulist, 1987); Bruce D. Chilton, *A Feast of Meanings: Eucharistic Theologies from Jesus through Johannine Circles*, NovTSup 72 (Leiden: E. J. Brill, 1994).

a ransom for many" (Mk 10:45); and the saying at the Last Supper: "This is my blood of the covenant, which is poured out for many" (Mk 14:24).

The narrative settings of these two sayings are important in two primary respects. First, the points at which a theology of the atonement is most transparent in the Gospel tradition are intimately related to scenes where the sorts of concerns with power- and status-seeking characteristic of the Roman Empire are on display among Jesus' followers. Second, in both instances the atonement theology to which Jesus bears witness is deeply rooted in Old Testament images and promise.

With regard to issues of power and status, it may be helpful first to paint a mural against which to read these scenes. With the rise of Caesar Augustus as ruler, Rome was unified not only by one emperor but also by a political order based on the ethics of patronage. Augustus assumed the role of benefactor or patron for all of the Roman world; in doing so, he adopted a role for himself that was formalized as one of the most prominent taken-for-granted ingredients of life throughout the Empire. Slaves were indebted to their masters. Sons were under the rule of their fathers. Clients were bound to their patrons and often had clients of their own. The resulting network of overlapping obligation was spun like a web throughout the Empire, with everyone ultimately indebted to the emperor—either as a result of his direct patronage or indirectly through the complex threads of obligation that found their way back to him.

Of course, even the emperor had client status of a sort, for the hierarchy of patronal relations extended beyond the human sphere to include the gods. Although he was not himself divine, the emperor was the recipient of the gods' patronage and served as their special agent. Thus the reciprocity of patronal relations that obligated slaves to masters, sons to fathers, the elite to the emperor and so on, was an extension of the emperor's (and with him, all of Rome's) indebtedness to the gods. In this way the political order found its legitimation in the gods themselves. It was sacred.

Against such a world order, Jesus' message stands in stark contrast. For example, Jesus' disciples are said repeatedly to have struggled with the question of who among them was the greatest. Jesus' response was to reject such maneuvering and to assert that the dominion of God belonged to little children. He further insisted that status in the community must be measured by one's role as a servant. Service, of course, was expected when relating to people of higher status, but Jesus, even while acknowledging his own superior status when measured in the company of his followers, communicated by word and deed that service was to be given to those of lower status, including little children.

Jesus further undermined patronal ethics by insisting that people give without expectation of return. Within normal social roles, gifts brought with them expectations of reciprocity; this was the way of the Roman household whose father was Caesar. Jesus set forth for his listeners an alternative household, not run by relations of debt and obligation. The household he imagined was one in which people would be treated as family, with services performed and goods shared without the attachment of reciprocal obligation. As Jesus summarized, "Love your enemies, do good, and lend, expecting nothing in return" (Lk 6:35). What is more, Jesus rooted this subversive ethic in the human vocation to imitate God: "Be merciful, even as your Father is merciful" (Lk 6:36).

In this way, Jesus opposed the Roman order at the most fundamental of levels, substituting for a pervasive worldview grounded in debt and obligation with roots in the favor of the gods a way of being in the world that took as its starting point the beneficence of God, the merciful Father who extends grace even to the ungrateful and the wicked. Jesus' message thus crossed the grain of the Roman political order not only at the level of practices and attitudes but also with respect to the most basic questions about "how the world works."

What, then, is significant about the narrative setting in which Jesus interprets his death as having saving significance? On the one hand, these scenes indicate how pervasive "politics as usual" would have been, even to the point of infiltrating the inner circle of Jesus' disciples. Those who follow Jesus are not immune to the struggle for power and quest for status as measured by the standards of public opinion. The narrative cotext of the ransom saying in both Matthew and Mark features a bid for recognition and honor, in the form of requests for the two primary seats of honor, on either side of the host in the kingdom banquet, for the sons of Zebedee, James and John. The anger of the other followers of Jesus on hearing of this surreptitious bid for distinction is likewise rooted in the ancient, agonistic game of status-seeking. If James and John were granted the highest positions, what rank would be left for the others?

On the other hand, the correlation here of atonement theology and scenes displaying deep-rooted dispositions toward acquiring, claiming and maintaining relative status and power evidences the depth of Jesus' unwavering posture over against those dispositions. These qualities and the behaviors they sponsor surface throughout the Gospel tradition, and Jesus consistently censures them—for example, when he gives advice on dinner invitations and seating arrangements (Lk 14:1-24) and when he urges hospitality to the least impressive inhabitants of the Roman social world, little children (e.g., Mk 9:33-37; 10:13-16). In the ransom saying, Jesus profoundly subverts status-seeking practices.

Jesus then illustrates his teaching with reference to his own mission. Consequently, the ransom saying functions both as an example that confirms the ethic he has just proposed and as Jesus' self-disclosure of the life goal given him by God. The climax of his mission, the reason for his having "come," is this: "to give his life as a ransom for many." In other words, Jesus' death demonstrates the distance between God's ways and the ways typical of human communities. Top-down relations of power, social obligations, struggling for honor and recognition—these patterns of behavior are opposed by the cross at the most basic level.

"Ransom," or better, "means of release" (*lytron*), belongs to the semantic domain of "deliverance" or "salvation." Jesus' counsel to his quarreling disciples that they comport themselves as slaves rather than despotic rulers brings two images onto the interpretive stage. The most immediate is borrowed from the Roman slave trade, where a ransom might serve as the price of emancipation, after which the one freed belonged to the one who paid the price. The second is of at least equal, perhaps even greater importance, and derives from Israel's own past; God, it is said in the LXX, ransomed Israel. It is important for our understanding of the message of Jesus that we notice that God ransoms Israel not by "paying someone off" but by delivering the people from slavery in Egypt (Ex 6:6; 16:13).

These two overlapping images, from the slave trade and from this formative experience of Israel's life, remind us that metaphors like ransom can hold many meanings, not all of which are realized in a given context. Methodologically, one must differentiate between possible or virtual properties and actual ones.[8] In Jesus' message, for example, we hear nothing that might help us answer the question, To whom is the ransom paid? Nor do we hear him speculate on who pays the ransom. This aspect of the metaphorical range of "ransom" is not even broached. Subsequent theories of atonement that have as their centerpiece God's providing the devil with a payoff in the form of Jesus' death, or that view Jesus' death as a means of providing a ransom to the angry God or gods, may find support in the traditions of ancient Greece or even ancient Israel[9] but not in the Gospel tradition. Conceptually, the portrait Jesus provides is more akin to the servant in Isaiah, whose death is efficacious for the salvation of the many. Just as he has instructed his followers to devote their lives to the service of others, so now he reveals the purpose of his own coming in the same terms, even to the point that he will embrace death on behalf of others. In his death Jesus incarnates his own message concerning the living of life oriented toward God's purpose and thus toward the welfare of others.

Concerning the Last Supper tradition, it is significant that Luke again

---

[8]See Umberto Eco, *Semiotics and the Philosophy of Language*, AS (Bloomington: Indiana University Press, 1984), pp. 97-129.

[9]See Ceslas Spicq, *Theological Lexicon of the New Testament* (Peabody, Mass.: Hendrickson, 1994), 2:428; Jon D. Levenson, *The Death and Resurrection of the Beloved Son: The Transformation of Child Sacrifice in Judaism and Christianity* (New Haven, Conn.: Yale University Press, 1993).

portrays the disciples squabbling over relative greatness. Similarly, Paul presents the Last Supper material within an epistolary argument against factionalism within the Corinthian community. Again, then, Jesus' representation of the atoning significance of his impending death is set in a context in which it provides a stark alternative to the world system to which his followers continually fall prey. Here, in elucidating the significance of his looming death, Jesus pushed backward into Israel's history and embraced Israel's expectations for deliverance. At the table he intimated that the new exodus, God's decisive act of deliverance, was coming to fruition now, in his death, in the climax of his mission. Moreover, he developed the sense of his death in terms borrowed from the constitution of Israel as the covenant people of God (Ex 24:8), the conclusion of the exile (see Zech 9:9-11) and the hope of a renewal of the covenant (Jer 31:31-33), so as to mark his death as the inaugural event of covenant renewal. How could Jesus contemplate such thoughts? Taken together with his prophetic action in the temple, the symbolic actions at the table of Jesus' last meal with his disciples suggest that he viewed himself as the focal point of God's great act of deliverance; in his death the temple and all that it signified regarding the ordering of Israel's life were invalidated, and his own life and death were to be the basis of Israel's life before God.

We may take as axiomatic that Jesus did anticipate his death; in the charged environment of Roman Palestine how could he not have done so? To admit this is to open the door to its corollary—namely, the probability that he reflected on its significance and did so in a way that intimately related it to his mission to redeem the people of God. By this we mean, on the one hand, that Jesus was no masochist looking for an opportunity to suffer and die, but he did see that his absolute commitment to the purpose of God might lead, in the context of "this adulterous and wicked generation" (Mk 8:38), to his death. On the other hand, this means that Jesus was able to gather together Israel's history and hopes and from them forge a view of himself as the one through whose suffering Israel, and through Israel the nations, would experience divine redemption. As Ben Meyer has insisted, "Jesus did not aim to be repudiated and killed; he aimed to charge with meaning his being repudiated and killed."[10]

Where might Jesus have gone for resources to construct such a view? Attempts to find in Israel's history a "suffering messiah" figure have thus far proven fruitless, yet this does not preclude the possibility that Jesus could have pioneered this combination of images. Given what we know of Jesus, the issue is not whether we can allow for innovation on his part. We must ask instead whether the raw materials for innovation were at hand, as well as whether any proposed innovation could be understood by those around Jesus. With respect to this last question, the Gospels repeatedly witness the obtuseness of Jesus' followers in getting the connection between divine mission and shameful demise. This suggests that, even if the raw materials had been readily available, such a connection would not have been easy for even his closest followers.

With regard to the presence of interpretive resources, one can with relative ease sketch three interrelated, traditional phenomena.[11]

☐ The first is the tradition of the suffering of God's messengers, the prophets.[12] The presumed destiny of divine prophets was consistently that of rejection and death, and it is not coincidental that Jesus both identified himself in prophetic terms and presaged his solidarity with the prophets in their having been spurned and killed.

☐ The second is the tradition of the suffering righteous, with deep roots in the Scriptures of Israel and ongoing development in the Second Temple period. Again, it is not coincidental that the Synoptic Gospels portray the death of Jesus in terms that reflect the influence of the pattern of the suffering righteous one, nor that this pattern was itself shaped under the influence of Isaiah's portrayal of the suffering servant.[13]

---

[10]Ben F. Meyer, *The Aims of Jesus* (London: SCM, 1979), p. 218.

[11]For greater detail and nuance, see the related analysis in N. T. Wright, *Christian Origins and the Question of God*, vol. 2: *Jesus and the Victory of God* (Minneapolis: Fortress, 1996), pp. 576-92.

[12]See, for example, Nehemiah 9:26; Jeremiah 2:30.

[13]See especially George W. E. Nickelsburg Jr., *Resurrection, Immortality, and Eternal Life in Intertestamental Judaism*, HTS 26 (Cambridge, Mass.: Harvard University Press, 1972).

◻ Finally, one finds in significant strands of Second Temple Judaism the promise that the restoration of Israel as a people was related fundamentally to Israel's reconciliation with God and that Israel's deliverance would come by means of great suffering.[14]

Here then are the raw materials from within Israel's own story and traditions for the construction of a soteriology in which affliction might be understood not only as a condition from which to be delivered but also as the means by which deliverance might come.

Imagining the ensuing theology of atonement as a quilt will help to qualify this interpretation of the Gospel material in three ways. First, as has already become clear, many pieces of patchwork from the story of Israel and its traditions have been stitched together with Jesus' career to form one whole, with the result that these two stories, Israel's and Jesus', become mutually interpreting. Second, the redemptive interpretation of Jesus' death does not depend on one image, one scriptural text or one particular cord of Jewish tradition. Although the concept of atonement in the Gospels points to the efficacy of Jesus' death in redemption, its content remains amorphous, especially when compared to the more developed Pauline notions of sacrifice, redemption, reconciliation and justification, and to the manifold theories of atonement developed in subsequent Christian theology. In other words, the line from the scant evidence for an atonement message in Jesus' own words to the later atonement theories of Anselm or Luther is neither straight nor easily drawn.

Third, and perhaps most important, we do not need to insist that Jesus bequeathed this interpretive quilt to his followers in completed form. We may perceive creativity and innovation on Jesus' part in drawing together material stamped with the divine purpose and with suffering and repulsive death, while leaving room for Jesus' followers to add even more mate-

---

[14]That is, the suffering of the righteous would be regarded as the means by which the people might be forgiven—see Dale C. Allison Jr., *The End of the Ages Has Come: An Early Interpretation of the Passion and Resurrection of Jesus* (Philadelphia: Fortress, 1985), pp. 5-25; Max Turner, *Power from on High: The Spirit in Israel's Restoration and Witness in Luke-Acts*, JPSSup 9 (Sheffield: Sheffield Academic Press, 1996), pp. 119-37.

rial, more colors, more squares to the cloth. The Gospels themselves suggest that this was so when they show the difficulty with which Jesus' followers came to understand his reflections on these intertwined motifs.

One more aspect of this portrait of the saving significance of Jesus' death needs to be made plain. *This is its orientation to the salvation of the people of God, not simply to the salvation of individuals.* The modern tendency to separate the religious and the political leads inevitably to an anachronistic sundering of "forgiveness of sins" and "restoration of the people." In Second Temple Judaism, however, these two could not have been separated, and Jesus could not have aimed to renew Israel without raising the issue of how forgiveness was to be gained. His mission as this is known to us in the Gospels is directed toward revitalizing Israel as the people of God. Pursuing this aim compelled him to proclaim and embody an ethic grounded in divine dispositions and brought him into conflict with the conveyers of Roman and Jewish religious and political worldviews and practices. It led him to a form of execution emblematic of a way of life that rejected the value of public opinion in the determination of status before God and inspired interpretations of his death that highlighted the redemptive power of righteous suffering.

Paul and the Saving Significance of the Death of Christ

As rare as talk of the salvific meaning of the cross might be in the Gospels, the opposite is true of the Pauline letters. Paul turns repeatedly to the cross, often interpreting its significance as atoning. To speak of atonement theology in Paul is to bring a number of intimately related issues onto the table, in addition to the cross itself. These include the nature of God according to Paul, the human condition and the character of "divine wrath." What is more, for Paul, the concept of "atonement" actually comprises a constellation of images—each with its own integrity, even when correlated with others. In this section we must touch on all of these matters. At the outset, though, we need to address in a provisional way the importance of the concept of "sacrifice"—an issue to which we first turn, then return in our discussion of the saving significance of the death of Christ in Paul.

Sacrifice and Paul's World

What is Paul's approach to the atonement? Answers to this question typically build on important, though often undeveloped, presuppositions about Paul's world of thought. First, it is generally assumed that Paul's theological categories were grounded in Jewish thought and that Jewish thought in some significant sense was concerned with sacrifice for sins. Accordingly, for Paul, Jesus' death is best interpreted in sacrificial terms. While we may agree that Paul is best read against the horizons provided by Second Temple Judaism, this does not detract from the need additionally to inquire into how Paul's more pervasively Gentile audiences, scattered around the Mediterranean, might have heard his speech about the significance of Jesus' death. It is another thing, too, simply to assume that the determinative narrative for ordering God-human relations was or must be grounded in the notion of sacrifice for sins.

For example, we have already seen that, with respect to the portrait of Jesus in the Synoptic Gospels, the two most clear references to the atoning death of Jesus are determined elsewhere than in a soteriological scheme grounded in ancient Jewish ideas of sacrifice for sins. The controlling images found in both the ransom saying and the words of Jesus at the Last Supper derive from reflection on the exodus story. The most prominent echoes of Israel's past, then, would center not on the problem of sins per se—nor, then, on the need for a sacrifice to cover sins. What is at stake, rather, are images of deliverance, the generation of the community of God's people and the delineation of the identity of that community.

It is true, of course, that in the Matthean version of the Last Supper, Jesus speaks of "my blood of the covenant, which is poured out for many for the forgiveness of sins" (Matt 26:28). The primary point here is the metaphorical affirmation of the basis of the covenant with God in Jesus' violent, sacrificial death.[15] As Moses made a sacrifice for the people in order that they might enter into the divine covenant (Ex 24:8), so Jesus ratifies the covenant by offering up his life. Jewish tradition had already made the link between Moses' "covenant" sacrifice and atonement; for example, an early, interpretive translation of Exodus 24:6-8 reads:

> And Moses took half of the blood and set it in basins, and half the blood he sprinkled upon the altar. He took the Book of the Covenant of the Law and read before the people; and they said, "All of the words that the Lord has spoken we will perform and obey." Then Moses took the blood and sprinkled it upon the altar to atone for the people, and said, "Behold, this is the blood of the covenant that the Lord has made with you upon all of these words."[16]

Evidently the path from "covenant sacrifice" to "forgiveness of sins" had already been blazed, though it is of interest that this path was not taken by Mark, Luke or Paul, at least not so explicitly, in their records of the words spoken at the Last Supper.

Moreover, not all, nor even most, sacrifices, whether in the Old Testament or in Second Temple Judaism, were "for sins," nor was sacrifice the exclusive way to deal with sin. The purpose for which sacrifices were to be offered in ancient Israel is not always specified clearly. When it is, thanksgiving, worship, communion with God and feasting function as category headings alongside atonement for sin. Even "sin offerings," as they are usually translated, need not be related to "sin"—at least not as we would think of sin—but rather might relate to religious impurity, including that brought about by, for example, menstruation or nocturnal emission. And the prophetic tradition repeatedly accentuates contrition and acts of justice over against the cult of sacrificial practices (e.g., Is 1:10-20).

However one reads the significance of sacrifice in the Jewish temple in

---

[15]This affirmation is "metaphorical" because the outpouring of blood is neither a central nor even necessary feature of death by crucifixion.
[16]*Tg. Ps.-J.* Ex 24:8; similarly, *Tg. Onq.*

Judaism in the first century, then, two points are clear. First, animal sacrifices were not the only means by which right relations with God might be restored or maintained—a reality that comes into sharp focus in the vitality of Judaism following the demise of the temple in A.D. 70. If it is true that selected passages in Israel's Scriptures had already criticized and in some cases abandoned the sacrificial system,[17] it may well be that Israel found in its own history the capacity to survive and thrive with no (literal) altar of sacrifice at all. Forgiveness grounded in penitential prayer, repentance and acts of charity would, in developing rabbinic Judaism, not only replace the now-razed temple but actually render the sacrificial altar obsolete. But this innovation, however extraordinary it might at first appear, was presaged in the psalmic and prophetic tradition of Israel's Scriptures and in such expressions of Second Temple Judaism as the Jewish sect at Qumran.[18]

Second, many sacrifices offered in the temple—indeed, most sacrifices that were offered in the temple—had nothing to do with sinful activity consciously committed or with its consequences. This is not to detract from the atoning significance of the sin offering and guilt offerings, for which Leviticus 4—5 supplies the repeated litany of interpretation: "In this way, the priest will make atonement on his behalf for his sins, and he shall be forgiven" (Lev 4:26, 31, 35; 5:10, 16, 18). The map of Israel's sacrificial system is more complex than even the designation "sin offering" might suggest. Although, for example, a sacrificial offering might be made

---

[17]See Johannes Behm, "θύω κτλ.," in *TDNT*, 3:183.

[18]This is not to say that one finds in the prophets or subsequent literature an outright rejection of the temple. What is at issue, typically, is the legitimacy of the priesthood or the degree to which sacrificial offerings genuinely represented personal or communal dispositions. For example, Isaiah 66:3 reads, "Whoever slaughters an ox is like one who kills a human being; whoever sacrifices a lamb, like one who breaks a dog's neck; whoever presents a grain offering, like one who offers swine's blood; whoever makes a memorial offering of frankincense, like who one blesses an idol" (NRSV). For the author, the practices of the priesthood in Jerusalem had resulted in an illegitimate sacrificial system. Similarly at Qumran, though one finds a rejection of the validity of the sanctuary in Jerusalem and a refusal to participate in its rites of worship, the temple (or the idea of the temple—cf. 11QTS, which sketches the plans for a new temple [also 5Q15]) was not beyond rehabilitation; until the rededication (or rebuilding) of the temple, however, true worship was to be offered within the Qumran community (e.g., 1QS 8.8-9; 9.4-5).

so that a woman who had recently given birth might be pronounced ritually clean (see Lk 2:22; see also Lev 12)—and in this way she would be restored to her relationship with God—this hardly broaches the need for atonement as this need is usually articulated today.

In this context it is worth reflecting briefly on the motivations of those outside the Jewish faith who made pilgrimage to the Jerusalem temple, an activity for which there is wide-ranging evidence during our period. "Proselytes" and "God fearers," of course, given their own social and religious proclivities, would have come to Jerusalem for their own reasons. What of those who had no particular or special devotion to the God of Israel? In the ancient Roman world it was not uncommon that a prestigious foreign deity might be "summoned" in the case of tragedies or simply pacified through homage and sacrifice.

Indeed, for Romans the gods were, so to speak, companions or fellow participants in the stuff of common life; consequently, city structures included provision of personnel to maintain good relations with the gods. Magistrates had cultic responsibilities in their own cities. Among Greeks and Romans, then, sacrifices were offered in recognition of the supremacy of the gods and in exchange for their favors. Walter Burkert refers to this function of worship as "crisis management." Although he is aware that, in ancient Greece, sacrificial rites fostered fellowship among the worshipers who shared in the sacrificial meal, he also recognizes that "adversity teaches prayer."

> All the great crises that leave men helpless even when united may be interpreted as caused by the wrath of the Stronger Ones, gods and heroes: bad harvests and infertility of the soil, diseases of men and cattle, barrenness of women and abnormal offspring, civil wars and defeat by a foreign army. Conversely, if these powers are appeased, all kinds of blessings must return, rich harvests, healthy children, and civil order. The traditional means to secure the one and prevent the other are sacrifice and prayer, especially in the form of vows.[19]

---

[19]Walter Burkert, *Greek Religion* (Cambridge, Mass.: Harvard University Press, 1985), p. 264.

This does not mean that the Gentiles among whom Paul proclaimed, and to whom he wrote, concerning the cross of Christ were well-prepared culturally for this message. Greek and Roman mythology and drama had included portraits of heroic self-giving and human sacrifice on behalf of one's city, for example, but in Paul's day such representations would have appeared barbaric, excessive.[20] Paul himself could write of the ridiculous character of the cross, when viewed from the perspective of the Greco-Roman world (1 Cor 1:18-25). It does mean, however, that Paul's Gentile audiences were likely to read the story of the cross with certain guiding presuppositions. Chief among these would have been the arbitrariness of the gods, whose anger must be turned away and whose benefits must be sought. It is puzzling that many of our American readers share these same assumptions about God—in spite of the fact that neither the Scriptures of Israel nor Paul himself supports this view.

The Graciousness of God

Whatever meaning atonement might have, it would be a grave error to imagine that it focused on assuaging God's anger or winning God's merciful attention. One by one, the stories of human rebellion in Genesis 3—11 (Adam and Eve, Cain and Abel, Noah and the ark, Babel) indicate that the human proclivity toward sin is not matched by God's withdrawal. Rather, God draws near to see what humankind has done and does pronounce judgment, but then, in gracious optimism and mercy, tries again. The Scriptures as a whole provide no ground for a portrait of an angry God needing to be appeased in atoning sacrifice.

One line of thought must suffice to ground this assertion. Chief among the qualities of Yahweh in both Old and New Testaments is his graciousness. One notable witness to this characterization of God is the self-revelation of God in Exodus 34:6-7:

---

[20]So Martin Hengel, *The Atonement: The Origins of the Doctrine in the New Testament* (Philadelphia: Fortress, 1981), pp. 1-32.

The LORD, the LORD,
a God merciful and gracious,
slow to anger,
and abounding in steadfast love
  and faithfulness,
keeping steadfast love for the
  thousandth generation,
forgiving iniquity and
  transgression and sin,
yet by no means clearing the
  guilty.

The importance of this pronouncement is underscored first by its status as Yahweh's self-revelation and second by its numerous reappearances in the Scriptures (Num 14:17-19; Deut 5:9-10; 7:9-13; 2 Chr 30:9; Neh 9:17-19, 31-32; Ps 77:9-10; 86:5, 15; 103:8-12, 17-18; 111:4; 116:5; 145:8-9; Joel 2:12-14; Jon 3:10—4:3). A series of important affirmations flow from this confession, the most basic being that God's graciousness is foundational to his character; hence, it outlasts his wrath and spills over in abundance in activity that saves and sustains life. It is significant, too, that Yahweh thus attributes "steadfast love and faithfulness" to himself in the immediate aftermath of the episode involving the golden calf (Ex 32). This points to the persistent, everlasting quality of the love he lavishes on his people, even when rebuffed by humanity. God's graciousness is thus neither rooted in nor dependent on people's prior acts or presumed responses, nor subject to human calculation. God's gracious acts grow out of his own dispositions, and he can be graciously disposed even toward the unrighteous (see Jon 4:2, 11; Lk 6:35-36).

The whole of salvation rests on God's initiative, the single source of salvation is God, and God's salvific purpose comes to expression in the one event of grace, the redemptive act of Christ—one finds such pivotal affirmations as these in Paul. For James, God is the giver of every perfect gift; God's generosity extends above all to those who are poor according to worldly standards (Jas 1:5, 17-18; 2:5; 4:6; cf. Prov 3:34; 1 Pet 5:5). The epistles of John emphasize both the priority and primacy of God's love and its implications for morality: "God is love," John writes (1 Jn 4:16), summarizing the essence of the portrayal of the gracious God in Scripture.

Human Sin and the Wrath of God

What, then, of the "wrath" of God? In ancient and classical Greek literature, the gods were often characterized by a certain arbitrariness of personality and action, and were prone to anger, grudge and punishment. Against this backdrop it is not surprising to see human acts of worship aimed at mitigating divine acrimony or winning divine consent. The gods, it would seem, required to be pampered. This was in spite of the reality that, for many in the classical and Roman periods, emotions and rationality were polarized; if "wrath" might easily be understood as mindless rage, it is not easy to see how human acts aimed at second-guessing the gods so as to appease their anger might have utility. Can whimsical anger or pleasure be manipulated? Nevertheless, in similar fashion, it is not uncommon to find among our contemporaries persons who live under the threat or wrestle regularly with images of God becoming angry. Undoubtedly the widespread popularity of penal substitutionary atonement is built in part on the base of human fear of God, combined with the perceived necessity of placating an emotion-laden God ever on the verge of striking out against any who disobey his every will.

In spite of popular views of "the Old Testament God," divine wrath in the Old Testament is not well represented by views of this kind. The wrath of God is present, of course, and when it is present, it is typically a response to Israel's failure to maintain the covenant and is presented as a corollary of God's righteousness. God's "personality" is not one quickly or impulsively given to anger or retribution. Rather, he is "slow to anger and abounding in steadfast love" (e.g., Ex 34:6; Num 14:18). In fact, Old Testament scholars today continue to debate in what sense it is appropriate to attribute anger to God in any way other than metaphorical. That is, given our limited vantage point as human beings (and so the human perspectives from which the books of the Old Testament were written), perhaps we attribute "anger" to God only because we have no language other than human language with which to comprehend God."[21]

In any case, clearly, for Paul, wrath is not a divine property or essential attribute of God.[22] As he develops this concept in Romans 1, "wrath" is, rather, the active presence of God's judgment toward "all ungodliness and wickedness" (Rom 1:18). The wrath of God is not vindictive indignation or the anger of divine retribution, but the divine response to human unfaithfulness. God's wrath may be future, eschatological (Rom 2:5, 8; 1 Thess 1:10; 5:9; Col 3:6), but it is also already present, for God is now handing people over to experience the consequences of the sin they choose (Rom 1:18, 24, 26, 28; cf. Wis 11:15-16; 12:23). In what sense, then, can Paul speak of the "wrath to come"? What does it mean for human beings to be rescued from the coming wrath, as 1 Thessalonians 1:9-10 has it? Even in this context, divine anger or retributive justice are alien concepts, since these assume that something in God's own self must be altered (i.e., his anger transformed into love) or that God's sense of holiness must be requited. Paul's point lies elsewhere, however, in the need for human transformation. The wrath to come refers to the climactic, end-time scene of judgment when those who prefer to worship idols rather than the living God receive the fruits of their own misplaced hopes and commitments.

In Romans 1:18-32, Paul's anthropology comes into special focus in a way that sheds light not only on the human condition but also on the Pauline notion of divine wrath. Here *sin* (in the broad sense; the language Paul uses in 1:18 is *ungodliness* and *unrighteousness*) is identified not with individual acts of wickedness but with a general disposition to refuse to

---

[21]See Jan Bergman and Elsie Johnson, "Πνὰφ," in *TDOT*, 1:348-60; Gary A. Heron, "Wrath of God (OT)," in *ABD*, 6:989-96.

[22]The following represents an expansion of Joel B. Green, "Death of Christ," in *DPL*, pp. 201-9.

honor God as God and to render him thanks. Sin is the proclivity to act as though things created, including ourselves, were the Creator. To sin, then, is to turn away from authentic human existence by turning away from God.

Four aspects of Paul's reflections in this passage need to be sketched. First, Paul is not giving the autobiography of individual persons; he is not bent on outlining how each person in his or her own experience comes to be implicated in sin. Instead, his is a universalistic presentation, a diagnosis of the condition of the human family taken as a whole (cf. Rom 3:9). Second, the acts of wickedness that Paul goes on to enumerate by way of illustration are not themselves *the* problem. Lust, gossip, envy, deceit, same-sex relations, rebelliousness toward parents, and the rest—these are expressions of *sin*. Third, within the fabric of Paul's argument, these activities are themselves already expressions of the wrath of God. They evidence the moral integrity of a God who takes *sin* seriously. It is this, God's moral character, that Paul is defending here, and he does so by showing the progression from (1) the human refusal to honor God, with its consequent denial of the human vocation to live in relation to God; to (2) God's giving humanity over to its own desires—giving humanity, as it were, the life it sought apart from God; and from this to (3) human acts of wickedness—which do not arouse the wrath of God but are themselves already the consequences of its active presence.

To put it pointedly, here Paul has nothing to do with an emotion-laden God who strikes out in frustration or vengeance against we who are implicated in sin. Sinful activity is the result of God's letting us go our own way—and this "letting us go our own way" constitutes God's wrath. In Paul's own words, the wrath of God is revealed in God's giving humanity over to their lusts, over to their degrading passions and over to their debasement of mind (Rom 1:18, 24, 26, 28). Or to use language from another Jewish writing from roughly this period, God "torments" those who live unrighteously by allowing them their own atrocities (Wis 12:23). *Our sinful acts do not invite God's wrath but prove that God's wrath is already active.*

Finally, for Paul, *sin* marks a rupture in the divine-human relationship, but it also manifests itself in human relations and in relations between humanity and the material creation. *Sin* in this broad sense can never be understood as something private or individualistic, for it always manifests itself in relation to others and to the cosmos (see Rom 1:26-32). Clearly, then, the soteriological effects of Jesus' death must be understood in relational, communal and even cosmological terms.

What is more, Paul recognizes that ungodliness and unrighteousness have as their object their own self-legitimation: humanity embraces a lie (Rom 1:25) and receives a corrupt mind (Rom 1:28), with the consequence that it defines its unjust ways as just. Consequently, it is small wonder that Paul's preaching of and identification with the cross would excite opposition and misunderstanding. A humanity that has turned against itself as it turned against God will not easily sanction so revolutionary a reordering of the world as would be required by this exposition of the crucified Christ.

Paul's portrait of God is not that of an angry deity requiring mollification. Divine wrath is not an affective quality or "feeling" on the part of God. Rather, it is a means of underscoring how seriously God takes sin. The righteousness of God is effective in the present to save, but as men and women resist it, they experience God's righteousness as condemnation. Whatever else can be made of Paul's understanding of the death of Jesus, his theology of the cross lacks any developed sense of divine retribution. Quite the contrary, according to such texts as Romans 5:6-8, the death of Christ is the ultimate expression of the boundless love of God: "But God demonstrates his love for us in that while we were still sinners Christ died for us" (Rom 5:8).

Within its context, this affirmation in Romans 5 brings to the fore three crucial declarations that help us to gain even better perspective on Paul's theology of the cross. First, the love of God for humanity is immeasurable, for there are no human parallels by which to plumb its depths. Even though someone might dare to die on behalf of a righteous person

(Rom 5:7), Christ died for "the ungodly" (Rom 5:6), for "sinners" (Rom 5:8), for "enemies" of God (Rom 5:10). Second, Paul's audience can be certain that their suffering (cf. Rom 5:1-5) has significance because the suffering of Christ has proven to be so meaningful. Through his death "we have been *justified*," "*saved* from the wrath of God," "*reconciled* to God" (Rom 5:9-11). In the midst of our impotence, Christ took on the measure of our powerlessness and died in our place; as a result of his death, we share in his life, *and* we find that our own suffering has significance.

Third, in a crucial though perhaps unexpected turn of phrase (Rom 5:8), we are told that *God* demonstrates his love by means of what *Christ* did. We might have anticipated that God's love would be manifest best in God's own deed. This would certainly be the case if Paul were sketching an atonement theology oriented toward divine recrimination, since in this case the cross would be nothing more or less than a divine lashing out against Jesus (rather than against all of humanity). Paul's way of putting things, however, certifies that "Christ's death does not merely express his own sentiment, . . . but God's; or to put it another way, God's stance toward the world is quintessentially demonstrated in the action of Christ."[23] In the end we find in Pauline discourse the unrelenting affirmation of the oneness of purpose and activity of God and God's Son in the cross. Thus any atonement theology that assumes, against Paul, that in the cross God did something "to" Jesus is not only an affront to the Christian doctrine of the triune God but also misrepresents Paul's clear affirmation in Romans 5.

At the same time, as we have seen, the priority of God's initiative in Paul's thought does not completely overshadow his understanding of the need for atonement from the human side of the equation. Quite the contrary, Paul's orientation toward God serves to introduce the sharp contrast Paul sees between God and humanity—that is, between the

---

[23]Charles B. Cousar, *A Theology of the Cross: The Death of Jesus in the Pauline Letters*, OBT (Minneapolis: Fortress, 1990), p. 45.

faithfulness of God and human unfaithfulness (e.g., cf. Rom 1:17-18). Paul's portrait of humanity "before Christ" is that of persons, collectively and individually, ensnared in sin, enslaved to powers from which they are impotent to escape.

Images of Atonement

In explicating the significance of Jesus' crucifixion, Paul never seems to tire of adding new images to his repertoire. In fact, Paul tailors his representation of the significance of the death of Jesus to the needs of his audience in particular circumstances. Given what we have just seen, this is not surprising. Paul needs to communicate not only that salvation has come in the cross of Christ but also how this act of atonement pulls the rug out from under the way we typically organize the world and our lives in the world. Of the several dozen metaphors Paul employs to lay bare the benefits of the death of Christ, only a handful can be mentioned here. These are conveniently assembled in two Pauline texts: 2 Corinthians 5:14—6:2 and Galatians 3:10-14.

An examination of the presentation of the effects of Jesus' death in 2 Corinthians 5:14—6:2 underscores the degree to which the various categories by which Paul drew out the significance of the cross overlap with one another. Even though *reconciliation* stands at the center of this passage (2 Cor 5:18-20), other categories are mentioned as well: *vicarious substitution* ("for us," 2 Cor 5:14, 15), *representation* (2 Cor 5:14, 21) or *interchange*,[24] *sacrifice* (2 Cor 5:21),[25] *justification* (implicitly, 2 Cor 5:19, 21), *forgiveness* (2 Cor 5:19), and *new creation* (2 Cor 5:16-17). Moreover, the cross and resurrection of Christ appear in tandem as salvific events (2 Cor 5:15).

Reconciliation as a term is not found very often in the Pauline corpus.

---

[24]See Morna D. Hooker, "Interchange and Atonement," *BJRL* 60 (1978): 462-81; "Interchange in Christ," *JTS* 22 (1974): 349-61; and more recently, *Not Ashamed of the Gospel: New Testament Interpretations of the Death of Christ* (Grand Rapids, Mich.: Eerdmans, 1994), pp. 20-46.

[25]See James D. G. Dunn, "Paul's Understanding of the Death of Jesus as Sacrifice," in *Sacrifice and Redemption: Durham Essays in Theology*, ed. S. W. Sykes (Cambridge: Cambridge University Press, 1991), pp. 35-56.

Apart from this passage it appears in Romans 5:10-11 with reference to the reconciliation of humanity to God, Colossians 1:20 with reference to the reconciliation of the cosmos to God, and in Ephesians 2:16 with reference to the reconciliation of both Jew and Gentile to God and one another. Whether Ephesians is judged to have been written by Paul, its message at this juncture is clearly Pauline, for this notion of "restored relationship" in Paul consistently embraces the dynamic presence of love active to restore the divine-human relationship and both to call for and to enable persons to exhibit toward one another this same restoration. Moreover, especially in 2 Corinthians and Colossians, the work of reconciliation is extended to the entire creation.

Importantly, Paul does not speak here of any need for mutual reconciliation. "The world" is estranged from God and needs to be brought back into relationship with God. God, however, is not estranged from "the world." For this reason, Paul has no need to show how God can be appeased, how God might be empowered to love again, how God might overcome having been so often scorned and so on. "God was in Christ, reconciling the world to himself"—this affirmation demonstrates that God's love has the upper hand in divine-human relations and that the work of Christ had as its effect the bringing of "the world" back to God (and not vice versa). This is supported by verse 17, wherein it is evident that the death of Christ has as its further effect the miracle of new creation. God has not been "made over," for the difficulty does not lie at his feet. Rather, "the world" needs this "make over," and this is what the cross accomplishes.

In 2 Corinthians 5, Paul's choice of terminology and logic of argumentation is context-specific. He has chosen his words carefully. Paul's need is to counter the triumphalistic boasting of his opponents at Corinth as well as to overcome the disharmony between himself and his "children" at Corinth. Rooting the message of reconciliation fundamentally in the sacrificial death of Jesus and asserting that reconciliation entails living no longer for oneself but for Christ (and thus for others), he addresses his first aim. His impassioned appeal to the Corinthians to be reconciled to God (2 Cor 5:20; 6:1-2), followed by an affirmation of his own open-handedness to the Corinthians (2 Cor 6:11-13; 7:2), deals with the second.

Similarly, Galatians 3:10-14 consists of a combination of images or theological categories by which Paul expounds the salvific character of the cross of Christ. The larger unit, Galatians 3:1-14, contends that the Galatians' experience of receiving the Spirit by faith signified the fulfillment of God's promise to bless the Gentiles through Abraham, and this fulfillment was made possible through the death of Christ. The benefits of the death of Christ are presented in Galatians 3:10-14 through a fusion of images: Christ as the *representative* of Israel in whose death the *covenant* reaches its climax;[26] *justification* (Gal 3:11); *redemption* (Gal 3:13), evoking exodus and exilic themes (cf. the corollary of *adoption* in Gal 3:26-29); *substitution* ("for us," Gal 3:13); *sacrifice* (implicitly, Gal 3:13); the *promise of the Spirit* (Gal 3:14); and the *triumph over the powers.*

As in 2 Corinthians 5, here Paul has also chosen his categories carefully. At this juncture in his argument with those Galatian Christians who are enamored with legal observance, Paul needs to overcome the obvious problem of the fundamental distinction between Jew and Gentile—a distinction that centered on the status of the *law-abiding* Jew in contrast to the *law-less* Gentile. Such a distinction had already caused Peter and Barnabas, along with other Jewish Christians, to withdraw from table fellowship with Gentiles, according to Galatians 2:11-14. And Paul writes as though it were a commonplace among the Galatian Christians that distinctions were made on the basis of who was circumcised (e.g., Gal 5:11-12; 6:11-16). Gentiles, in this way of thinking, lived under the divine curse as persons outside the law; how could they share equally in the blessings of Abraham? Paul's first answer, as shocking as it might have

---

[26]See N. T. Wright, *The Climax of the Covenant: Christ and the Law in Pauline Theology* (Minneapolis: Fortress, 1991), pp. 137-56.

seemed to Jewish Christians, was that those who use the law to drive a wedge between Jews and Gentiles have abused the law and, therefore, fall under the same curse as that assumed to accrue to Gentiles on account of their lawlessness. With the playing field now leveled—with both Gentile and Jew equally the objects of divine curse—the question remains, how can anyone participate in the blessings of Abraham? Paul's answer focuses our attention on the crucifixion of Jesus. Borrowing the imagery of Deuteronomy 21:22-23, he writes that Jesus has in his crucifixion borne the curse of God—he has been placed outside the community of God's covenant. More than this, he has done so "on our behalf"—in his death he has enacted the destiny of a humanity alienated from God, thus exhausting the power of the law to segregate people from the covenant. It is not accidental that, in constructing his argument, Paul refers to "Christ" bearing the "curse," for this places in provocative juxtaposition two profoundly contradictory images: the one "anointed by God" is the one "cursed by God." If Jesus has identified with humanity in having been placed outside the covenant of God's people as one who bears the divine curse, his divine "anointing" signifies the acceptance of the "outsider," both Jew and Gentile.

Here we have a specimen of Paul's ongoing reflection on Israel and particularly his inclusion of believing Gentiles in the "Israel of God" (Gal 6:10). For Paul, believers share in the benefits of the new creation and are counted as the people of God because of their inclusion in the salvific work of Christ. As Paul acknowledges, "I have been crucified with Christ. It is no longer I who live, but Christ who lives in me" (Gal 2:19-20). Even if the eschatological role of Israel in Pauline thought is not thus settled, it is nonetheless apparent that the death of Christ marks the new aeon in which Gentiles may be embraced, in Christ, as children of Abraham.

The sheer diversity of interpretive categories or images used in these two Pauline passages to describe the significance of Jesus' death heralds something of the plethora of images we might have mentioned from within the Pauline letters. Indeed, Paul makes use of a rich variety of metaphors by way of comprehending the cross and encouraging both understanding and response among his varied audiences. This multiplicity raises a caution against moving too quickly to positing for Paul a single (or any one as *the* central) theory of the atonement or interpretation of Jesus' passion.

Reflection on these two representative texts in 2 Corinthians and Galatians raises another issue of importance in Paul's theology of the cross—namely, Paul's apocalyptic horizon. The cross has cosmic repercussions. This is the importance of the use of such language as "new creation" in 2 Corinthians 5:17 and Galatians 6:15. These texts must be understood not as in some modern translations as individual-focused ("If anyone is in Christ, that person is a new creation!"—cf., e.g., NIV, NASB). Instead, Paul's words signify the role of Jesus' death in the termination of the old epoch and the presentation of the new ("If anyone is in Christ, there is a new creation!"—e.g., NRSV, NCV). Galatians 3:10-14 points similarly to the death of Jesus as the defeat of the powers—a motif that emerges also in Ephesians 2:14-15. In this letter, the law appears as a barrier separating Jew and Gentile, and the death of Christ abolishes this "dividing wall." In Galatians, however, the law is characterized more as a force, like the elemental spirits of this world, holding the Jewish people captive (Gal 4:1, 3). In a context-specific way, Paul insists that the death of Christ has triumphed—not by denying the law but by demonstrating its validity and executing the blessing of the covenant.

Elsewhere in Paul's writings we continue to read that the death of Christ marks the end of the rule of the apocalyptic powers (e.g., Col 2:15) and deliverance "from the present evil age" (Gal 1:4). In Colossians this is the result not of the annihilation of the powers but of their restoration to their purpose in creation. Stripped of the garments of their dominion (Col 2:15), they have been reconciled by the instrumentality of Jesus' death on the cross (Col 1:20). The intrusion of the new world into contemporary life has for Paul far-reaching consequences for those who would follow the crucified Christ and embody in their lives together the new creation revealed in the cross. Old ways of relating to one another (e.g., boasting in a continuous game of one-upmanship in the service of status-seeking) and of drawing lines between Jew and Gentile, slave and free, male and female are shown to be just that—old, out of date and thus condemned (cf., e.g., Gal 3:26-29; Philem).

The Death of Jesus as Sacrifice

Reflection on these two representative texts, 2 Corinthians 5:14—6:2 and Galatians 3:10-14, also suggests the importance for Paul of the imagery of sacrifice borrowed from within the history of the covenant of God with Israel. Elsewhere Paul can refer to the death of Christ as a *hilastērion*—that is, the "mercy seat" or cover of the ark of the covenant (Rom 3:25). It was here that the sacrificial blood was sprinkled annually on the Day of Atonement, so that atonement might be made for the people (Lev 16).[27] Also in Romans, Paul apparently thinks of the death of Jesus in terms borrowed from legislation concerning the sin offering in Leviticus 5:6-7, 11: "God sent his own son in the likeness of sinful humanity—that is, as a sin offering *(peri hamartias)*, and he condemned sin in sinful humanity" (Rom 8:3). The sacrifice thus offered by Jesus is understood by Paul to entail the final solution to the problem of the human bias toward sin. This does not mean that Paul thinks of Christ's having been punished by execution on the cross so as to satisfy the rancor of God.[28] What is at stake is the mediation of restored relationships, the mediation of God's holy presence among those whose holiness is lacking. In Israel's Scriptures, one formidable medium for accomplishing restoration was sacrifice, and it is within the matrix of the Old Testament conception of sacrifice that Paul develops the substitutionary nature of the cross of Christ.

---

[27]On Romans 3:25, see further, chapter four.

[28]See the helpful discussion in Stephen H. Travis, "Christ as Bearer of Divine Judgment in Paul's Thought About the Atonement," in *Jesus of Nazareth: Lord and Christ: Essays on the Historical Jesus and New Testament Christology*, ed. Joel B. Green and Max Turner (Grand Rapids, Mich.: Eerdmans, 1994), pp. 332-45.

The rationale for the sacrificial system in Israel is not worked out fully in the Old Testament and may forever elude our full comprehension. That is, although Israel's Scriptures provide great detail regarding how to offer sacrifices and when, they do little to explain the mechanics of how sacrifices "work." James Dunn has argued that the notion of "identification" or "representation" is basic. That is, the sin offering in some way came to represent the sinners in their sin. Thus, by laying hands on the beast's head in the ritual of sacrifice, sinners identified themselves with the beast, indicating that the beast now represented the sinner *in his or her sin* (i.e., *qua* sinner); the same may be said of other ritual actions, such as sprinkling the blood of the animal on the people on whose behalf the sacrifice is offered or placing the blood of the sacrificed on their ear lobes, right thumb and right big toe (e.g., Ex 24:8; 29:10, 15, 19-20; Lev 3:2, 8, 13; 14:14). In God's sacrificial economy, Israelites were allowed to do to their animals what they were not to do to themselves or their children. This reminder of God's capacity to forgive human failure is grounded in the metaphoric relationship between Israel and the herds and flocks that the sacrificial system takes for granted. Therein, the sinner's sin was identified with the beast, and its life became forfeit—"Just as Christ, taking the initiative from the other side, identified himself with [human beings] in their fallenness (Rom. 8:3), and was made sin (2 Cor. 5:21)."[29]

This logic introduces Christ's dual role in his death—his substitution *for humanity* before God and in the face of God's justice, but also his substitution *for God* in the face of human sin. The language of representation to assist our understanding of substitution is not designed to deny the sense of Christ's having achieved something objective in his death. Indeed, according to Paul, Christ gave himself up for us *so that* we might live in him (cf. Rom 8:3-4; 14:9; 2 Cor 5:15, 21; 1 Thess 5:9-10). As significant as the theme of participation in Christ's death (and resurrection) is for Paul (cf., e.g., Phil 3:10), the possibility

---

[29]Dunn, "Paul's Understanding," p. 44.

of such participation is grounded in his first dying "for us."

Paul and the Significance of Jesus' Death

Here, then, lies the crux of Paul's interest in the cross: at the intersection of the objective reality of the cross as saving event and the subjective means by which he comprehends and communicates that reality. By "subjective" we do not mean "impressionistic" or "individualistic"; rather, we want to draw attention to the context-specific ways in which Paul has chosen to articulate the nature of his atonement theology. Taking seriously this subjective dimension of Paul's message, we should not be tempted to confuse the various metaphors he uses for describing the death of Jesus and its effects—sacrifice, for example, or justification—with the actuality of the atonement.

In order to understand better the profundity of Paul's message—as well as the depth of Paul's challenge to our own contemporary discourse concerning the cross—it may be helpful to return briefly to 2 Corinthians 5:16-17. Here Paul outlines the world-order change made effective in Christ's death. "New creation" is the phrase Paul uses to mark the cosmic shift he envisages on account of the advent of Christ. Previously, Paul admits, he thought of Christ "from a human point of view," unenlightened, determined by the old order of things. Now, however, Paul says, "We no longer know him in that way." "Look! Everything has become new!" This commentary on the cross points to the rhetorical edge of Paul's cross talk. The cross-as-atonement is an invitation to salvation, to be sure. But it also defines the nature of salvation and the life of salvation. And the life of salvation is as distinct from former ways of living as the humiliation and folly of the cross is bizarre according to normal patterns of thought. Paul's message underscores more than the objective side of the atonement. He is after a conversion of the imagination, a transformation of ideals and perceptions, and a resocialization into a new community of reference and faithfulness. By means of his "word of the cross" he hopes to induct his audiences into a way of living, into a community that is cruciform. He wants, through his preaching, whether oral or written, to decimate those ideals, norms, values and behaviors that stand in conflict with the community of God's people oriented around the cross of Christ. The word of the cross undermines all other words.

As he moves from community to community, Paul weaves a theological language that moves between the story of Israel as this is reflected in and interpreted by the advent of Christ, on the one hand, and the exigencies and settings of his audiences on the other. In this way, language takes shape within an ongoing conversation,[30] as language is adopted and adapted that both fits the particular circumstances to which Paul addresses himself and toils to reconfigure experienced reality so that it accounts more fully for what God has done in Christ. This means that Paul can use one set of metaphors with the Colossians, another with the Galatians, while remaining true to the gospel and bearing witness to the same actuality.

To put it differently, the battle in which Paul is engaged is in an important sense one of rhetoric. Who controls the metaphors that shape our lives? Working especially among Gentiles, relative upstarts within the story of Israel, he throws himself into the difficult but crucial task of serving as midwife to a conversion of worldview. These new believers need new ways of organizing the world, new canons by which to evaluate what is meaningful, and new practices that reflect their new commitments and dispositions. His references to the death of Jesus thus serve to deconstruct the old and reconstruct the new.

For Paul, as for Jesus, the cross is the new foundation on which the identity and practices of God's people can be built. Through his language concerning the atonement, the saving significance of Jesus' death, Paul

---

[30]Colin Gunton (*The Actuality of the Atonement: A Study of Metaphor, Rationality and the Christian Tradition* [Grand Rapids, Mich.: Eerdmans, 1989], p. 48) observes "that traditional atonement metaphor is particularly well suited to show that language takes shape in a kind of conversation." Our language, he goes on to suggest, "must take a metaphorical shape corresponding to the changes brought about by the incarnation, cross and resurrection of Jesus" (p. 49).

was able to ground the Christian faith and the formation and life of the people of God in the ancient story of God's people, while at the same time inviting—one might say, provoking—those people more fully to embrace and more faithfully to reflect the new era occasioned by the cross.

3

THE CROSS &
THE NEW TESTAMENT

A Mélange of Voices
(Part Two)

*M*any of us have been to a carnival—either in reality or through the virtuality of television—and have experienced that clever act where a dressed-up wooden dummy is enabled to "speak" by means of a ventriloquist's talent. In recent decades among evangelicals, Christian reflection on the atonement has had a touch of the carnivalesque, with Luke or Peter or some other New Testament writer made to speak in someone else's voice. In this vaudevillian act Luke is the mannequin, and the levers of his mouth are controlled by the Pauline interpreter. Dressed up to resemble another New Testament writer like Paul or attached by puppet strings to a historical Christian figure like Anselm or Martin Luther, many New Testament writers lose their distinctive presence. They are not allowed to speak with their own voices.

Carnivals serve a useful purpose, of course, but most of us do not live in them. When our money is gone and our tickets spent, we return to our cars and reenter a world of many voices and sometimes complex communication styles. Focusing on Paul has been instrumental in shaping our Christian identity, and we have reason to celebrate many of the distinctives we have learned from Paul that now characterize our faith. However, we are in danger of turning a choir of New Testament voices into a solo performance with regard to our understanding of Jesus' death as a saving event. Such a transformation has proven dangerous not only to our sense of Christian identity within the church but also to our mission as the church.

Continuing the exploration begun in chapter two, we now need to attend to additional New Testament voices related to the theology of the atonement. We have already seen how Jesus' own understanding of his death is both like and unlike the emphases we find in Paul's letters. Additionally, we have seen that Paul himself has not one but multiple ways of articulating the significance of the cross for salvation. The possibility of diverse witnesses to the atonement is thus fully present, and this variety can only be broadened by accounting for the viewpoints of other New Testament materials—materials that, in their own ways, are equally as profound and certainly as definitive for Christian faith and life as those evident in the Pauline documents. In this chapter, then, we continue to survey the New Testament for its teaching on the saving significance of Jesus' death by lifting up the contributions of Luke, John, Hebrews and 1 Peter.

The Messiah Must Suffer and Enter into His Glory: The Death of Jesus and the Offer of Salvation in Luke-Acts

It is clear from the prefaces to both volumes, Luke 1:1-4 and Acts 1:1-2, that the Acts of the Apostles continues the narrative begun in the Gospel of Luke. Hence, we refer to these two books as Luke-Acts. Together they comprise well over one-fourth of the New Testament, contributing significantly more in terms of sheer words than any other writer. This, combined with the uniqueness of Luke's decision among the Gospel writers, or Evangelists, to continue the story of Jesus into the story of the early church, makes our taking his witness seriously all the more crucial. Luke recounts the beginnings of the early church and on several occasions sketches the content of early missionary preaching; in the theological presentation of his historical narrative, what role does the death of Jesus play?

To those reared on a steady diet of Pauline theology, the evidence in Luke-Acts may be surprising. Though his narrative spans the period from Jesus' birth to Paul's imprisonment, Luke devotes only three partial verses, some nineteen of his almost thirty-eight thousand words, to the atoning significance of Jesus' death. What is more, both of these texts, Luke 22:19-20 and Acts 20:28, are shrouded in controversy. Scholars continue to debate whether Luke 22:19-20 is original to the Gospel of Luke or added later by scribes who wanted to bring the scene of the Last Supper in Luke into harmony with that in the Gospels of Matthew and Mark. Even if these words were written by Luke, as we think highly probable, it is nonetheless interesting that Luke has neither developed the concept of the redemptive death of Jesus more fully nor integrated it more fully into his narrative. As a quick comparison of different English translations will show, Acts 20:28 has presented its own set of problems. In Paul's speech to the Ephesian elders as Luke records it, does Paul refer to "the church of the Lord" or "the church of God"? Is that church purchased with "his own blood" or with "the blood of his own [Son]"? The difficulty here is that a plain reading of the text would have Paul affirming that God purchased the church with his (God's!) own blood; stated in this way, this expression would be without precedent or analogy in any other biblical text.[1] As New Testament scholar Eduard Schweizer has observed, "[Luke] quotes this phrase as if it were some foreign language."[2]

How could Luke not have more fully developed the saving significance

---

[1]Although the metaphor of "purchasing with blood" (i.e., with death) is used with reference to the atonement in the New Testament, the death is always that of Jesus, not of God.

[2]Eduard Schweizer, *Luke: A Challenge to Present Theology* (London: SPCK, 1982), p. 45.

of Jesus' death? The urgency of this question grows when we remember that Acts portrays Peter and Paul outlining the gospel of Jesus Christ in missionary speeches to Jew, Gentile and mixed audiences, but *never* in those speeches do we hear of the atoning death of Jesus. Why not?

Sometimes this question is put forward in ways that suggest that Luke somehow did not understand well the apostolic message. In such circumstances we do well to look more carefully, to observe whether Luke has not been turned into a carnivalesque sideshow, with the Pauline ventriloquist working all of the levers and pulling all of the strings. The question is rather, What does Luke contribute to our understanding of the apostolic message?

How Is Salvation Available?

If Luke-Acts is fundamentally concerned with the message of salvation, and if salvation is not at a basic level interwoven into the significance of Jesus' death, how is salvation made available? On this question, Luke is quite clear. Salvation is available through Jesus on account of his resurrection and ascension—that is, on account of his exaltation to the right hand of God. Three texts in particular underscore this Lukan emphasis.

The first is the Pentecost speech in Acts 2.[3] Luke portrays the outpouring of the Holy Spirit, leading eventually to the question of the gathered crowds, "What does this mean?" Peter replies in terms of the expected era of salvation sketched in Joel 2:28-32, which he interprets in relation to Psalms 16 and 110. We can trace his argument in three steps.

1. What has happened on this day of Pentecost is nothing less than the fresh work of the Holy Spirit, poured out in fulfillment of Joel's promise of restoration.

2. The spectacular phenomena recounted in Acts 2:1-13 join other forms of "witness"—namely, the Psalms and the followers of Jesus—in

---

[3]On what follows, see Joel B. Green, *The Acts of the Apostles*, NICNT (Grand Rapids, Mich.: Eerdmans, forthcoming).

demonstrating that Jesus has divine prerogatives so that he is able to dispense the blessings of salvation, the gift of the Holy Spirit being chief among these.

3. These events mark the onset of "the last days," which are marked by the universal offer of salvation and threat of judgment, so that all are called to contrition and repentance.

For our purposes, the central point in Peter's logic is the crucial one. According to the citation from Joel, "all who call on the name of the Lord will be saved." Who is this "Lord"? For Joel, of course, the Lord is Yahweh, God of Israel. For Peter, however, the exaltation of Jesus to God's right hand proves that "God has made him both Lord and Christ, this Jesus whom you yourselves crucified" (Acts 2:36). Raised up, the Lord Jesus now serves as coregent with God and in this capacity administers the promise of the Father, the gift of the Spirit.

Having established the relation between the phrase "the name of the Lord," Jesus' exaltation, and salvation, Luke can build on this new understanding. Thus, for example, the "complete health" of the man born lame is attributed to the efficacy of "the name" (Acts 3:16)—a conclusion that is reached through a rehearsal of the theological significance of Jesus' resurrection (Acts 3:13-15). Later, in Acts 4:11-12, a statement regarding God's vindication of Jesus (that is, Jesus' resurrection [see Acts 4:10]) leads into a declaration of the universal significance of Jesus' name for salvation.

A second, central affirmation of the redemptive significance of Jesus' exaltation comes in Peter's speech to the Jerusalem council in Acts 5:30-31: "The God of our ancestors raised up Jesus. . . . God exalted him at his right hand as Leader and Savior, to give repentance to Israel and the forgiveness of sins." Here we have a straightforward affirmation that Jesus' exaltation has as its consequence his confirmation as Savior and that it is as Savior that he "gives" repentance and forgiveness of sins. This is another instance of synecdoche (where a part is allowed to represent the whole), which is common in Acts: as the gift of the Holy Spirit signified the whole of salvation in Acts 2, so here repentance and forgiveness of sins is allowed to do so.

The third text is less direct but similar. In the midst of his preaching at the home of Cornelius, Peter proclaims, "All the prophets testify about him that everyone who believes in him receives forgiveness of sins through his name" (Acts 10:43). Again, forgiveness of sins is synecdoche for salvation. Peter's logic is not straightforward because his argument is missing a central element. The prophets (like the Old Testament as a whole) do proclaim the forgiveness of sins but invariably identify Yahweh as the one who offers pardon. Never do the prophets speak of a time when Jesus (or the Messiah) would offer the forgiveness of sins. How is it that prophetic testimony concerning Yahweh is transferred to Jesus? The answer can only be that, according to the consistent view in the book of Acts, on account of his exaltation Jesus is Lord; as Lord, he assumes the divine prerogative to administer the benefits of salvation, here represented as forgiveness of sins.

Summarizing, we see that the means of salvation for Luke is the exaltation of Jesus. Before taking the next step it may be useful to remind ourselves that the salvation of which Luke writes may appear to us, erroneously, to be focused on individual persons. "Forgiveness of sins" has come to be associated with individual salvation in our world, when in fact divine pardon is a profoundly social occasion. This is true, first, because sin is that which excludes us from the community of God's people, so that forgiveness would be the way in which we (re)gain entry into that community. Forgiveness and reconciliation are fundamentally *social* realities. It is also true, second, that in Second Temple Judaism, Israel's hopes for restoration as the people of God were interwoven with the promise and expectation that Yahweh would forgive the people of Israel. Similarly, even if individuals receive the gift of the Spirit, the consistent testimony of Acts is that reception of the Spirit has as its immediate effect incorporation into and participation with the multiethnic community of God's people (see, e.g., Acts 2:37-47; 15:6-11).

What of Jesus' Death?

What, then, of the death of Jesus?[4] The sheer frequency of times that we read in Luke-Acts of the divine necessity of the suffering and death of Jesus the Messiah is warning enough that salvation has not come *in spite of* the crucifixion. In fact, it is of great interest that Jesus in the Third Gospel and his witnesses in the book of Acts repeatedly insist that the suffering of the Messiah is declared in Scripture, yet neither Jesus nor his witnesses have much to say about the purpose of that suffering. Of course, as we have seen, the salvific effect of the cross is not altogether absent from Luke's narrative, which introduces two traditional metaphors for the atonement: sacrifice (Lk 22:19-20) and business transaction (Acts 20:28); at the same time, these have not been woven fully into the fabric of Luke's narrative theology. Can more be said?

We may gain our bearings by noting how Luke has staged the episode of Jesus' death in Luke 23:44-49, indicating how opposition to Jesus (symbolized for Luke in the darkness/failure of the sun—cf. Lk 22:53) led to Jesus' death. Luke records the results of Jesus' death as the repentance of the Jewish crowds and the exemplary confession of the Gentile centurion. In other words, the rejection of Jesus by the Jewish leadership in Jerusalem leads to the widening of the mission to embrace all peoples, Jew and Gentile.[5] Earlier in the Gospel, we are informed (cf. Lk. 21:13-19), suffering and rejection foster the propagation of the word. Similarly, in Acts, the rejection of Jesus—first by the Jewish leadership in Jerusalem, then by some Jews in other locales (e.g., Acts 13:44-49; 14:1-18; 18:2-6; 28:17-29)—leads to the spread of the mission. The missionary program of Acts 1:8 is grounded in this: Jerusalem is the place of Jesus' passion and the first locus of hostility toward the apostolic mission, and this hostility will fos-

---

[4]On what follows see Joel B. Green, "'Salvation to the End of the Earth': God as the Saviour in the Acts of the Apostles," in *Witness to the Gospel: The Theology of Acts*, ed. I. Howard Marshall and David Peterson (Grand Rapids, Mich.: Eerdmans, 1998), pp. 99-101.

[5]This is developed more fully in Joel B. Green, "The Demise of the Temple as Culture Center in Luke-Acts: An Exploration of the Rending of the Temple Veil (Luke 23.44-49)," *RB* 101 (1994): 495-515.

ter the spread of the gospel. As Luke is fond of narrating, struggle and opposition do not impede but seem actually to promote the progress of the gospel: "It is through many persecutions that we must enter the kingdom of God" (Acts 14:22; cf., e.g., Acts 6:1-7; 8:1-4). Persecution leads to the growth of the church and the spread of the good news, and this proves that the church is of God (see Acts 5:39).[6]

Second, these words of Paul cited in Acts 14:22, set as it is in the immediate aftermath of the stoning of Paul, urge a reading of the passion of Jesus as in some way paradigmatic for all of those who follow Jesus. As C. K. Barrett has demonstrated, Jesus' words to his disciples, "If any want to become my followers, let them . . . take up their cross day after day" (Lk 9:23), portend a lifetime of discipleship as cross-bearing, exemplified in the life of people like Paul in the narrative of Acts (cf. Lk 9:16). For Luke this theology of the cross is rooted not so much in a theory of the atonement but in a narrative portrayal of the life of faithful discipleship as the way of the cross.[7]

Third, in describing Jesus' crucifixion, Acts echoes the words of Deuteronomy 21:22-23:

The God of our ancestors raised up Jesus, whom you had killed by hanging him on a tree. (Acts 5:30)

The Jewish leaders in Jerusalem had Jesus put to death by hanging him on a tree. (Acts 10:39)

They took him down from the tree. (Acts 13:29)

When someone is convicted of a crime punishable by death and is executed, and you hang him on a tree, his corpse must not remain all night

---

[6]This and related motifs are developed in Scott Cunningham, *"Through Many Tribulations": The Theology of Persecution in Luke-Acts*, JSNTSup 142 (Sheffield: Sheffield Academic Press, 1997).

[7]C. K. Barrett, "*Theologia Crucis*—in Acts?", in *Theologia Crucis—Signum Crucis: Festschrift für Erich Dinkler zum 70. Geburtstag*, ed. by C. Andersen and G. Klein (Tübingen: J.C.B. Mohr [Paul Siebeck], 1979), pp. 73-84. Cf. Manfred Korn, *Die Geschichte Jesu in veränderter Zeit: Studien zur bleibenden Bedeutung Jesu im lukanischen Doppelwerk*, WUNT 2:51 (Tübingen: J.C.B. Mohr [Paul Siebeck], 1993), pp. 242-59; John T. Carroll and Joel B. Green, *The Death of Jesus in Early Christianity* (Peabody, Mass.: Hendrickson, 1995), chap. 4.

upon the tree; you shall bury him that same day, for anyone hung on a tree is under God's curse. (Deut 21:22-23 NRSV)

Luke-Acts (cf. Lk 23:39) accounts for four of the six New Testament uses of the verb "to hang," a term that is also found in this text from Deuteronomy.[8] This suggests the formative influence of the Greek text of Deuteronomy 21:22-23 on Luke's understanding of the cross.[9] No doubt in conversation with early Christian use of Deuteronomy 21:22-23 in the interpretation of the cross of Jesus, Luke thus signaled his awareness of the disgrace of Jesus' execution. He does not employ Deuteronomy 21:23 in order to repudiate this shame, however, but in order to acknowledge it. These allusions serve to locate Jesus' death firmly in the necessity of God's purpose. The ultimate disgrace, the curse from God, leads to exaltation. The text of Deuteronomy is thus used in an ironic way, transforming the earlier passage beyond what one might regard as its original aim by applying it to God's Anointed One. The execution of Jesus on a cross, then, was shameful in every way, and from both Roman and Jewish points of view.[10]

This means that Jesus embodies in his own career the drama of salvation as Luke portrays it throughout his Gospel and Acts. This drama is one of transposition, status reversal, the lifting up of the lowly, good news to the poor. Indeed, the act of salvation itself can be represented as "being raised up," using the same language used of Jesus' own resurrection. For example, Luke uses these words to narrate the event when a crippled man receives salvation: "Peter took him by the right hand *and raised him up*" (Acts 3:7, emphasis added). That this restoration to health signified salvation in the most holistic sense is then evidenced by the man's walking, his

---

[8] κρεμάννυμι; cf. Galatians 3:13; 1 Peter 2:24.

[9] This passage from Deuteronomy does not envision crucifixion per se but rather impalement of the body of the executed after death. Nevertheless, in pre-Christian times it was already being applied to the victims of crucifixion. See, for example, Philo *Spec. Leg.* 3.152; *Post. C.* 61; *Somn.* 2.213; 4QpNah 3-4.1.7-8; 11QTS 64.6-13. For discussion, see Joseph A. Fitzmyer, "Crucifixion in Ancient Palestine, Qumran Literature, and the New Testament," in *To Advance the Gospel* (New York: Crossroad, 1981), pp. 125-46; Max Wilcox, "'Upon the Tree: Deuteronomy 21:22-23 in the New Testament," *JBL* 96 (1977): 85-99.

[10] See Carroll and Green, *Death of Jesus*, chap. 9.

praising God and his entry into the temple precincts from which he had previously been excluded on account of his malady (Acts 3:8-10, 16). In Jesus' being raised up, so also are those who are beaten down, who live on the bottom rungs of society's ladder, raised to life. Jesus has blazed the trail of new life (Acts 3:15).

These two—the cross of Jesus and the cross-bearing of those who follow him—are intimately related. In his suffering and resurrection, Jesus embodied the fullness of salvation interpreted as status reversal; his death was the center point of the divine-human struggle over how life is to be lived, in humility or self-glorification. Though anointed by God, though righteous before God, though innocent, he is put to death. Rejected by people, he is raised up by God—and with him the least, the lost, the left out are also raised. In his death, and in consequence of his resurrection by God, the way of salvation is exemplified and made accessible to all those who will follow.

The Son of Man Must Be Lifted Up: The Significance of the Cross in the Writings of John

In studies of the theology of the New Testament, John has been the one figure to stand alongside Paul as a great theologian of the New Testament era. At times this has meant John's presence has been eclipsed by Paul's shadow, however, so it is important that we let John be John. In this section we will explore the significance of the death of Jesus in the Johannine material, which includes for the sake of convenience the Gospel of John (sometimes called the Fourth Gospel), the letters of John (in this context, 1 John in particular), and the book of Revelation. These five documents are associated with the same name, John, and in important ways share a common perspective, but they are not likely to have been written by the same person.

The Fourth Gospel

The major preoccupation of the Fourth Gospel is Christology, and this is focused in John's case on the nature of Jesus and his mission. John 3:16-17 helpfully summarizes that mission: "That whoever believes in him should not perish but have eternal life. For I did not come to judge the world but to save it." Jesus came into the world to give life. More often than not in the Gospel of John, this "mission statement" appears in texts that are bundled together with talk of Jesus' "giving life" by giving up his own life. Clearly for John, the death of Jesus has saving significance.

How does John develop this atonement theology? He draws his metaphors especially from the Scriptures of Israel. For example, in disclosures regarding the "giving" of the Son of God may be heard echoes of the "binding of Isaac" of Genesis 22 (see Jn 1:29; 3:16; 19:17). This is important because the binding of Isaac, also known as the *Akedah*, had become for Second Temple Judaism a way of speaking of death on behalf of others. Other texts point in this general direction as well—for example, Jesus is the Good Shepherd who lays down his life on behalf of the sheep (Jn 10:11-18). Even more interesting is the association of Jesus with the theological world of the Passover lamb. In the Gospel's opening chapter, John speaks of Jesus as the lamb of God who brings forgiveness of sins (Jn 1:29, 36), reflecting the development of Jewish thought which came in the Second Temple period to interpret the Passover as an atoning sacrifice. On a related note, Jesus' death according to the Fourth Gospel coincided with the time of the Passover sacrifice (Jn 18:28; 19:14); the hyssop and basin are present at the cross (Jn 19:29; cp. Ex 12:22); the *seeing* of the blood flow from the side of Jesus is emphasized (Jn 19:35; cp. Ex 12:13); and the soldiers do not break Jesus' legs (Jn 19:31-37; cp. Ex 12:46). The world of the exodus is continued in John 6, where in an extended discourse Jesus compares himself to the "bread from heaven" that fed Israel; now, however, those who ingest his life will have life. Even the footwashing of the disciples by Jesus has become in John's hands a metaphor of the giving of Jesus' life on behalf of others (Jn 13:8-11).

One of the more distinctive aspects of John's presentation of the death of Jesus is his focus on the motif of "raising up" or "exaltation." This image appears first in John 3:14-15: "Just as Moses lifted up the snake in the wilderness, so the Son of Man must be lifted up, that everyone who believes in him may have eternal life" (see Jn 8:28; 12:32-33). Precisely in what way the Son of Man is to be "lifted up" is obscure this early in the Gospel. There is no ambiguity, however, in the purpose of that lifting up; it is salvific, life-giving for all who believe. Only with the progression of the Gospel do we come to understand the double meaning of this exaltation. "Lifting up" expresses John's theology of the glory of the Son, but it also points to the means by which Jesus will be executed—namely, by being "lifted up" on a cross (see Jn 12:33; 18:32). As tragic and humiliating as the cross might be in the eyes of some, in John's narrative the cross is nothing less than the actualization of God's purpose in sending Jesus; hence, Jesus' last words from the cross are not sorrowful or reserved. "It is finished," Jesus announces (Jn 19:30), speaking not so much of the end of his natural life but of the completion of his mission.

Salvation is life, of course, but for John it is also light. That is, for John a cornerstone image of salvation is revelation. For John, terms like *believing, understanding, seeing* and *knowing* are far more than cognitive exercises; they refer to the transformation of people as children of God. And this transformation is effected through the revelation of God in Jesus. In Jesus we see the Father (Jn 14:1-11), and in the cross the fullness of his love is disclosed. These two perspectives—the cross as atoning sacrifice and as redemptive revelation—are not competitors within the Fourth Gospel but complementary.[11]

1 John

The motif of revelation is continued in the opening of 1 John, where it appears in tandem with an unambiguous reference to the cleansing effect

---

[11]Max Turner, "Atonement and the Death of Jesus in John: Some Questions to Bultmann and Forestell," *EvQ* 62 (1990): 99-122. For atonement theology in John's Gospel more broadly, see George L. Carey, "The Lamb of God and Atonement Theories," *TynB* 32 (1981): 97-122; Bruce H. Grigsby, "The Cross as an Expiatory Sacrifice in the Fourth Gospel," *JSNT* 15 (1982): 51-80.

of Jesus' death (1 Jn 1:5-2:2; cf. 5:6-8). Here the author is on the offensive, countering claims of sinlessness, claims that do not take the power of sin seriously enough. Against such claims, he asserts the reality of sin and affirms the greater power of the death of Jesus to cleanse us from sin. The image he employs, translated in the NRSV as "atoning sacrifice" (1 Jn 2:2), is drawn from Israel's history—the sin offering (Lev 25:9) and especially the Day of Atonement (Lev 16:16).

The importance of the connection of this text with the Day of Atonement is suggested by the relationship between impurity and sin, addressed in the rite of the Day of Atonement described in Leviticus 16. Sin results in impurity in the temple, so the ritual prescribed for the Day of Atonement calls for purification of the sanctuary/temple and the use of a scapegoat. Immediately following the purgation of the sanctuary, the high priest places his hands on the goat's head, confesses over it the sins of Israel and sends the goat into the wilderness. Thus is the sanctuary cleansed and the people's sins banished. Note that, in this rite, the scape-goat is not butchered and presented as a sacrificial offering, and there is no attempt (or necessity) to appease God. God is not the problem, but sin is, for it defiles us for communion with God. The death of Jesus, according to the deployment of this imagery in 1 John, cleanses us and thus readies us for unfettered fellowship with God.

Elsewhere in 1 John, the significance of Jesus' death is worked out in exemplary terms. Christians are to replicate in their own lives the self-giving love expressed in the cross (1 Jn 3:18-22; 4:7-12).

The Book of Revelation

The central christological image in the book of Revelation is the Lamb, and this portrait is centered in chapter 5. The author of Revelation, whose name is John (Rev 1:9), narrates a scene of high drama, initially tragic in its attempt to locate the one authorized to break the seal and open the scroll held in God's right hand. How will the sovereignty of God be established if no one can open the scroll and reveal its contents? There is only one who is qualified, and he is identified first as "the Lion of the tribe of Judah, the Root of David"—that is, the triumphant and militaristic Messiah of God (Rev 5:5). When John focuses his eyes on this Lion, however, what he sees is a slaughtered Lamb, whose worthiness to open the scroll, we quickly discover, is grounded in the manner and significance of his death:

> You are worthy to take the scroll
>   and to open its seals,
> for you were slaughtered and by
>   your blood you ransomed for God
> saints from every tribe and language and people
>   and nation. (Rev 5:9 NRSV)

What is fascinating about this paradox of images is that they coexist without contradiction in one person. Jesus is the conquering Messiah, and the manner of his victory is his slaughter. Jesus' death is evil's defeat.

The images John employs to develop the significance of Jesus' death are varied. Jesus' death liberates from sin and, like a covenant sacrifice, creates a people of God (Rev 1:5; 5:9-10). In Revelation 5:9-10, the central image is borrowed from the marketplace: Jesus "purchased" a people for God. To whom did Jesus "pay" the price of his own blood (that is, his own death)? This aspect of the metaphor is not developed, with the result that we should probably understand this image as a way of underscoring the seriousness (or costliness) of rebellion against God and his purposes. In Revelation 7:9-17, the death of Jesus is portrayed as a cleansing or sanctifying agent.

A further key component of John's interpretation of the death of Jesus is its effectiveness in defeating evil. Revelation places the drama of salvation on the cosmic stage, so that the slaughter of the Lamb wins a cosmic victory. The technology of this warfare goes unidentified; specifically *how* the cross overcomes evil is not developed. What is clear is that the faithfulness of Jesus in his life-giving death is a faithfulness to the eternal will of God. The death of Jesus shows how God measures fidelity and triumph and, because God is the uncontested sovereign of the universe, Jesus' faithfulness in the cross repeals all other powers, all other purposes.

As pivotal as the death of Jesus is to the realization of God's kingdom and the formation of his people, for John's Revelation Jesus' death has another role. Those who worship the Lamb are called to embrace the way of the Lamb, to emulate in their lives the faithful witness of the Lamb—even to the death. This note is sounded especially in Revelation 12:11:

> They have conquered Satan by the blood of the Lamb
> > and by the word of their testimony,
> for they did not cling to life even in the face of death.

John presents here no call to masochistic martyrdom; he does not idealize suffering and death. Instead, he insists that faithful witness in the world requires prophetic engagement with the world, irrespective of the consequences. We may recall that John himself had been exiled to Patmos "because of the word of God and the testimony of Jesus" (Rev 1:9). Although he had not been martyred, John's own faithful witness had invited the malevolent attention of the same forces that had placed Jesus on the cross.

To Remove Sin by His Own Sacrifice: The Saving Significance of Jesus' Death in Hebrews

Hebrews refers to itself as a "message of exhortation" (Heb 13:22)—a sermon of sorts, which is pervaded by reflection on the death of Jesus.[12] Especially potent is the dual image of Jesus as both the perfect sacrificial victim and the high priest who offers the sacrifice. The thought world of Israel's Scriptures is transparent throughout the book.

---

[12]See Morna D. Hooker, *Not Ashamed of the Gospel: New Testament Interpretations of the Death of Christ* (Grand Rapids, Mich.: Eerdmans, 1994), pp. 112-24; Carroll and Green, *Death of Jesus*, pp. 133-39.

Forgiveness, according to Hebrews, has as its prerequisite the shedding of blood (Heb 9:22). The shedding of blood, or death, in mind here is the offering of the new covenant sacrifice that frees God's people from the rule of sin so that they might participate in authentic worship with a cleansed conscience. Here then the author weaves together two distinctive images. On the one hand, the death of Jesus ratifies the new covenant. On the other, the author writes of "expiatory sacrifice": Jesus bears the sins of humanity on their behalf.

Jesus is not only the sacrificial offering but is also the high priest. Unlike priests who carried on their work in the Jerusalem temple, however, Jesus has no need to sacrifice for his own sins because he is without sin. Yet, as one who stands in solidarity with humanity, he is able to embody the mediatorial role of a priest. As the perfect priest and the perfect sacrifice, his death obviates the need for additional sacrificial offerings (see Heb 9:25-28; 10:10, 12-14).

If the perfection of Jesus as a high priest untainted by sin and as an unblemished sacrificial victim comprises the leitmotif of this "written sermon," room is left in the author's reflection on Jesus' death for a second image. In Hebrews 2:14-15 the death of Jesus is also positioned over against the life-threatening powers of evil. Jesus' death, that is, declares the power of the devil null and void.

He Bore Our Sins . . . So That We Might Live to Righteousness: The Death of Jesus in 1 Peter

In this first letter attributed to Peter, the author, whom we regard as the apostle, draws heavily on imagery from the Scriptures of Israel in order to demonstrate that the church *is* the people of God, without remainder. We should not be surprised to discover, then, the significant degree to which the roots of his depiction of Jesus' death are entangled with Old Testament images—especially the Passover lamb and the suffering servant of Yahweh. Peter is concerned above all to demonstrate the *manner* of Jesus' death, which becomes the basis for discussing both the ground of our salvation and the nature of authentic discipleship. His theological reflections on the death of Jesus are hardly of a speculative nature, however. As the message of the letter unfolds, it becomes obvious that Peter is writing to Christians who are themselves suffering and who therefore require help in articulating the foundation of their faith in the death of Jesus.

The pivotal role of the death of Jesus in Peter's message is signaled immediately in the letter's opening. Peter's audience are those who have been "sprinkled with his blood" (1 Pet 1:2). Here is a reminder of the covenant Moses ratified with the people of Israel on Sinai, when he sprinkled them with blood as a symbol of the sealing of the covenant (Ex 24:7-8). Exodus images are suggested in 1 Peter 1:14-20 as well, where Jesus' death ("the precious blood of Christ") is described as the means by which people were delivered from the bondage of their past. "To deliver" can be translated differently, so as to suggest a metaphor from the marketplace: "to redeem" or "to ransom." Verse 18 pushes this image further, insisting that the "cost" of redemption had to be paid not in the currency of silver and gold but with blood—that is, with death. Precious metals are useless in this transaction. However, as in the narrative of Israel's deliverance from Egypt in Exodus, there is no hint of *payment* rendered to secure the release of these people from bondage. Otherwise, though Peter never develops fully its significance, he does employ sacrificial imagery as he reflects on the cross (see 1 Pet 2:21, 24; 3:18).

More pervasive in the letter is the author's concern with the exemplary character of Jesus' suffering. This interest is most fully present in 1 Peter 2:21-25:

> Because it was to this very thing that you were called, because Christ also suffered for you, leaving you a pattern so that you should follow in his footsteps. "He committed no sin, and no deceit was found in his mouth." When he was reviled, he did not revile in retaliation; when he suffered, he did not threaten, but rather entrusted himself to the One who judges justly. He himself bore our sins in his body on the cross, so that, being dead to sin, we might live to righteousness. By his wounds you were

healed. For you were going astray like sheep, but now you have turned to the shepherd and guardian of your lives.

This section of Peter's letter is fascinating for the way it weaves together the text of Isaiah 53:3-6, concerning the suffering servant of Yahweh, and the message Peter develops throughout the letter. "This very thing" refers to the larger concerns of 1 Peter 2:13—3:7, where Peter sketches the behavior appropriate to Christians—behavior that is consistently marked by nonviolence and undeserved suffering. Peter seems to address his Christian audience as though they were all people of low status, like slaves, and indeed this is consistent with his opening address to them as "aliens" (1 Pet 1:1). One of the pressing realities of Christian life to which Peter addresses this letter is that conformity to Christ has the effect of marginalizing Christians in the larger world. Adopting commitments and practices consistent with the example of Jesus, his disciples find themselves less and less "at home" in the world. The result is rejection, revilement and suffering, but even here Jesus' followers may find in him a pattern worthy of emulation. Jesus was himself a victim of injustice; should Christians be surprised that they suffer unjustly (1 Pet 4:12-19)?

In his passion and death, then, Jesus is the model of innocent suffering. In his passion and death, he models faithful obedience and trust in God. This is key to Peter's message, but it is not the whole message. As important as the exemplary character of Jesus' death is, the utility of the cross of Christ as a pattern to follow depends on the actuality of the atonement. On account of Jesus' death, and only because of it, Peter insists, you are now able to live faithfully as he did. That is, the pattern of Jesus' faithfulness in the midst of suffering and death can be followed only because his suffering and death brings with it our restoration to fellowship with God. The image Peter uses here is not strictly "sacrificial," since it is related more closely to the scapegoat—which, we may recall, is not slaughtered but consigned to the wilderness (Lev 16). The effect is nonetheless one of freedom to live apart from sin.

Conclusion

The voices we have heard derive from different parts of the New Testament canon and different venues in the ancient Roman world. Given the different needs to which they are addressed, we should not be surprised to hear among them differences of insight and nuance. Heard together, their harmony is sometimes delicate. At other times the effect is more complex, with wonderful hints of powerful melodies contending with countermelodies. That all belong in the same choir is nonetheless assured.

In the next chapter we will explore more fully the various points of unity and diversity that characterize the New Testament witness to the cross of Christ. Here it is enough to remember that no one view—not that of Paul, not that of Peter, and so on—presents us with "the correct view." Indeed, as we have seen in this chapter, Peter is capable of more than one way of focusing the importance of Jesus' death. Yet all of his images of the cross and images of salvation belong together, and all of those we have surveyed in this and the previous chapter belong to the larger witness of the New Testament to the saving significance of Jesus' death. The impression with which we are left is that the death of Jesus is an historical event of such profundity that we can only do it violence by narrowing its meaning to one interpretation or by privileging one interpretation over all the others.

4

THE SAVING SIGNIFICANCE
OF JESUS' DEATH IN
THE NEW TESTAMENT

What would happen if theology took the mission of the church seriously? Theologian Clark Pinnock raises this important question in his introduction to the current theological scene. Such a theology, he contends, would require a renovation in theological language, focus and thought patterns, for it would have to be more concerned with being understood by outsiders.[1]

Of course, the same might be said for a theology more sensitive to the down-to-earth lives of those who are in the church. What would happen if theology took the everyday realities being faced by Christians more seriously? One answer would clearly be that we would find our theological reflections more fully aligned with the theology of the New Testament materials. After all, writers of the books of the New Testament were not concerned to set forth the content of the faith for all time, and what they

---

[1]Clark H. Pinnock, *Tracking the Maze: Finding Our Way through Modern Theology from an Evangelical Perspective* (San Francisco: Harper & Row, 1990), pp. 5-7.

have written does not provide us with systems of theological thought. Peter, Paul and others were concerned to communicate the Christian message to be sure, but New Testament documents are all, to varying degrees, "occasional" in character. That is, whether written to address concerns in a particular household (Philemon) or to Christians in a particular region (Galatia) or with no audience specified (Luke-Acts), the New Testament materials are located first in a particular social world with its own patterns of speech, needs and cultural assumptions. The books of the New Testament were shaped by that world at the same time that they aimed to shape that world.

The contextual rootedness of the New Testament is perhaps nowhere on display more than in its atonement theology. Drawing on the language and thought patterns of Israel's religion and life experiences within the larger Greco-Roman world, these writers struggled to make sense of Jesus' crucifixion. They did not have to provide manuals of cultural practices for their audience but could assume that "sacrifice" or "ransom" belonged to the collective knowledge of their readers. One of the particular challenges for those of us who attempt to articulate an atonement theology at the turn of the twenty-first century is that the encyclopedia of our everyday lives has a different set of entries than those shared by people of the ancient Mediterranean. We easily misconstrue their words. And perhaps more importantly, we misconstrue the aim of those materials— an aim toward shaping Christian faith and life in the Mediterranean world.

Our Contemporary Dilemma

In fact, a prominent difficulty we face today with regard to atonement theology is the problem of misunderstanding. On the one hand, we find Christians whose notions of the atonement bear little resemblance to the message of Scripture. They tend to think of God as an angry man or a vindictive judge whose wrath must be averted by the death of his Son lest it be vented on us, his children. On the other, for an increasing number of persons and faith communities, atonement theology is irrelevant, for it represents for them a barbaric faith.

Rejection of atonement theology by some is not because traditional models of redemption—for example, those of Luther and Anselm and Irenaeus—have become obsolete. We may have difficulty understanding them in our contemporary contexts, but this is reason only to interpret them anew, not to reject them. As Herman-Emiel Mertens has suggested, "The one who accepts these traditional models without reserve and passes them on untranslated, does not at all serve the religious community well."[2] Criticism of atonement teaching typically takes a different turn. Especially for many feminist theologians, but not only for them, the message of the cross does not simply stand in need of reinterpretation; the cross itself and the divine drama it represents—therein lies the problem. Unlike some liberation theologies, where those New Testament materials struggling to make sense of the death of Jesus are important precisely for the seriousness with which they grapple with suffering,[3] feminist theologies generally find atonement imagery offensive. Does not biblical imagery perpetuate patriarchal patterns of power and encourage victims of abuse to submit to unjust suffering? Can the New Testament understanding of the atonement have relevance at the turn of the twenty-first century?

For many Christians, this more radical critique of atonement theology may be surprising. In fact, we want to suggest that feminist criticisms of atonement theology help admirably to focus important issues that need further reflection.

The Saving Death of Jesus in the Dock

According to the earliest tradition, Jesus' death was "for us." That is, the

---

[2]Herman-Emiel Mertens, *Not the Cross, but the Crucified: An Essay in Soteriology*, LTPM 11 (Grand Rapids, Mich.: Eerdmans, 1992), p. 85.

[3]Compare, for example, Boff, who writes in the introduction to his study of Jesus' passion, "I hope that my experiment will be a help to those who, in their pain, seek to confer a meaning on the painful passion of the world" (Leonardo Boff, *Passion of Christ, Passion of the World: The Facts, Their Interpretation, and Their Meaning Yesterday and Today* [Maryknoll, N.Y.: Orbis, 1987], p. xiii).

followers of Jesus have never been content with the "brute" fact that Jesus died but have always been concerned with the interpretation of this fact. "Christianity proclaims not merely that Christ died, but that his death had significance for the otherwise apparently absurd course of human history."[4] Throughout the history of the Christian church, beginning with the apostolic era itself, theologians have formulated theories to explain how Jesus' death is effective for our salvation. What is the association of liberation with violent, unjust death? Margo Houts helpfully contends, "There are no pat answers. There are only theories which try to assimilate a wide array of biblical images, theories which try to explain a mystery, theories which fit some cultural milieus better than others, theories which all have their flaws and glitches."[5]

Numerous models have been proposed—for example, incarnational, satisfaction, moral influence, dramatic, governmental, mimetic, ransom, penal substitution and so on—and these will be explored more fully in the next chapter. The history and variety of theories of atonement notwithstanding, one has come to dominate the landscape of Christian faith in America, especially in its more popular expressions. This is the model of penal substitution, often attributed to Anselm or at least understood as having its derivation in his theory of satisfaction. According to this theory, humanity has, in its sin, turned away from God and so merits divine punishment. Jesus, in his death on the cross, died in place of (as a substitution for) sinful humanity at God's behest, and in doing so he took upon himself the punishment humanity ought to have suffered.

The most adamant objections to atonement theology, understood popularly as penal substitution, have come from feminist theologians. This is not to say that feminist theologians are the first to raise questions against

---

[4]Thomas C. Oden, *The Word of Life*, Systematic Theology 2 (San Francisco: Harper & Row, 1989), p. 345. What follows is an adaptation of John T. Carroll and Joel B. Green, *The Death of Jesus in Early Christianity* (Peabody, Mass.: Hendrickson, 1995), chap. 13.

[5]Margo G. Houts, "Classical Atonement Imagery: Feminist and Evangelical Challenges," *Catalyst* 19, no. 3 (1993): 1.

this atonement imagery, nor is it to say that feminist theologians are univocal in their assessment of atonement theology. Nevertheless, feminist theologians have raised two broad concerns that help to focus our thinking here.[6]

First, for many feminist theologians, atonement imagery raises important questions about the nature of God. Second, and intimately related, the troublesome metaphors concerning the character of God that are accorded privilege in atonement theology lead easily and naturally to the incarnation of those characteristics in human relationships—that is, among those whose vocation is to reflect the divine image.

What, according to feminist theological analysis, does atonement theology teach about God's character? According to the predominant model, God is envisaged as the powerful patriarch in the greater household of the human family. This God demands absolute allegiance and punishes any act of disobedience. The cross of Christ, according to this model, becomes a manifestation of God's wrath and a paradigm of parental punishment: God is the patriarch who punishes his son in order to satisfy God's own parental honor and sense of justice. Atonement theology may urge images of the grace of God, but, according to Rita Nakashima Brock, it can do so only at the expense of "the abuse of the one perfect child." She writes, "The experience of grace is lodged here, I believe, in a sense of relief at being relieved of punishment for one's inevitable failings and not in a clear sense of personal worth gained from an awareness of the unconditional nature of love. *The shadow of the punitive father must always lurk behind the atonement. He haunts images of forgiving grace.*"[7]

Pushing further, Beverly W. Harrison and Carter Heyward have insisted, "As the classical portrait of the punitive character of this divine-human transaction, Anselm of Canterbury's doctrine of atonement . . .

---

[6]Ibid., pp. 1, 5-6.

[7]Rita Nakashima Brock, "And a Little Child Will Lead Us: Christology and Child Abuse," in *Christianity, Patriarchy, and Abuse: A Feminist Critique*, ed. Joanne Carlson Brown and Carole R. Bohn (New York: Pilgrim, 1989), pp. 52-53; emphasis added.

probably represents the sadomasochism of Christian teaching at its most transparent."[8] God plays the role of the sadist who willfully inflicts punishment, and Jesus embraces the character of the masochist who willingly suffers it.

Where might this imagery lead? Feminist theologians have been quick to observe that atonement theology construed along these lines legitimates and perpetuates abuse in human relationships, not least in the home. What is more, locating Jesus, characterized as the willing victim of unjust suffering, at the heart of Christian faith is for some tantamount to idealizing the values of the victim and advising the abused to participate in their own victimization.[9]

Some Responses

What are we to make of these criticisms? First, it must be acknowledged that legitimate concerns lie behind these objections. However we might want to urge (as we will do momentarily) that atonement theology, either biblically or classically understood, is misappropriated and misrepresented when coerced into the popular mold of the model of penal substitution, the fact remains that study groups, songs and other manifestations of popular church life in America often represent this model as nothing less than *the* historical teaching of the Christian church. As such, when criticisms of this view are raised, we can do nothing less than admit straightforwardly that, on biblical and traditional grounds, this contemporary manifestation of atonement theology is both deficient and disturbing. That atonement theology might be placed in the service of abusive behavior, and indeed serve to provide the divine imprimatur for that behavior, is a scandal that calls for repentance and repudiation. (But is the

---

[8]Beverly W. Harrison and Carter Heyward, "Pain and Pleasure: Avoiding the Confusions of Christian Tradition in Feminist Theory," in *Christianity, Patriarchy, and Abuse: A Feminist Critique*, ed. Joanne Carlson Brown and Carole R. Bohn (New York: Pilgrim, 1989), p. 153.

[9]Cf. Joanne Carlson Brown and Rebecca Parker, "For God So Loved the World?" in *Christianity, Patriarchy, and Abuse: A Feminist Critique*, ed. Joanne Carlson Brown and Carole R. Bohn (New York: Pilgrim, 1989).

culprit atonement theology per se?)

Second, though, it is important to remember that the classical view of the atonement put forward by Anselm is not the penal-substitutionary theory popularized in our day. That is, it is a mistake to think that to reject penal-substitutionary atonement is to reject Anselm's or any other of the primary classical atonement models. A closer reading of history is in order.

Third, thoroughgoing criticism of atonement theology by some feminist theologians reflects our common problem of dependence on metaphorical language to communicate what is beyond language.[10] Especially from feminist quarters we have been cautioned about the limits of our religious language. Hence, it is ironic that some of those same feminist theologians are themselves guilty of treating as literal the metaphorical language of atonement theology. Alternatively, it might better be said that metaphorical language related to the atonement has been literalized in popular expressions of American Christianity, but in this case, instead of addressing the problem of metaphor in communicating the atonement, some feminists have demonized the doctrine of atonement itself. Perhaps people on all sides are implicated in a common refusal to recognize the limits of language or, more particularly, the reach of metaphor.[11]

Metaphors are two-edged: they reveal and conceal, highlight and hide. This means, first, that no one metaphor will capture the reality of the atonement. Metaphors from Israel's sacrificial system communicate something important about the death of Jesus, but they cannot contain the profundity of the cross of Christ.

The nature of metaphor suggests another interpretive imperative: not all properties are necessarily embraced or legitimated in a given use of a metaphor.[12] Mark 10:45 ("For the Son of Man came not to be served but

---

[10]Cf. Colin Gunton, *The Actuality of the Atonement: A Study of Metaphor, Rationality and the Christian Tradition* (Grand Rapids, Mich.: Eerdmans, 1989), esp. chap. 2.

[11]Cf. George Lakoff and Mark Johnson, *Metaphors We Live By* (Chicago: University of Chicago Press, 1980).

[12]Cf. Umberto Eco, *Semiotics and the Philosophy of Language*, AS (Bloomington: Indiana University Press, 1984), chap. 3.

to serve and to give his life a ransom for many") employs the metaphor of ransom, but this usage need not encourage speculation on the nature of this business transaction. Who pays the ransom? To whom is it paid? These questions are not addressed by the text, either by this verse or by the larger narrative of Mark's Gospel. This may well be because, as we saw in chapter two, in Israel's historical exodus from Egyptian bondage, "ransom" is understood primarily as "release" (and not as "payment").

Umberto Eco provides an interesting example of this problem by referring to a medieval encyclopedia, where everything that exists is nothing other than "an emanative outpouring" of God. In this shared understanding of the world, "every being functions as a synecdoche or metonymy of the One." The code, however, is ambiguous. Is the lion a figure of Christ or of antichrist? On the one hand, "the lion erases his tracks with his tail … and is thus a figure of Christ canceling the traces of sin." On the other, according to a medieval exegesis of Psalm 21, the "terrible maw of the beast … becomes a metaphor of Hell" and, thus, of the antichrist. How might a person disambiguate any particular usage of the lion metaphor? "In order to decide whether the lion must be seen as a *figura Christi* or as a figure of the Antichrist, a *co-text* was necessary."[13] That is, the person must refer to the sentences and larger textual units surrounding the metaphorical reference and relating to it so as to constrain its interpretation.

Of course, Eco's example raises another issue. Apart from avid readers of the book of Revelation or of C. S. Lewis's Chronicles of Narnia, not many of our contemporaries would struggle with the aforementioned ambiguity at all. We do not as a matter of course employ the metaphor of "lion" in order to refer to Christ (or the antichrist). Hence, the success of a metaphor is a function not only of interpretive attention being paid to cotext but also of shared sociohistorical presuppositions. Anselm's model of the atonement arose out of and reflects a particular sociohistorical moment relatively foreign to us. One important mode of analysis of his

---

[13]Ibid., pp. 103-4.

model would therefore be to inquire into its ability to communicate within or against the world in which Anselm worked.

The same might be said of Paul's metaphors of course, and this is our fourth point of response. It is certainly of interest that, although Paul uses an almost inexhaustible series of metaphors to represent the significance of Jesus' death, penal substitution (at least as popularly defined) is not one of them.[14]

We can go further, highlighting key points developed more fully above, in chapter two. (1) It is not only that Paul commissions a wide array of metaphors for communicating the significance of Jesus' death to his diverse audiences. (2) It is also that Paul never operates with the picture of God or the God-Jesus relationship attributed to Paul by many of his recent critics. For Paul, notions of punishment and retribution are peripheral at best. As Stephen Travis has argued, "He understands both salvation and condemnation primarily in relational terms: people's destinies will be a confirmation and intensification of the relationship with God or alienation from him which has been their experience in this life."[15] The "wrath of God" is, for Paul, not an affective response on the part of God, not the striking out of a vengeful God. As we have indicated, Paul's concern is not with retributive punishment.

Moreover, (3) Paul's conception of "sin" is not one that accords particular emphasis to individual sinful acts, each of which, it might be thought, attracts divine punishment. Sin, rather, is a general disposition of hostility toward God and God's purpose, a refusal to honor God as God. Sin is a

---

[14]Paul S. Fiddes notes that Paul has a "penal view" of Christ's suffering and that he conceives of Christ as a substitute and representative of humankind, but he denies that these two concepts can be joined in Paul into a theory of "penal substitution," in which atonement is achieved via a transfer of penalty (*Past Event and Present Salvation: The Christian Idea of Atonement* [Louisville: Westminster John Knox, 1989], p. 98). The phrase "penal substitution" is thus a mixing of Pauline metaphors.

[15]Stephen H. Travis, "Christ as Bearer of Divine Judgment in Paul's Thought about the Atonement," in *Jesus of Nazareth: Lord and Christ. Essays on the Historical Jesus and New Testament Christology*, ed. Joel B. Green and Max Turner (Grand Rapids, Mich.: Eerdmans, 1994), p. 332; Travis, *Christ and the Judgment of God* (Basingstoke, U.K.: Marshall, Morgan and Scott, 1986); Travis, "Wrath of God (NT)," in *ABD*, 6:996-98. Contra (among recent interpreters), Leon Morris, *The Cross in the New Testament* (Grand Rapids, Mich.: Eerdmans, 1965), pp. 382-88.

relational problem. Hence, although Paul's notion of atonement takes sin with utmost seriousness, it is concerned above all with the restoration of the divine-human relationship, not with the mollification of a God angered by masses of misdeeds.

Similarly, (4) Paul does not treat God as the subject and Jesus as the object of the cross. S. W. Sykes has suggested that the New Testament juxtaposes two principal narrative sequences in its representation of Jesus' death as a sacrifice. Each of these storylines has its own primary actors—for the one, God; for the other, Jesus. Although these two are not independent of each other, inasmuch as they both focus on the cross of Christ, neither is the one assimilated into the other.

> The one story has to do with God's appointment of Jesus as his "means of dealing with sin." The other story has to do with Jesus' own voluntary self-offering. Told as a single trinitarian drama, this becomes all too easily a monstrous saga in which the Father plans the immolation of his own Son in appeasement of his wrathful rejection of the human race. *But it is highly significant that at no stage is this inference explicitly drawn in the New Testament, where the two narrative sequences tend to occur in somewhat different contexts.*[16]

Jesus, then, is not a victim only but is himself the offerant. (5) What is more, Jesus' self-offering was not the courageous exploit of one who sought his own death, in the same way that the suffering Paul experienced was not suffering for its own sake. Neither Jesus nor Paul was committed to agony and pain, nor did they idolize unjust suffering. In Jesus' commitment to the divine, redemptive purpose, in his solidarity with God's project and with those suffering in a world hostile to God's purpose, Jesus encountered pain in the form of a Roman cross.

Taken on its own terms, then, Paul's theology of the atonement, and that of the New Testament as a whole, is not as susceptible to the charge

---

[16]S. W. Sykes, "Outline of a Theology of Sacrifice," in *Sacrifice and Redemption: Durham Essays in Theology*, ed. S. W. Sykes (Cambridge: Cambridge University Press, 1991), pp. 294-95; emphasis added. See also his earlier essay, "Sacrifice in the New Testament and Christian Theology," in *Sacrifice*, ed. M. F. C. Bourdillon and Meyer Fortes (London: Academic Press, 1980), pp. 61-83.

of glorifying abuse as some have thought. Having raised the issue of faithful engagement with the biblical materials, we are now in a position to turn our attention more directly to the atonement in New Testament teaching.

The Atonement in the New Testament
Within the pages of the New Testament, the saving significance of the death of Jesus is represented chiefly (though not exclusively) via five constellations of images. These are each borrowed from significant spheres of public life in ancient Palestine and the larger Greco-Roman world: the court of law (e.g., justification), commercial dealings (e.g., redemption), personal relationships (whether among individuals or groups—e.g., reconciliation), worship (e.g., sacrifice), and the battleground (e.g., triumph over evil). Each of these examples provides a window into a cluster of terms and concepts that relate to that particular sphere of public life.

For example, without using the actual term *sacrifice* (which, in any case, might be used to refer to a variety of cult-related practices, each with its own aim), Paul and John can refer to Jesus as the "Passover Lamb" (1 Cor 5:7) and "the lamb of God who takes away the sin of the world" (Jn 1:29; cf. Jn 1:36; Rev 5:6); Peter can relate how Jesus "bore our sins in his body on the tree" (1 Pet 2:24; cf. 1:19); Jesus' death can be characterized by New Testament writers as "first fruits" (1 Cor 15:20, 23; cf. Lev 23; Deut 16) and the "blood of the covenant" (Mk 14:23; cf. Ex 24:8); and the handing over of Jesus can recall the binding of Isaac (Rom 8:32; cf. Gen 22). The writer of Hebrews qualifies the salvific significance of Jesus' death specifically in terms borrowed from Israel's sacrificial cult (cf., e.g., Heb 9:11-14). Similarly, "reconciliation" can be represented by the specific language of reconciliation (Mt 5:24; Rom 5:10-11; 11:15; 1 Cor 7:11; 2 Cor 5:18-20; Eph 2:16; Col 1:20, 22), but also by the terminology of peace (Eph 2:14-18) and the many acts (e.g., Rom 16:16), pleas (e.g., Philem), and testimonies (e.g., Acts 15:8-9; Gal 3:26-29) of reconciliation that dot the landscape of the New Testament.

Why are so many images enlisted in the atonement theology of the New Testament? Our earlier reflections point immediately to one reason for this plurality. Language for the atonement is metaphorical;[17] given the nature of metaphor, it is unthinkable that one soteriological model could express all of the truth. Hence, even if Christians have always spoken with one voice in their affirmation of Jesus as our Savior, already in the New Testament and certainly since, this affirmation has been understood in a variety of ways.

A second reason for this plurality is pastoral. In what language a person construes the efficacy of Jesus' death is dependent in part on the needs the person hopes to address. "Very different models and categories are used to describe the 'lost' condition of the human race prior to Christ. . . . Different descriptions of the human situation inevitably lead to different explanations of how this has been altered by the work of Christ."[18] If people are lost, they need to be found. If they are oppressed by hostile powers, they need to be delivered. If they exist in a state of enmity, they need to be reconciled. And so on.

More particularly, images of atonement are often used in the New Testament because of the specific needs of a local congregation.[19] The image of reconciliation, for example, which comes very much to the fore in 2 Corinthians 5:14—6:13, helps Paul to lay bare the nexus between the Corinthians' relationship toward him and their status before God. In this context, reconciliation with God would work itself out also in reconciliation with Paul. This lies behind Paul's dual request: "Be reconciled to God!" and "Open wide your hearts [to us]!"

Third, a plurality of metaphors is used to draw out the salvific signifi-

---

[17]See, though, the concreteness of the concept of "reconciliation" as a description of the new relationship between God and humanity that follows from the cross of Christ (I. Howard Marshall, "The Meaning of 'Reconciliation'," in *Jesus the Saviour: Studies in New Testament Theology* [Downers Grove, Ill.: InterVarsity Press, 1990], pp. 258-74).

[18]C. M. Tuckett, "Atonement in the NT," in *ABD*, 1:518.

[19]Cf. John Driver, *Understanding the Atonement for the Mission of the Church* (Scottdale, Penn.: Herald, 1986); Boff, *Passion of Christ*, pp. 78-84.

cance of Jesus' death because of wider cultural considerations. If the message of salvation is universal, and this is one of the constants in New Testament atonement theology, and if that message is to be grasped in ever-expanding cultural circles, then that message must be articulated in culture-specific ways. As Mertens observes, "Images of Christ and conceptions of salvation bear the mark of the prevailing cultural consciousness and are only temporarily relevant. They do not remain always and everywhere equally useful. Some 'age' quicker than others."[20] Merten's choice of words, "temporarily relevant," helpfully underscores the cultural rootedness of christological images but too easily masks the possibility of our understanding in our contexts images initially set in others. To affirm biblical books as Scripture is itself to embrace the ongoing relevance of their message, including their metaphors. At the same time, even these metaphors have a context—including their cultural rootedness as well as their significance within the ongoing narrative of God's engagement with his people. The point here is that, in the case of the atonement in the New Testament, images are drawn from and shaped by a range of possibilities constrained by Israel's own Scriptures and religious life, as well as the wider public discourse of Roman antiquity. Even if they are to varying degrees transformed by their association with the crucifixion of Jesus of Nazareth, they nevertheless take their interpretive point of departure from prominent, shared, social intercourse.

By way of rooting ourselves more fully in the atonement theology of the New Testament, we may examine selected images employed by various New Testament writers. Following this, we will turn finally to some preliminary implications of this discussion for atonement thought today.

Redemption

In their Greek-English lexicon, Louw and Nida identify the key terms for "redemption"—*lytroomai* ("to release or set free"), *lytrōsis* ("redemption"),

---

[20]Mertens, *Not the Cross*, pp. 63-64.

apolytrōsis ("redemption"), *lytrōtēs* ("redeemer"), *lytron* ("means of release," "ransom"), and *antilytron* ("ransom")—in the semantic subdomain of "release, set free," together with a number of other terms the usage of which in the New Testament sometimes pertains to salvation: *luō, apoluō, apallassō* ("to release, to set free"); *agorazō, exagorazō* ("to purchase, to redeem"); *aphesis* ("the process of setting free or liberating"); *eleutheria, eleutheros, eleutheroō* ("to be free," "to set free").[21] We list these terms to illustrate again the linguistic variety available to early Christians as they sought to articulate the significance of Jesus' death—in this case even within the general framework of "redemption."[22]

Luke-Acts collects a number of these terms (cf. Lk 1:68, 77; 2:38 [cf. 2:25]; 21:28; 24:21; Acts 7:35) in such a way as to link the concept of redemption with the prototypical act of deliverance in the Old Testament: the liberation of God's people from Egypt. This is accomplished in a way that underscores the agency of Jesus (like Moses) as "deliverer" and that identifies God's action in Jesus as deliverance from sociopolitical oppression and as the forgiveness of sins. Interestingly, however, rather than draw a bridge from Jesus' death to this full-bodied notion of redemption, characters within Luke's story understand the crucifixion as a denial of their hope that Jesus would be the one to redeem Israel (Lk 24:19-21). Even though the narrator labels this view as a profound misunderstanding, he goes on to show only that the cross was not a contradiction of such longings, not that the cross was directly instrumental in instigating God's redemption. For Luke, the totality of Jesus' ministry—his coming, his public mission, his death, his exaltation and present activity via the Spirit—play this role.

More to the point in discerning the role of the concept of redemption in

---

[21] Johannes P. Louw and Eugene A. Nida, eds., *Greek-English Lexicon of the New Testament Based on Semantic Domains*, 2 vols. (New York: United Bible Societies, 1988), 1 §§37.127-38. They also mention δικαιοὸ—usually "to justify" but in Romans 6:7 "to release [from the power of sin]."

[22] See I. Howard Marshall, "The Development of the Concept of Redemption in the New Testament," in *Jesus the Saviour* (Downers Grove, Ill.: InterVarsity Press, 1990), pp. 239-57.

the larger drama of the atonement in the New Testament are data from other New Testament writers. Immediately coming to mind is the concept of "ransom saying" ("For the Son of Man came not to be served but to serve and to give his life a ransom [*lytron*] for many"—Mt 20:28; Mk 10:45; cp. 1 Tim 2:6; Tit 2:14), which plays a central role in the Gospels of Matthew and Mark. This saying identifies the cardinal purpose of Jesus' mission as service toward others, then identifies the death of Jesus as the ultimate expression of a life lived on behalf of others. The author of 1 Timothy makes a similar point, identifying Jesus' death as the means of deliverance and clarifying with the use of "all" that, in his death, Jesus was the mediator between God and the whole of humanity.

Paul uses the language of redemption (*apolytrōsis*) in Romans 3:21-26 (esp. vv. 24-25) where the primary emphasis is on God's own integrity, but where God's integrity is certified by the assertion that redemption is in Christ, through his death now understood as an atoning act. In Romans 8:23 the term is used in a different, eschatological sense for the divine consummation of God's deliverance on a cosmological scale. According to Colossians 1:13-14, redemption is related to the forgiveness of sins but is also developed in the context of talk of competing kingdoms. Redemption entails freedom from the "power of darkness" for new life and loyalty to God's Son. In other cases, Paul employs the language of purchase leading to the release of slaves to represent the salvific effect of the cross. "You have been bought with a price," he writes to the Corinthians, reminding them that through Christ's death they have been set free from bondage to sin but now belong to the Lord (1 Cor 6:20; 7:23). In this context, Paul insists that Christians have been freed through the cross for service to Christ. Elsewhere he writes, "Christ has redeemed you from the curse of the law" (Gal 3:13). Among the Galatians, then, Paul portrays the law as a powerful force holding the Jewish people captive; in his death, the apostle argues, Christ has set them free by putting into effect the universal blessing of the divine covenant (to both Jew *and* Gentile). The law has not been destroyed, as though the freedom won in Christ might lead to gratification of "fleshly desires": "Do not use your freedom as an opportunity for self-indulgence, but through love become slaves to one another" (Gal 5:13).

Likewise, the book of Revelation communicates the idea of the "purchase" of believers through the death of Jesus (e.g., Rev 5:9); ransomed, they are made into a new people serving God. Given the content of Revelation as a whole, redemption must be understood as deliverance from evil powers, together with unyielding allegiance to the Lamb. First Peter 1:18-19 affirms that believers were "ransomed" from the futile ways of their ancestors "with the precious blood of Christ" (cf. Eph 1:7; 2 Pet 2:1). In these and related passages, New Testament writers are drawing on a wealth of what would have been shared experience in the larger Greco-Roman world. Those familiar with the history of Israel, of course, would have heard reverberations of the story of the exodus in the background of such references (e.g., Ex 6:6; cf. Is 51:11). Others, however, might have been led to conjure up images of the "redemption" of slaves or of prisoners of war.

This raises the question, If Jesus' death "purchased" believers, to whom was the purchase price paid? The devil? The demonic world? It is here, at this juncture, that we encounter the limits of the metaphor of redemption. Israel might think of God's redeeming them from Egypt without assuming thereby that God actually paid Pharaoh a price for his former slaves. In the same way, a number of New Testament texts present Jesus' death as a ransom without identifying or indeed without even conveying the notion of a recipient of that "price." Underscored instead are the result of being purchased—namely, service to Christ—and the high cost of the deliverance that Christ's death wins.

Sacrifice

The importance of this category for explicating the death of Jesus in the New Testament is intimated simply by its prevalence and the variety of ways it appears. The formulaic expression "Christ died for all" and its many variants (cf., e.g., Mk 10:45; 14:24; Rom 5:6, 8; 1 Cor 8:11; 15:3; Gal 2:21; 1 Thess 5:10; 1 Pet 3:18) points to an understanding of Jesus' death as sacrificial in some sense. This is also true of references to his blood (e.g., Acts 20:28; Rom 5:9; Col 1:20), a graphic way of referring to sacrificial death. Jesus' death is interpreted as a covenant sacrifice (e.g., Mk 14:24; 1 Cor 11:25; Heb 7:22; 8:6; 9:15), a Passover sacrifice (e.g., Jn 19:14; 1 Cor 5:7-8), the sin offering (Rom 8:3; 2 Cor 5:21), the offering of first fruits (1 Cor 15:20, 23), the ritual of the Day of Atonement (Hebrews 9—10), and an offering like that of Isaac by Abraham (e.g., Rom 8:32). As the writer of Ephesians affirms, "Christ loved us and gave himself up for us as a fragrant offering and sacrifice to God" (Eph 5:2).

Of course, "sacrifice" has no monolithic meaning in ancient Israel. One must not only think of the various types of regular and special sacrifices (e.g., the burnt offering, the cereal offering, the guilt offering, the Passover sacrifice). One must also keep in mind the development of the "sacrifice of obedience"—the preference in some prophetic literature for obedience over sacrifice (e.g., Is 1:10-17; Amos 5:21-25; Mic 6:6-8). This latter development is explicitly highlighted by the author of Hebrews (Heb 10:5-10) and is not far from the background of an overall New Testament witness to the faithfulness/obedience of Jesus Christ.[23] Complicating this picture further, sacrifice was a category known to people in the larger Greco-Roman world quite apart from the sacrificial cult of Israel. Indeed, the idea of *human* sacrifice, the more specific way in which Jesus' death is understood in various New Testament writings, is known best outside of narrowly defined Jewish circles. This does not mean that one must step outside of the trajectories of Israel's religion to come to terms with Jesus' death as a sacrifice. After all, within Hellenistic Judaism one finds precursors to the sacrificial interpretation of Jesus' death, above all in the effective deaths of martyrs as narrated in 1 Maccabees 2:7-38; 2 Maccabees

---

[23]See Richard N. Longenecker, "The Foundational Conviction of New Testament Christology: The Obedience/Faithfulness/Sonship of Christ," in *Jesus of Nazareth: Lord and Christ. Essays on the Historical Jesus and New Testament Christology*, ed. Joel B. Green and Max Turner (Grand Rapids, Mich.: Eerdmans, 1994), pp. 473-88.

6:18—7:42; 4 Maccabees 6:24-30. In these texts the execution of the faithful is given special meaning in God's purpose—for example, as a means of resisting evil, of bringing forward God's vindication of his people, and even as an act atoning for one's own sins or sins of the nation.[24]

In what way(s) is Jesus' death presented as a sacrifice in the New Testament? We have already collected a number of pertinent references, but it will be helpful to examine in brief detail the sacrificial imagery of a few New Testament writers. In Romans 3:25, Paul can hardly have anything in mind other than Jesus' death as a sacrifice, referring as he does to the lid of the ark, the *hilastērion:* "The place at which atonement was made for the entire community of Israel on the great Day of Atonement in accordance with God's ordinance."[25] In Romans 3 Paul's usage of this term probably refers not so much to the "place" of atonement as its "means."[26] This is a much-debated text, and many interpreters have found here a Pauline affirmation of Christ's appeasement of God's wrath, called forth by human sin, by Christ's death. Such an interpretation helpfully underscores the righteousness of God but places the transformative significance of Christ's death in the wrong place. What is required is not a transformation within God's heart toward sinners but a transformation of their sinful existence before God.[27] The sacrificial character of Jesus' death in this context does bring God's holiness to expression, then, but by dealing with human sin. Here, as in Romans 8:3 and 2 Corinthians 5:21, where Jesus' death is likened to the sin offering, Paul underscores the magnitude of sin's reach and power. God's condemnation of sin is effected via the death of Jesus, and the death of Jesus marks the end of sin's power.

---

[24]Moreover, the interpretations of the deaths of the martyrs as atoning, as narrated in 2 and 4 Maccabees, themselves build on scriptural images of sacrifice and the Isaianic portrayal of the Servant of Yahweh whose suffering would be for the benefit of God's people. This reality is typically not taken with sufficient gravity by those who attempt to locate the immediate background to Paul's atonement theology in 4 Maccabees. Would not Jesus and his followers be capable of participating in a similar, parallel creative appropriation of those sacrificial metaphors and Servant passages?

[25]Jürgen Roloff, "ἱλαστήριον," in *EDNT,* 2:185-86.

[26]See the discussion in James D. G. Dunn, *Romans,* WBC 38a (Dallas: Word, 1988), pp. 170-72.

[27]So Judith M. Gundry-Volf, "Expiation, Propitiation, Mercy Seat," in *DPL,* p. 282.

The Fourth Gospel identifies Jesus' death as sacrificial in three related passages. First, in greeting Jesus, John the Baptist identifies him as "the Lamb of God who takes away the sin of the whole world" (Jn 1:29, 35). A clue to the appropriate interpretation of this identification appears much later, in John 19:14 (cf. Jn 18:28; 19:31), where the fourth evangelist emphasizes that Jesus' execution took place at the time of the slaughter of the Passover sacrifice. Hence, even though other interpretations might be suggested by the currency of the phrase "lamb of God" in contemporary literature (e.g., the lamb sacrificed in the burnt offering, the messianic lamb/ram of apocalyptic literature, the lamb/Servant of Yahweh silent before the shearers, et al.), the image of Jesus as Passover lamb is paramount.[28]

In chapter 5 of the book of Revelation, John records a crisis around the quandary of who might be able to open the scroll containing the hidden purpose of God. The initial identification of the one determined to be worthy to open the scroll, "the Lion of the Tribe of Judah" and "the Root of David," suggests powerful images of the Davidic Messiah, the conquering one. This is all immediately and radically reinterpreted, however, as this messianic figure is further identified as the Lamb whose sacrificial death has redeemed people from all nations (Rev 5:5-10). The victory of the Messiah—and, indeed, of the people of God—is won through a sacrificial death. Following this, "lamb" serves as a chief christological image for the book as a whole. From this text onward, however, we understand that the defeat of all that opposes the rule of God, portrayed throughout Revelation, has been accomplished by his sacrificial death.

Finally, it is imperative that we recall the sacrificial interpretation of Jesus' death that pervades the letter to the Hebrews. The author of Hebrews observes that "without the shedding of blood there can be no forgiveness of sins" (Heb 9:22), and builds a case that in his role as both

---

[28]Cf. the helpful discussion in Rudolf Schnackenburg, *The Gospel According to St. John* (New York: Crossroad, 1990), 1:297-301; I. Howard Marshall, "Lamb of God," in *DJG*, pp. 432-34.

priest and sacrificial victim, Jesus has "appeared once for all at the end of the age to remove sin by his own sacrifice" (Heb 9:26). Importantly, though, this author has not set for himself the task of defending or explicating the sacrificial system of Israel. Quite the contrary, he uses Israel's categories in order to show how Israel's past has been superseded by the work of Christ. Jesus' death has instituted a new covenant—one in continuity with but superior to the former covenant.

Revelation

The concept of atonement is not often developed in terms of the revelatory character of Jesus' death, but in significant strands of New Testament thought, the cross has this function. In this case, the human predicament is imagined in terms of "blindness" or "lack of perception." It is striking, for example, that human beings in the Gospel of Mark struggle from the beginning of the narrative with the question of Jesus' identity. Finally, having seen the manner of Jesus' death, the centurion recognizes what the narrator and God have been saying all along—namely, that Jesus is the Son of God (Mk 1:1, 9-11; 9:2-8; 15:39). Not only in his powerful and authoritative teaching but also in light of his death, Jesus and his mission must be understood.

The Third Evangelist has his own way of presenting the revelatory character of Jesus' mission. By bringing repeatedly into the foreground the question of the quality of life within the community of believers, Luke draws particular attention to Jesus' life of service toward others. In affirmations of Jesus' present orientation toward service (Lk 22:24-27) and his future, eschatological forms of service (Lk 12:35-38), we gain a glimpse of the character of God—known not for "lording it over" others or otherwise taking advantage of humans through abusive expressions of power but for mercy and grace. As we have intimated, though, this emphasis on revelation is not focused for Luke narrowly on the death of Jesus.

The Fourth Gospel, on the other hand, does point in a more emphatic way to the revelatory character of the cross. John's overarching concern with the theme of revelation is transparent in his ample use of the language of ignorance and knowing, blindness and seeing, and so on. Of Jesus John writes, "The true light, which enlightens everyone, was coming into the world" (Jn 1:9). The drama of the Fourth Gospel develops more pointedly around the theme of the coming of the "hour," however, and this is the "hour" of Jesus' being "lifted up," his glorification, his return to the Father. And these images reach their acme for John in the crucifixion of God's Son. What about God is revealed in the cross? In a passage with interesting parallels to the hymn to Christ in Philippians 2:6-11, John interprets the purpose of the incarnation in Jesus' self-giving (Jn 13:1-17). This self-giving is expressed both in the disgraceful act of a Teacher and Lord washing the feet of his followers and in his life-giving death (Jn 13:1-17). If, then, the cross is the moment in which the full glory of God is revealed (Jn 17:1), this glory is framed in the majesty of other-centered love.

Reconciliation

Our final example is one that may seem best suited to our present age, given our heightened concerns with social psychology and experience of community on the one hand, and our increased awareness of our connectedness to the whole cosmos on the other. Reconciliation as a term is not prominent in the New Testament, but as a conceptual umbrella it has wide currency among the New Testament writings. As an image, reconciliation assumes a state of hostility, and in the New Testament this hostility is understood to be present in a variety of relationships—that is, between God and humanity; between humanity and the rest of creation, including the earth but also supernatural powers and principalities; and between humans—master and slave, male and female, Jew and Gentile, the sick and the well, Paul and his churches, rich and poor, and so on. The work of Jesus is effective in bringing peace in all of these arenas and more.

In Paul and the wider Pauline circle, the language of reconciliation proves to be remarkably elastic.[29] In Paul's hands, reconciliation underscores the primacy of God's initiative in providing for salvation and promoting human recovery. Centered on the crucifixion of Jesus in human history, the act of reconciliation nevertheless has eschatological and cosmic ramifications. Just as cosmic forces were created through the agency of Christ, so in his death are they reconciled to God, restored to their authentic vocation in God's divine purpose. Reconciliation is a past event, since it is rooted in the cross, but the work of reconciliation continues until the eschaton. Paul urges the family of God, then, to ongoing reconciliation with God and in ethical comportment. Paul himself writes his job description in such terms: his is a "ministry of reconciliation" (2 Cor 5:18). The apostle lays the conceptual groundwork, but the writer of Ephesians makes explicit the connection between the vocabulary of reconciliation and the destruction of the barriers that separate Jewish from Gentile people. Salvation as portrayed in the Pauline concept of reconciliation, then, has personal and social, human and cosmic, spiritual and material, religious and ethnic meaning.

As we have outlined, many other images for explicating the significance of Jesus' death are noted in the New Testament and might have been explored here. Enough of these have been probed to indicate our great loss when the atonement theology of the New Testament writings is collapsed into one model or metaphor. And enough has been said to lay the groundwork for our final remarks on the constructive theological task.

The New Testament and Atonement Theology Today: Pointing the Way Forward

Our discussion of the significance of the death of Jesus in representative New Testament materials and our survey of a number of models for the

---

[29]Cf. Romans 5:10, 11; 11:15; 1 Corinthians 7:11; 2 Corinthians 5:18, 19, 20; Ephesians 2:16; Colossians 1:20, 22; Ralph P. Martin, *Reconciliation: A Study of Paul's Theology*, rev. ed. (Grand Rapids, Mich.: Zondervan, 1990); Victor Paul Furnish, "The Ministry of Reconciliation," *CurTM* 14 (1977): 204-18; Marshall, "Meaning of 'Reconciliation'."

atonement that appear in the pages of the New Testament have indicated the degree to which atonement theology is capable of being represented in a variety of ways. In fact, a plurality of metaphors has been used in Christian communities since the beginning of the Christian movement. Hence, we have no need to argue for the need to discern new models or transforming old ones for use in communicating the saving significance of Jesus' death today. Our concern lies elsewhere. First, today we must grapple with appropriating language suitable to communicating the profundity of Jesus' salvific work to people outside the Christian faith as well as those inside the church. Second, we must do so in ways that do justice to the biblical presentation of the work of Jesus.

This means, first and foremost, that the cross can never be neglected or marginalized in Christian proclamation, given the centrality of the cross to the writings of the New Testament. If, according to the Gospel of Mark, Jesus cannot be understood as Son of God apart from the cross; if, according to Paul, the messiahship of Jesus is radically nuanced by the adjective *crucified*; if, according to the book of Revelation, the Lion of Judah not only appears but triumphs over evil in all of its guises as the slain Lamb, then we today can scarcely attempt to think and act Christianly in ways that are not fundamentally informed and shaped by the cross. In fact, it is precisely the theology of the cross—that mystery of God at work against all human expectations, the foolishness that reveals the wisdom of God—that works continuously to unseat our own pretensions and efforts to accord privilege to our own agenda over against the way of God's mercy.

Reminding ourselves of the centrality of the cross for Christian faith and life does not mean that we should glorify suffering or justify abuse and victimization, however. For this reason it may be helpful to modify our terminology as Mertens has suggested: "Not the cross, but the Crucified."

"Not the cross, but the Crucified" is our hope. This distinction is extremely important. We must not hope to find our own calvary, nor long for another Golgotha. . . . Well-understood, "cross-faith" does not at all affect the lust for life. But it surely illuminates the evangelical paradox that "whoever loses his life . . . will save it" (Mk 8:35).[30]

Beyond this, how might we engage in a reflective, critical appropriation of New Testament atonement theology? First, this involves our respecting the integrity of the various New Testament writings, accepting their invitations to enter into their worlds and to adopt a perspective from within those writings. We come to appreciate how those writers sought to communicate in language appropriate to their life situations, while at the same time leaving ourselves open to being challenged by their visions of reality and of the purpose of God. This requires that we decenter our own self-interests so as to be addressed by the text as "other," to allow it to engage us in creative discourse, to take the risk of being shaped, indeed transformed in our encounter with Scripture. That is, we allow Scripture to be Scripture in our lives, including our reflections on the cross of Christ.

On the other hand, this does not mean that we lose ourselves in the various New Testament documents. These are first-century documents from the Mediterranean world; we live at the turn of the twenty-first century, many of us from quite different worlds. Understanding how the message of these ancient writers articulates with and challenges their world may shed light on our own experience of the world and of God. Yet we come to these texts as people with our own needs and questions, inquiring into the strategies, sources of authority and contours of those presentations that might inform our own communities of the faithful.

To put this last point more forcefully, we engage in a reflective appropriation of the New Testament message of atonement message not simply (and sometimes not at all) by reading its content directly into our world but also (and sometimes only) by inquiring into how those writers have engaged in the task of theology and ethics. This is true because Paul, Luke, John and the others were concerned to shape a community that

---

[30]Mertens, *Not the Cross*, p. 171.

serves God's aims in particular contexts. We may learn from them, then, how to be faithful to the grace of God and to embody the gospel of God in particular life-situations, but in order to do so we must move beyond the temptation simply to read their words and metaphors into our contemporary world. Sharply put, to speak of "sacrifice" today may be to use the same terms as those used in the first-century world, but spoken in the context of modern-day America those words can hardly mean the same thing. Unlike those who trafficked in the temples of Israel and the Roman world, we are people for whom the butchery of animals lies outside the realm of common experience.

In his study *Communities of Discourse*, Robert Wuthnow has drawn attention to a helpful approach to questions of this sort. Although his direct concerns lie outside of biblical studies, his methodological considerations are equally apropos a reading of atonement theology in the New Testament.[31] He characterizes his investigation as a study of the problem of articulation—that is, how ideas can both be shaped by their social situations and yet manage to disengage from and often challenge those very situations. In the case of atonement theology, we might ask, How can a given New Testament writer be situated in and reflect a particular sociohistorical environment while at the same time working to shape and perhaps to undermine that environment? What strategies does he adopt? How has he engaged in theological and ethical reflection? How has he invited his audience into the reflective and constructive task of discourse on the meaning of Jesus' death and its implications for discipleship? And what can we learn from this New Testament writer about engaging in the same theological task today, in our own social worlds?

To think along these lines is immediately to realize, first, that the models championed in the New Testament for expounding the meaning of Jesus' suffering may not (all) be suited to our day. We realize, second, that

---

[31]Robert Wuthnow, *Communities of Discourse: Ideology and Social Structure in the Reformation, the Enlightenment, and European Socialism* (Cambridge, Mass.: Harvard University Press, 1989).

we must inquire into how those models were used in, say, Paul's world and in his discourse, this by way of perceiving how Paul has adopted *and adapted* that language, those metaphors. Placing them within the divine drama, exegeting them in his letters, he is able to draw on shared experience and vocabulary without being ruled by their currency in the world at large. Having borrowed the language of purchasing slaves or prisoners of war, how then does he mold that language to his own ends? As Marshall observes, "A preacher would surely have delighted to point out the differences between sacral manumission and Christian redemption, and especially to contrast the price paid by the slave in the secular world with the free gift of God in Christ."[32]

Some Central Themes

In our attempt to engage the New Testament faithfully within the integrity of its own discourse and world, as well as to grapple with the needs, vocabulary and values of our own communities, we can be guided by additional themes that are central to atonement thought in the New Testament. Scripture, so to speak, provides us with a particular set of questions to ask as we work to articulate the meaning of Jesus' death in new contexts. Although they leave plenty of room for creative theological reflection, they also provide crucial points of orientation in our reflection.

The first of these turns the spotlight on the human predicament. "Lostness" may be articulated in a variety of ways—blindness, deafness, hard-heartedness, slavery to an evil power, enmity and so on—but one of the constants in the equation of New Testament thinking about the atonement is the acute need of the human community. Humanity does not have the wherewithal to save itself but needs help (salvation, redemption, deliverance and so on) from the outside, from God.

A second coordinate is the necessity of human response that flows out of the gracious act of God. The salvific work of God has not yet run its full

---

[32]Marshall, "Development of the Concept of Redemption," p. 242.

course, but the lives of God's people must already begin to reflect the new reality (new creation) to which God is moving history. We are saved *from*, it is true, but we are also saved *for*. Atonement theology in the New Testament does not simply hold tightly to the work of Christ but opens wide its arms to embrace and guide the lives of Christians. Believers—having been redeemed, reconciled, delivered, bought, justified and so on—are now released and empowered to reflect in their lives the quality of life exemplified by their Savior. This life is modeled after the cross and has service as its basic orientation. Atonement *theology* cannot be separated from *ethics*.

Between the human predicament and the imperative of human response is the divine drama, the ultimate manifestation of the love of God. This is the third coordinate: God, acting on the basis of his covenant love, on his own initiative, was at work in the cross of Christ for human salvation. The New Testament portrays Golgotha along two story lines—one with God as subject, the other with Jesus as subject. It will not do, therefore, to characterize the atonement as God's punishment falling on Christ (i.e., God as subject, Christ as object) or as Christ's appeasement or persuasion of God (Christ as subject, God as object). At the same time, however paradoxical it may seem, what happened on the cross for our atonement was, according to the New Testament, a consequence of God's initiative, a demonstration of divine love. As Paul summarizes, employing one model among many possibilities, "God was in Christ reconciling the world to himself" (2 Cor 5:19). Again, "God displays his love for us in that while we were still sinners Christ died for us" (Rom 5:8).

Fourth, and as a corollary to the three previous themes, New Testament atonement theology accords privilege to no one group over another. What happened on the cross was of universal significance—in the language of the day, for Jew and Gentile, for slave and free, for male and female. The cross was the expression of God's grace for all, for all persons as well as for all creation. Atonement theology thus repudiates ancient and modern attempts at segregating people away from the gracious invitation of God or otherwise possessing as one's own the gift of God available to all humanity.

Conclusion

What would happen if our thinking about the atonement took the church's mission seriously? If the New Testament provides any model in this respect, then one prominent answer would be that we would be dissatisfied with the narrow, even parochial views of the atonement that have become traditional in recent years. This is partially because what we now take to be the traditional view of the atonement employs language and depends on a model of divine-human interaction that is alien to the lives of huge numbers of those to whom the church's mission is directed. Must those outside the church first take a course in Christian theology before they can understand what Christ has done for them?

What is remarkable about the New Testament writers is how they drew on images from the everyday experience of people's lives—the marketplace, for example, or human relationships—in order to portray for them something of what in the end cannot be captured by language or images, the mystery of the saving significance of Jesus' death. This means, second, that our reflection on the atonement would have more of a creative quality about it, as we, following in the footsteps of Peter or Paul, cast about for metaphors and models that speak of this mystery to the people around us. Of course, because we are concerned here with the church's mission, we would take care to ground our reflection in Scripture and the theological and missionary tradition of the church, but this requires that we learn from them the theological and missionary task, not that we mimic their words and repeat their metaphors.

Views of the atonement as set forth by the various New Testament writings are the product of mission mindedness, of working to articulate the nature of the faith in terms that made sense to persons seeking to live in missionary outposts in the ancient world. The significance of Jesus' death "for us" can never be exhausted or captured, so early theologians searched the conceptual encyclopedia of their day in order to communicate in ever-widening circles the nature of God's good news in Christ. Such a range of metaphors was useful not only in proclaiming the meaning of the cross to potential Christians but was also serviceable in the resulting archipelago of local Christian communities.

If we would be faithful to Scripture, we too must continuously seek out metaphors, new and old, that speak effectively and specifically to our various worlds. If we would follow in the path of the New Testament writers, the metaphors we deploy would be at home, but never too comfortable, in our settings. Those writers sought, and we seek, not only to be understood by but also to shape people and social systems around us. Moreover, we would not eschew earlier models or the reality to which they point, but would carry on our constructive work fully in conversation with and under the guidance of the Scriptures of Israel and the church, and of apostolic testimony.

5

MODELS OF
THE ATONEMENT

A History & Assessment

R *eflection on the significance* of the death of Jesus did not come to a standstill at the end of the first century, nor even with the coalescing of narratives, epistles and apocalypse into the canon of the New Testament. Although it is true that the canon-making process placed certain parameters around the paths Christians might take and how far they might take them in their exploration of the meaning of the atonement, it is also true that subsequent centuries saw the development of further ways of thinking about the saving significance of the cross. That is, though the diversity of thinking about Jesus' death has been constrained by the patterns and witness of the New Testament documents, Christian reflection on the atonement has been a fertile field nonetheless.

Having observed something of the range of interpretations of Jesus' death in the New Testament, we are now in a position to see how the atonement has fared in the centuries after the era of Paul, Peter and John. We are also in a better position to evaluate these subsequent developments in light of both the range of possibilities witnessed in the New Testament and the important commonalities those New Testament witnesses share. How have Christian theologians interpreted the atonement in and for their own days? Our aim is not to choose the one best explanation of the atonement but first to present several of these models and theories and then to assess their strengths and weaknesses. This will help us to gain our bearings further as we seek to proclaim the saving significance of the cross in the differing contexts of the church's mission in the world today.

Our discussion will focus on four major models or explanations of the atonement: *Christus Victor*, satisfaction, moral influence and penal substitution. We recognize that throughout church history many church leaders, missionaries and theologians have combined elements from more than one of these categories in their teaching about the cross, and within each category we could explore any number of variations. Our interest, however, is not so much to catalog information about atonement theories but to develop a practice of thinking critically about explanations of the atonement. Therefore we will look at a major proponent of each model—summarizing their thought and evaluating their work in the light of the insights and norms developed in our study of the New Testament.

The *Christus Victor* Model

The writers of the immediate postapostolic period proclaimed salvation by the cross but offered little explanation on how the cross provided salvation.[1] By the late second century, church leaders like Irenaeus began com-

---

[1]In addition to the primary documents cited below, this section is developed in conversation with Gustaf Aulén, *Christus Victor: An Historical Study of the Three Main Types of the Idea of the Atonement* (London: SPCK, 1953); John Driver, *Understanding the Atonement for the Mission of the Church* (Scottdale, Penn.: Herald, 1986), pp. 39-44; H. D. McDonald, *The Atonement of the Death of Christ: In Faith, Revelation, and History* (Grand Rapids, Mich.: Baker, 1985), pp. 125-46.

bining proclamation of the saving significance of the cross with explanations of why Jesus had to die on the cross and how that effected our salvation.

Irenaeus and the next few generations of Christians thought about the cross in a context of conflict with the powers of the day. They participated in a Christian church that asserted that Jesus Christ was Lord, and thus they lived in tension with the dominant social structure of the day that declared Caesar was Lord. Both the church and empire solicited ultimate loyalty. At various times throughout the first three centuries of the church's history, Christian believers experienced both local and empire-wide persecution.[2] The cosmology of that era also led people to understand conflicts on earth as related to and intertwined with conflict between celestial powers. Therefore it is not surprising that Christians framed their discussion of the cross and resurrection in terms of a cosmic conflict between God and the forces of evil with the resurrection sealing Jesus Christ's victory over sin, the devil and powers of evil. Theologians today commonly follow Gustaf Aulén, who in a series of lectures delivered in 1930 labeled this the *Christus Victor* (Christ the Conqueror) model of the atonement.

The conflict-victory motif is common throughout those writing about the atonement in the second through fourth centuries. It is misleading, however, to say that the writers shared a single common theory of the atonement, because in their writings they included a variety of images and metaphors of the atonement. In addition, although they wrote about the atonement within a common framework of conflict victory, they did so in different ways. We will look at two of the main descriptions of the atonement developed within the *Christus Victor* framework.

---

[2]J. Denny Weaver argues that we must understand the historical matrix of church confronting empire as influencing the development of *Christus Victor* motif of the atonement and also see the rise of the Constantinian synthesis of church and empire as causing the abandonment of the *Christus Victor* explanation of the atonement (*Keeping Salvation Ethical: Mennonite and Amish Atonement Theology in the Late Nineteenth Century* [Scottdale, Penn.: Herald, 1997], pp. 39-49).

Irenaeus: *Christus Victor* as Recapitulation

Irenaeus (ca. 130-202), the bishop of Lyons, wrote in the late second century, when Gnostic sects and ideas were widespread. He sought to counter the Gnostic idea that evil had its source in matter and that salvation or escape from the corrupted body was through special knowledge. Like the Gnostics, Irenaeus understood humans as naturally mortal but stated that God had granted humans immortality as a special favor. Adam and Eve's sin corrupted humanity, so that they lost their immortality. In contrast to the Gnostics, therefore, for Irenaeus the root problem was not matter itself but a willful action by Adam and Eve—a disobedience in which each human has participated. Irenaeus argued that humans cannot, through knowledge or any other means of their own, escape their corrupted state. Salvation can only be through Christ.

Irenaeus, stressing the Pauline parallelism between Adam and Christ, emphasized that Adam was the originator of a disobedient race, and Christ inaugurated a new redeemed humanity. Central to his thinking was an idea he calls "recapitulation."[3] He writes, "God recapitulated in Himself the ancient formation of man and woman, that He might kill sin, deprive death of its power and vivify humanity."[4] Here the entire human race is represented in Jesus. Just as all humans were somehow present in Adam, so they can be present in the second Adam.

> For by no other means could we have obtained to incorruption and immortality, unless we had been united to incorruptibility and immortality. But how could we be joined to incorruptibility and immortality, unless, first, incorruptibility and immortality had become that which we also are, so that the corruptible might be swallowed up by incorruptibility, and the mortal by immortality, that we might receive the adoption of sons and daughters?[5]

---

[3] Also called the *physical theory of the atonement*.

[4] Irenaeus *Against Heresies* 3.18.7. In older texts that are in the public domain, such as this one, we have adapted the translations by using inclusive language when referring to humans.

[5] Ibid., 3.19.1.

In recapitulation Christ both sums up and restores humanity. Irenaeus placed great importance on the incarnation—Christ becoming human so that he could fill the representative role and so that he could pass through every stage of life. Adam lived making wrong choices, but Christ lived making right choices. Christ as a human could both resist and conquer the devil, where the human Adam did not.

> In such wise, then, was His triumph of our redemption, and His fulfilment of the promise to the patriarchs, and His doing away with the primal disobedience: the Son of God became a son of David and a son of Abraham; for in the accomplishment of these things, and in their summing up in Himself, in order to give us His own life, the Word of God was made flesh through the instrumentality of the Virgin, to undo death and work life in humans; for we were in the bonds of sin, and were to be born through sinfulness and to live with death. . . . [The Word] put Himself in our position, and in the same situation in which we lost life; and He loosed the prison-bonds, and His light appeared and dispelled the darkness in the prison, and He sanctified our birth and abolished death. . . . And He showed forth the resurrection, becoming Himself "the first-born from the dead," and raised in Himself prostrate humanity, being lifted up to the heights of heaven, at the right hand of the glory of the Father.[6]

In the context of Platonic realism, the idea of the Logos redeeming humanity by becoming human would have been an easily accessible and believable concept. Irenaeus' readers could think of humankind as a universal in which all individual people participated. So when Christ became human, he could suffuse the universal with immortality and thus redeem humanity. If Irenaeus had completely followed Platonic logic, however, then Christ would have simply been the bearer of a mysterious heavenly substance brought to earth to inoculate humanity with the Divine. In that case, the incarnation itself would have been sufficient for salvation. In the moment of assuming human flesh, Christ would have saved all human

---

[6]Irenaeus *Proof of the Apostolic Preaching* 37, 38.

flesh. Irenaeus clearly did not believe that. He discussed the role of human faith and choice in salvation,[7] and he also made clear that it was not just the incarnation of the Word that provides salvation but also Jesus Christ's death and resurrection.

> So, if He was not born, neither did He die; and if He did not die, neither was He raised from the dead; and if He was not raised from the dead, He has not conquered death, nor is its reign abolished; and if death is not conquered, how are we to mount on high into life, being subject from the beginning to death?[8]

Finally, it is important to observe that Irenaeus did not limit himself to only one model of the atonement. Mixed in with his talk of recapitulation are statements of propitiation,[9] and he also explored the meaning of Jesus' death in terms that would place him in the next subsection of this chapter: "[Christ] by his blood, gave himself as the ransom for those who had been carried into captivity."[10]

Gregory of Nyssa: *Christus Victor* as Ransom

Irenaeus and others mentioned ransom when they wrote about the cross since Jesus himself said that he had come to give his life as a ransom for many (Mk 10:45). The concept of ransom was also a part of everyday life at the time when theologians were using the *Christus Victor* model to explain the atonement. In spite of the efforts of the Roman emperors to establish peace and order, marauding gangs roamed the roads, capturing travelers and demanding a ransom payment for their release. Slaves lived in bondage but could be redeemed and freed for a price. Ambrose, bishop of Milan (ca. 345-407), spent all he had and melted the church's sacramental vessels in order to ransom those who had been captured in the battle of Adrianopole. Ransom and release were powerful and concrete

---

[7]Irenaeus *Against Heresies* 5.27.2; 5.28.
[8]Irenaeus *Proof of the Apostolic Preaching* 39.
[9]For example, Irenaeus *Against Heresies* 5.17.1.
[10]Irenaeus *Against Heresies* 1.1.

images for Christians in the early centuries of the church.

As theologians and preachers like Irenaeus spoke of Jesus Christ's saving work in terms of ransom, inevitably the question arose, To whom is the ransom paid? The most common answer was the devil. Origen of Alexandria (ca. 185-254) was the first who developed a detailed theory of how Jesus was a ransom payment to the devil.

> To whom did he give his life a ransom for many? Assuredly not to God, could it then be to the Evil One? For he was holding fast until the ransom should be given him, even the life of Jesus; being deceived with the idea that he could have dominion over it, and not seeing that he could not bear the torture in retaining it.[11]

The devil accepted the deal, but according to Origen, the goodness of Jesus was too much for the devil. He could not stand having Jesus in his grasp; this was torture. He let go and lost his ransom payment after having already given up his prisoners.

Origen pictures Jesus as conquering the devil through the devil's own miscalculation and self-deception. Gregory of Nyssa (330-ca. 395) describes God as conquering the devil through trickery; God deceived or tricked the devil. On the one hand, Gregory thought that God's justice would not allow God simply to rescue sinners by force; the devil had a right to adequate compensation for sinners who had sold themselves into slavery to him. He wrote, "It was requisite that no arbitrary method of recovery, but the one consonant with justice, should be devised by Him who in His goodness had undertaken our rescue."[12] Gregory describes the devil as thinking he was getting a good deal by taking Jesus as a ransom payment, "The Enemy saw . . . an opportunity for an advance, in the exchange, upon the value of what he held. For this reason he chose [Jesus] as a ransom for those who were shut up in the prison of death."[13] The

---

[11] Origen *In Matthaeum* 16.8.
[12] Gregory of Nyssa "The Great Catechism" 22.
[13] Ibid., 22.

devil, however, was tricked because he was unaware of the divinity of Jesus hidden under his human flesh.

> The Deity was hidden under the veil of our nature, that so, as with ravenous fish, the hook of the Deity might be gulped down along with the bait of flesh, and thus, life being introduced into the house of death, and light shining in darkness, that which is diametrically opposed to light and life might vanish; for it is not in the nature of darkness to remain when light is present, or of death to exist when life is active.[14]

In this way God triumphed over the devil and the power of death.

Gregory recognized that some may think it inappropriate for God to act in a deceiving way. He responds, however, that God's actions were appropriate because they achieved a just result and because the devil was getting what he deserved.[15] The devil himself had deceived humans by "spreading the glamour of beauty over the hook of vice like a bait."[16] Just as Irenaeus did not limit his discussion of atonement to recapitulation, so Gregory did not focus solely on the image of ransom. In fact, in the midst of his discussion of ransom, Gregory makes direct mention of the stages of Jesus' life, birth, rearing, growing up and advancing to death, and of the role of recapitulation in Christ's victory over evil and the evil one.[17]

Christus Victor: An Assessment

Irenaeus and Gregory of Nyssa offer explanations of the atonement born from the writings in the New Testament and from the context of their ministries. The image of the cross as a victory over the powers and the metaphor of ransom or redemption are explicitly developed in the New Testament, and the concept of recapitulation coheres well with Paul's

---

[14]Ibid., 24.
[15]Ibid., 26.
[16]Ibid., 21.
[17]Ibid., 26.

writing on Adam and Christ.[18] In their day the theme of conflict and victory was not only intelligible but had pastoral significance because of the cosmology and lived experience of the people. The ransom metaphor powerfully communicated the saving significance of the cross because people of their era had seen slaves and captives ransomed and liberated. These writers used thought forms of the day, like Platonic realism, but were not controlled by them. They resisted following Platonism to its logical conclusion, which would have implied that at the moment of the incarnation of the Logos all humanity was saved. They fully embraced the scandalous notion of God's becoming incarnate in human flesh and dying on a cross, and thus took a stand against Gnosticism.

These writers clearly communicate the acute need of humanity for liberation from enslavement to sin and the powers of evil at both a corporate and personal level, and they do so without presenting Christ's victory in a way that privileges certain persons or groups over others. Jesus' life of obedience, and not just the moment of crucifixion, is integral to both the recapitulation model and the ransom metaphor. Therefore, these theologians' teaching on the atonement easily lends itself to reflection on the ethical implications of Jesus' saving activity since the way he lived his life is an integral part of the saving work. Irenaeus, Origen and Gregory of Nyssa each avoid even hinting at Christ appeasing God the Father, or the Father punishing the Son. Indeed, in light of what we will see in later thinkers, it is interesting and significant to note that Origen strongly dismisses the notion that Jesus Christ was supplying a ransom payment to God the Father.

A person might critique the *Christus Victor* model by saying it does not capture all of the significance of the cross. However, Irenaeus and Gregory never claim that it does, and they include other images and metaphors in their writing about the cross. In that sense these early theologians follow the New Testament writers in not attempting to put forward a single

---

[18]For example, victory over the powers: Galatians 4:3-9; Ephesians 2:14-16; 3:7-13; Colossians 2:13-15; ransom/redemption: Matthew 20:28; 1 Corinthians 6:20; 7:23; Galatians 4:3-9; 1 Timothy 2:6; Titus 2:14; Revelation 5:9; recapitulation: Romans 5:12-21; 1 Corinthians 15:22, 45; Ephesians 1:10.

model as though it captured the whole meaning of the cross. At the same time, it is also true that when Gregory pushed beyond both the model and content of the New Testament and attempted to explain the details and mechanics of the ransom payment, he got into trouble. As others would do later, he found himself basing key parts of his explanation on what his logic led him to identify as acceptable and unacceptable behavior for God, and as he achieved greater clarity, he also ended up stating explicitly what others had avoided or left hazy—namely, that the devil had certain rights and powers that God must respect. These details make for a more complete explanation of how our salvation was achieved at the cross, but in the process Gregory develops a satanology that does not find support in the New Testament. He leans heavily on his imagination and allows the logic of his metaphors to take him further than can be supported.

Some have blamed the details of Gregory's explanation for the gradual decline of the popularity of the *Christus Victor* model. This is unlikely since other explanations of *Christus Victor* were available. For instance, although contemporaries of his, like Gregory of Nazianzus, did reject aspects of Gregory's depiction of salvation by ransom, many continued to write from within a *Christus Victor* framework. Like Origen, however, they placed more emphasis on the source of the devil's downfall in his own self-deception. God did not deceive him; rather, the devil overreached his own power, thinking that at the cross he had received a prize that would leave him in control, only to be surprised by the resurrection. Therefore, although the details surrounding the ransom metaphor may have contributed to the decline of the use of the *Christus Victor* motif after the sixth century, its decline was more likely caused by a changing cosmology and the Constantinian synthesis of church and state. The tension between the empire and the church had, in the early days of the church, funded an atonement theology grounded in the image of Christ conquering even in death. When the church became so closely linked with worldly powers, then a conflict-victory metaphor was less connected to people's daily lives.

Anselm: Satisfaction Model

Anselm of Canterbury (1033-1109) addresses the issue of the atonement in his book *Cur Deus Homo* (*Why Did God Become Human?*). Anselm rejects any notion of a debt to the devil (2.21)[19] and does not develop a recapitulation model of the atonement. He gives singular importance to a substitutionary motif in which Christ's sacrificial death offers satisfaction to God for the debt owed to God by sinful humanity. Although it may be true that penal substitution models that developed later have strong similarities with Anselm's satisfaction model of the atonement, there are also significant differences. We are unfair to Anselm if we simply lump him together with any approach that stresses that Jesus died in a substitutionary way to satisfy God the Father. Offering one blanket critique would not be accurate or appropriate, and we would lose the opportunity to learn valuable lessons if we do not read Anselm's work and evaluate it in terms of its own context.

Anselm's Medieval Setting

Before recreating the flow of Anselm's argument, we will quote a parable from near the end of his book. This parable offers a good summary of his argument, but more importantly it displays that Anselm is thinking about this whole issue in terms of medieval kings, lords and vassals.

> Let us suppose there is a king whom all the population of his state (except only one individual, who is, however, of the same race), has so often offended that not one of them, by any action of his own, can escape the penalty of death: but that he, who alone is innocent, is so high in the king's favor that he can, and bears so great a love to the culprits that he will, reconcile all who will believe in his advice, by a certain service which will greatly please the king, to be done on a day fixed according to the king's will. But since not all who need to be reconciled can assemble on that day, the king grants, on account of the magnitude of that service, that whoever,

---

[19]The in-text citations used throughout this section refer to the book and chapter of Anselm's *Cur Deus Homo.*

either before or after that day, shall have avowed their desire to ask for forgiveness through that service done on that day, and to adhere to the covenant thus made, shall be absolved from all past offenses; and that should it happen that after this pardon they transgress again, if they will worthily make satisfaction and thenceforward amend, they shall again receive forgiveness through the efficacy of the same covenant; only under this condition, that no one shall enter into his palace until that have been done whereby the guilt shall be forgiven. (2.16)

As this parable exemplifies, we can hardly overemphasize the importance of honor and satisfaction in Anselm's description of the atonement.

Both honor and satisfaction were of extreme significance in the medieval world of chivalry and feudalism, of knights, lords and vassals. It was a society of a carefully managed series of reciprocal obligations. The lord provided capital and protection; the serf provided honor, loyalty and tribute. Honor demanded that a lord do what was proper and act as a lord should act. For example, it would not be proper for a lord to fail to fulfill his pledge of protection to a vassal. Those under the lord must fulfill their oaths of loyalty. If a vassal did not fulfill the requirements of an oath, he must offer something to satisfy the offended lord. It was seen as unbefitting if a lord did not demand redress from a guilty vassal or did not take revenge against another lord who had in some way offended him. In Anselm's era, as in many others, the degree of punishment given for a crime depended not only on the severity of the crime but on the rank of the offended person: the higher the rank the higher the penalty. These medieval concepts and practices are evident throughout the pages of *Cur Deus Homo*.

In the religious realm Anselm lived in an age consumed by the seriousness of sin and fear of divine wrath. Recounting of sins, the means of their remission and procedures for absolution were pressing pastoral and theological issues. In this context it is noteworthy, as Ellen Charry points out, that in Anselm's pastoral work as an abbot, he saw gentleness and compassion, not stern discipline and threats, as the choice instruments in character formation. Moreover, in his devotional and theological writings he sought to encourage readers that they could trust in divine mercy. Anselm's writing emphasized that love does not arise out of fear of the wrath of God but in response to God's goodness.[20]

To say, however, that Anselm put the accent on God's love, not God's wrath, does not mean that he rejected the medieval penitential system. Penance was understood as a just or requisite payment of a penalty for a fault. According to the theological categories of his time, excess payment could be stored up as merit and transferred to cover what others owe. This concept is present in Anselm's prayers and is central to his thinking in *Cur Deus Homo*.[21]

Anselm's *Cur Deus Homo*

In this important treatise, Anselm seeks to answer the question "For by what reason, and by what necessity God was made man, and by His death, as we believe and confess gave life to the world?" (1.1). Why could God not have accomplished this through another human, or simply decreed it? Anselm states that he writes for apologetic reasons to address the questions of unbelievers (1.1). Therefore, although he does at times use Scripture, his aim is to present rationally argued answers to questions independent of one's knowledge of Christ through revelation.[22] *Cur Deus Homo* is divided into two small books. In the first book Anselm sets out to describe the situation without Christ. He explains what the human problem is and what is demanded for a solution. In the second book he shows how Jesus Christ meets the requirements demanded by the first book.

He begins by asking why God should have an interest in saving humanity. The answer is that God must save humans because they will

---

[20]Ellen T. Charry, *By the Renewing of Your Minds: The Pastoral Function of Christian Doctrine* (New York: Oxford, 1997), pp. 154-75.

[21]Ibid., pp. 168-69.

[22]Charry reports that Anselm cites or interpolates scriptural texts sixty-nine times in *Cur Deus Homo* (Charry, *By the Renewing of Your Minds*, p. 169).

belong to whoever saves them from eternal death. It would be inappropriate for humans to be servants to someone other than the one to whom they had been created to serve.

Anselm points out that the incarnation bothers some because they cannot conceive of God's becoming human and suffering—of the "Highest [stooping] to such indignities." Anselm seeks to calm these concerns by stating, "We assert the Divine Nature to be without doubt impassible, and in no way possibly to be brought down from its ineffable exaltation" (1.8). He affirms that Jesus Christ is true God and true Human and that it was the human nature of Jesus Christ that endured humiliation and infirmity, not the Divine.

Anselm also wants to protect God from the accusation of improperly forcing his innocent Son to die. God commanded Christ to die, willed him to die, but did not make Christ die. The Son obeyed the command but did not have to obey. "[He] willingly underwent death in order to save men and women" (1:8). Still one can ask, Is this any way for a father to treat a son? Anselm replies:

> Surely it is most consistent in such a Father to give His consent to such a Son, when He wills something laudably for the honor of God, and useful for the salvation of humans, which could not otherwise have been effected. (1:10)

Jesus Christ's ethical behavior is central to Anselm's argument. Although only in passing, he does state that Jesus' actions serve as a model for humans in encouraging people to act justly, not out of fear of punishment but from a desire to become an instrument of mercy. He writes, "So He gave us a far greater example to influence every person not to hesitate to give back to God, in his own name, when reason requires it, what he is sometime suddenly going to lose" (2:18).

Anselm thinks of sin in terms of not repaying a debt owed to God. If a person always repaid what was owed God, she or he would never sin.

What is the debt we owe to God? The whole will of a rational creature ought to be subject to the will of God. . . . This is the sole and whole honor we owe to God. . . . Whoever renders not unto God this due honor, takes away from God that which is His, and does God dishonor: and this is sin. (1:11)

F. W. Dillistone explains, "In the language of feudal tenure a man's honour was his estate. Normally this was a unit of land, but the term honour also embraced his title and status. The fundamental crime against a lord and against the social order, was to attempt to diminish the lord's honour. . . . It was the maintenance of a king's 'honour' which preserved his kingdom. . . . By withholding his service man is guilty of attempting to withdraw some part of God's 'honour'."[23]

Anselm states that "each sinner ought to repay the honor of which he has robbed God: and this is the satisfaction which every sinner ought to make to God" (1:11). More is required than simply paying for the damage done. It is only fitting to offer some compensation. For instance, if one damages someone's health, it is not enough simply to restore that person's health. One must also offer compensation for the suffering involved. In God's case we must offer compensation for the insult to God's honor (1:11). It is impossible for humans to offer this satisfaction to God. This is for two reasons, the first of which is the degree of sin. We have, in a sense, stolen our whole selves from God, depriving God of whatever he proposed to make of human nature (1:23). It is impossible for humans to compensate God, second, on account of the status of the one sinned against. Because we have sinned against God, whose status is immeasurable, the debt owed to God is likewise immense.

Could God forgive sin without satisfaction being paid? Anselm says no. "If [sin] be not punished, it is unjustly forgiven. . . . [And] it beseemeth not God to forgive anything in His realm illegally" (1:12). "It is . . . not consistent with God to take sinful humanity without reparation made" (1.19). God must preserve "the honor of His own dignity" (1:13).

---

[23] F. W. Dillistone, *The Christian Understanding of Atonement* (Philadelphia: Westminster Press, 1968), pp. 192-93.

Anselm puts the problem in one sentence when he writes, "It is needful that God should complete what He designed in human nature, but ... He cannot do this except through an entire satisfaction for sin, which no sinner can make" (2.4). The penalty can be paid by another person, but no human who already has a debt demanding death (the situation of all humans) can pay the debt for someone else. A sinless person, however, would be debt-free and could pay this debt. The debt payer would have to be human, since it is a human debt, but would have to be greater than human to make complete satisfaction and to make it for all humanity. Therefore, "the satisfaction whereby humanity can be saved can be effected only by One who is God and Human" (2.6). This one is Jesus Christ. "His death shall reconcile sinners to God" (2.15).

Anselm concludes, "What can be more just than that he, to whom is given a payment greater than all that is owing him, should, if this be given in payment of what is owing remit the whole debt?" (2.20).

Anselm's Satisfaction Model: An Assessment

Anselm achieved what he set out to do—namely, to write a logical explanation for the necessity of Jesus Christ's death on the cross. He used a framework and imagery taken, not from the Bible, but from the feudalistic system of his day. Anselm's work matches those of the New Testament writers in a key methodological way. Like them, he sought to interpret the cross with images easily intelligible to the people of his era. This is where Anselm offers us a positive model as he challenges us not to rely simply on the same metaphors that Paul or the author of Hebrews used in a culture and time very distant from his or ours. Also, however, it is at this same methodological point, of rooting his explanation of the atonement in the culture of the day, that Anselm stumbles and offers us a model of what to avoid. He does more than just use images and experiences from daily life to illustrate the atonement; he allows his experience of medieval life—its logic and conventional wisdom—to have an overwhelming influence in the shaping of his model of the atonement. Anselm offers a less-than-biblical view of the cross—not because he uses terms like *vassal* or *satisfaction* that are foreign to biblical writing on the cross but because he uses them in a way that gives the cross and the atonement a meaning at odds with that found in the Bible.

Anselm makes very clear that sin is a huge problem that necessitates extraordinary measures, yet his is a rather narrow view of sin. Because of his focus on honor, he emphasizes dealing with the debt of sin, not on eradicating sin itself. For Anselm, salvation is too easily equated with the remission of the debt. Because of Jesus' work, humans do not have to attempt what would be impossible—namely, to offer recompense and satisfy the huge hurt we caused to God. The biblical concept of salvation places more emphasis on the reestablishment of communion with God and entering a discipleship community. True, to a degree Anselm's concept of sin is relational. For Anselm, in contrast to later penal substitution theories of the atonement that focused on a courtroom setting and infractions against a legal code, the medieval offenses were centered in the relationship between lord and vassal. In the end, however, Anselm's focus on honor causes him to fall short of the relational understanding of sin so central to the biblical writings. The emphasis on meeting the debt to the honor of the offended lord places little importance on the relationship itself and gives no attention to the impact a restored relationship with God will have on a person's relationship with others.

It might appear to some that Anselm's satisfaction thinking lines up well with the biblical concept of redemption. However, for Anselm, redemption is to become free from indebtedness, whereas in the New Testament redemption is freedom from slavery, including slavery to sin. As John Driver observes, "Freed from the servitude of sin, we become servants of God. So biblical redemption is really a change of masters (cf. Ex. 3:12)."[24]

As we have noted, some contemporary theologians view Anselm as the author of a "divine child abuse model of the atonement"—one that pictures a wrathful God punishing his son. It is not clear to us, however, that theolo-

---

[24]Driver, *Understanding the Atonement*, p. 58.

gians of this ilk have engaged in a careful reading of Anselm's thought on its own terms and in its own sociohistorical context. In reality, Anselm differs significantly from those who would later develop penal substitutionary views of the cross. In our criminal-justice system "satisfaction" has to do with the apprehension and punishment of the guilty, whereas for Anselm and his contemporaries, satisfaction hinged on fulfillment of certain obligations to loyalty and honor. Therefore, Anselm does not present a wrathful God punishing Christ in our place; rather, Christ satisfies, or pays, a debt we owe.

Yet Anselm still has a son dying on the cross to satisfy a debt owed his father. So, although Anselm may avoid the extreme version of "divine child abuse" that we find in other satisfaction theories, his depiction could still have allowed the drama of the cross to develop in that way. He recognizes this potential problem and therefore emphasizes that Jesus Christ voluntarily went to the cross; God the Father did not force him to die on the cross. But does this solve the problem?

Answering that question brings us to the first of a number of ways that Anselm's thinking about the atonement is too entangled in his world. He uncritically allows his culture to have too great an influence on his description of the saving significance of the cross. Alternatively, he does not allow God's relation with Israel and the character of God as revealed through Jesus Christ fundamentally to shape his concept of God. That is, Anselm not only borrowed from his feudal society the example of lords and vassals to illustrate the debt we owe God, but he actually allowed medieval concepts of honor to define how God ought to act. When Anselm writes that God cannot simply forgive our sin, he draws his conclusion not from Scripture but from social conventions of his own day. Not in the pages of Scripture, but according to the social norms of his day it was unbefitting for a feudal lord simply to ignore or forgive a debt owed him by a vassal.[25] In addition, we must question the wisdom of his leaning

---

[25]Rowan Williams offers a contrasting view of God's ability and willingness to forgive in "The Forgiveness of Sins," in *A Ray of Darkness* (Boston: Cowley, 1995), pp. 49-53.

so heavily on concepts borrowed from the penance system—such as just payment for a fault and the possibility of earning excess merit—at a time when so many people understood that system as a way to avert the punishment of a wrathful God.

In Anselm's model the offended lord or king is the object of the payment of satisfaction, and, except for demanding this satisfaction, the lord is not an actor in the drama. Therefore, a great weakness of Anselm's model is that it loses the concept of God as actor, the One reconciling the world to himself. Anselm, of course, affirms the divinity of Jesus, so technically God is both subject and object in his model. Anselm, however, does very little to keep one from viewing this drama in a way that alienates the persons of the Trinity from one another. Readers could easily understand that Jesus provides them the merit they need to earn standing with a demanding God and thus think that forgiveness is earned from God by Jesus, whereas in the Bible, forgiveness is God's gracious gift.

Anselm potentially promotes a distorted concept of God not just because linking God with a feudal lord diminishes God's active role in reconciliation but also because readers may too easily associate God's character and practice with those of feudal lords. Certainly some lords treated humanely those on their estate, but many did not. For the latter, as Leonardo Boff observes, Anselm's God would bear little resemblance to the Father of Jesus. Rather,

> he epitomizes the figure of the absolute feudal lord, the master with the power of life and death over his vassals. God is endowed with the traits of a cruel, bloodthirsty judge, bound and determined to exact the last farthing owed by any debtor in justice. A horrible cruelty prevailed in Saint Anselm's time regarding payment of debts. This sociological context is reflected in Anselm's theological text, unfortunately contributing to the development of an image of a cruel, sanguinary, vindictive God, an image still present in many tormented, enslaved Christian minds.[26]

---

[26]Leonardo Boff, *Passion of Christ, Passion of the World: The Facts, Their Interpretation, and Their Meaning Yesterday and Today* (Maryknoll, N.Y.: Orbis, 1987), p. 97.

A significant contributing factor to the problems described in the preceding paragraphs is that Anselm not only used feudal culture to define how God must act, but like many others he accepted the Greek philosophical commitment to an impassible deity. This led Anselm to compartmentalize Jesus' divinity in a way that left it untouched by his human suffering. Anselm keeps the human Jesus at arm's length from God, and this contributes to the sense of division within the Trinity as well as limits the emphasis Anselm can place on Jesus serving as a representative of God to humanity. What the cross reveals to us about God may be as significant as what is accomplished on the cross. Anselm, however, circumvents the scandal of God incarnate on the cross by placing Jesus' divinity in a kind of protective bubble wrap. Anselm's commitment to an impassable God hinders him from using Jesus, the suffering lamb of God, as a corrective to people's concept of a distant, demanding God.

We applaud Anselm's efforts to encourage people to trust in divine mercy instead of living in fear of divine wrath. Yet by uncritically rooting his understanding of the atonement in feudalism, the penance system and Greek philosophy he too easily reinforces the common concept of God as an angry demanding figure. For the same reason, Anselm's work also has weaknesses in the ethical realm.

Anselm briefly mentions the ethical imperative of Jesus' life for Christians. Yet at the ethical level as well, his work fails to capture the scandal of the cross. Jesus' life and the cross challenged and contrasted the accepted systems of status, patronage and balanced reciprocity. Based on the Gospel portrait of Jesus' life, a person could offer a strong challenge to a feudal system that held certain members of society hostage to the debt obligations at the heart of relationships characterized by honor and shame, and challenge medieval attitudes that accepted the notion that a lord's life was of greater value than a peasant's life. Anselm did not challenge these attitudes or the feudal system. Rather, he vaunted them by presenting God in the guise of a feudal lord thus, even if inadvertently, providing divine sanction for the subjugation of human subjects on whose backs the system was built.

Reading Anselm instead of simply accepting a three-sentence summary that represents his work allows a person to recognize *Cur Deus Homo* for what it is: one theologian's attempt to make sense of the atonement by thinking of it not in biblical concepts but in terms of the legal and social norms of his day. As we have tried to make clear, the way he rooted the explanation in his culture is both its great strength and great weakness. The greatest problem in relation to the satisfaction model, however, is not Anselm but those who came after him and stripped his presentation of its medieval garb. These interpreters of Anselm perhaps unwittingly took from him certain core ideas and added from their own day legal terms and ideas alien to his, then presented the result as *the* biblical explanation of the atonement for all times and places. We will evaluate their work in the section on penal substitution, but first we turn to Abelard, a contemporary of Anselm.

Abelard: Moral Influence Model

Peter Abelard (1079-1142) asks the same question as Anselm, "Why . . . was it necessary for God to take human nature upon him so that he might redeem us by dying in the flesh?"[27] Abelard does not agree with Anselm's answer or the *Christus Victor* model. Instead, he uses an example from slavery to refute the idea that the devil deserved a ransom payment. First, Abelard asserts that in fact God still has the rights of ownership over humans. "For if any slave wanted to forsake his lord and put himself under the authority of another master, would he be allowed to act in such a way that his lord could not lawfully seek him out and bring him back, if he wanted to?"[28] Far from having the right to compensation, because of what he has done the devil has infringed upon the rights of God.

---

[27]Peter Abelard "Exposition of the Epistle to the Romans."
[28]Ibid.

Who indeed doubts that, if a slave of any master seduces his fellow slave by subtle suggestions and makes him depart from obedience to his true master, the seducer is looked upon by the slave's master as much more guilty than the seduced? And how unjust it would be that he who seduced the other should deserve, as a result, to have any special right or authority over him![29]

Abelard's main challenge to Anselm revolves around the issue of forgiveness. He first attempts to undercut Anselm by stating that God was free to forgive if God wished to forgive. Abelard asks, if Jesus pronounced forgiveness of people's sins before he went to the cross, then if by the same grace God wanted to forgive others, would not that be possible? Abelard also asks rhetorically, "And if that sin of Adam was so great that it could be expiated only by the death of Christ, what expiation will avail for that act of murder committed against Christ?"[30] In essence, he asks, if God could put up with this enormous sin of having his son killed, then would it not have been even easier simply to pardon other, lesser sins?

Confident that he has shown the inadequacy of other explanations of the atonement, Abelard moves on briefly to give his answer to the question: "In what manner have we been made more righteous through the death of the Son of God than we were before, so that we ought to be delivered from punishment?"[31] Rather than a payment to or victory over the devil, or a satisfaction of a debt owed to God, Abelard sees Jesus' life and death as a demonstration of God's love that moves sinners to repent and love God. He writes:

> Now it seems to us that we have been justified by the blood of Christ and reconciled to God in this way: through this unique act of grace manifested to us—in that his Son has taken upon himself our nature and persevered therein in teaching us by word and example even unto death—he has more fully bound us to himself by love; with the result that our hearts

[29]Ibid.
[30]Ibid.
[31]Ibid.

should be enkindled by such a gift of divine grace, and true charity should not now shrink from enduring anything for him.[32]

In relation to sin, Abelard focuses on the intention rather than the outward acts themselves. An act is good or bad because it flows from good intentions or bad. "It follows from this that the same thing may be done by the same person at different times, and yet that the action may sometimes be called good, sometimes bad, because of a difference of intention."[33] Thus he understands the work of Christ as reorienting our intentions "so that we do all things out of love rather than fear."[34]

In the other models of the atonement we discuss in this chapter, the saving action of the cross is directed at the devil or God and occurs primarily outside of us. In them, our status is changed because of Christ's victory over sin or the devil, or because Christ has paid a debt we owe or suffered a punishment we deserve. In contrast, for Abelard the saving action of the cross is primarily subjective, or a change that occurs within humans. The example of Jesus' life arouses within us a greater love of God, and we become more righteous. For Abelard, the cross was not so much about removing an objective barrier between God and humans but rather a demonstration to humanity of God's matchless love.

Abelard's Moral Influence Model: An Assessment

Abelard's argument has an almost timeless quality that would allow it to be understood equally in most, if not all, settings. That same timeless quality, however, means it remains at an ethereal level that does not deeply connect with any one context. He writes abstractly about both Jesus' life and the lives of the humans Jesus' example has influenced.

Abelard helpfully highlights the subjective aspect of Christ's atoning work that had received minimal attention in previous atonement writing

[32]Ibid.
[33]Peter Abelard "Know Thyself."
[34]Abelard "Exposition of Romans."

but is present in the Bible.[35] His work would be more acceptable, however, if he would have presented the subjective influence of the cross as a missing element from atonement thinking rather than *the* answer to the question of why God became a human. He has left a number of issues hanging in the air. For instance, although he does include Jesus' death as part of what moves us to love, he does not explain why Jesus' death on the cross was necessary. It appears his atonement model could function logically without the cross. He correctly contests the concept of a vindictive, punishing God, but he does so by speaking loudly of God's love and very softly of God's judgment instead of depicting God's judgment as part of God's love and distinguishing it from vindictive retribution.

Grace plays a significant role in his theory in that God takes the initiative to act in a way that will lead to our reconciliation. Yet Abelard displays an overconfidence in the human capacity to bring about our salvation. He assumes that, awakened by the example of God's love, we can arrive to a point of living righteously. Sin appears as a relative and surmountable barrier for Abelard in contrast to an absolute and insurmountable barrier in the other explanations.[36]

The ethical character of Abelard's work is more pronounced than the other models we are exploring because his model requires not only that Jesus lived an exemplary sinless life but also that humans live differently in response to the example of Jesus' life. In addition to the abstract nature of his description of these changes, a significant weakness of his model is its individualistic character. The focus is on Jesus' life and death moving individuals to love and to be reconciled with God. Of course, these individuals could then come together and form Christian community in a voluntary way, but the community-forming nature of Christ's work or the sense of

---

[35]For example, Romans 5:8; 8:32-39; 1 John 3:16; 4:10.

[36]In places it does appear that Abelard recognizes that even after being awakened to love by Jesus' example, humans will fall short and need the merit of Christ's perfect love. For example, he wrote: "That [Jesus] . . . might supply from his own what was wanting in our merits. . . . Otherwise what great thing did his holiness merit, if it availed only for his own, and not for others' salvation" (cited in McDonald, *Atonement*, p. 177).

reconciliation with others that is part of one's reconciliation with God do not appear to be integral to Abelard's explanation of the atonement.

Penal Substitution Model

One does not need to go to a theological library to encounter the penal substitution model of the atonement. Most Christians in the West have encountered it in Sunday school classes, heard it proclaimed by pastors and evangelists, sang it in hymns and read it in tracts or books of basic doctrines. We can also go to faraway lands where Western missionaries have preached and encounter the penal substitution model in places where its legal language and concept of justice are quite foreign—in Japan for instance, or in the jungles of Panama.

In fact, one of us was giving a class to a group of indigenous pastors in Panama. In response to the question of why Jesus died on the cross, these pastors responded with the following answer that communicates the heart of the penal substitution model of the atonement. They explained that God would like to be in relationship with humans and dwell together with us forever in heaven, but human sin does not allow for this since God is holy and cannot associate with anyone corrupted by sin. It is impossible for humans to achieve the sinless perfection necessary, and because God is just, he must punish us for our sin. God, however, provides a solution. God the Father sends his Son to earth to suffer the punishment we deserve by dying on the cross. Since Jesus has paid the penalty for us, God can regard us as not guilty. If we believe that we are sinners deserving of hell, but that Jesus died in our place, then we can be in relationship with God and go to heaven.

Although the exact legal mechanics of how one person could pay the penalty for everyone's crimes may be a little mind-boggling, the basic ideas of this model can be communicated even to children. Many of us may remember sitting in a class as a child or youth and hearing an example similar to this one: it is as if God is a judge sitting in court looking at a big book that lists all our sins, and God says, I must punish you for all these sins. If, however, a person accepts Jesus as Savior then Jesus will say, "No, I died on the cross to pay the penalty of those sins," and then when God looks at the book again the list of sins is gone, and the page with your name on it is totally blank. Similarly, some of us may remember hearing the more gruesome story that compares God to a railroad switchman who sees that his son has wandered on to the main track just as a passenger train is hurtling toward him. If the man throws the switch, his son will live, but the train will crash into freight cars parked on the siding, and many people will die. The father opts to leave the switch open and kill his son instead of killing the people on the train.

The railroad story succeeds in disturbing young listeners, but theologically does not communicate much more than that God the Father was willing to kill his son to save others. Adding more theological details to parables of penal substitution does not, however, lessen the distress in the minds of listeners. It simply adds further troubling images. For instance, Shirley Guthrie recounts how the following example left a young listener filled with questions and fear.

> The preacher held up a dirty glass. "See this glass? That's you. Filthy, stained with sin, inside and outside."
>
> He picked up a hammer. "This hammer is the righteousness of God. It is the instrument of God's wrath against sinners. God's justice can be satisfied only by punishing and destroying people whose lives are filled with vileness and corruption."
>
> The preacher put the glass on the pulpit and slowly, deliberately drew back the hammer, took deadly aim, and with all his might let the blow fall.
>
> But a miracle happened! At the last moment he covered the glass with a pan. The hammer struck with a crash that echoed through the hushed church. He held up the untouched glass with one hand and the mangled pan with the other.
>
> Jesus Christ died for your sins. He took the punishment that ought to have fallen on you. He satisfied the righteousness of God so that you might go free if you believe in him.[37]

---

[37]Shirley Guthrie, *Christian Doctrine*, rev. ed. (Louisville, Ky.: Westminster John Knox, 1994), p. 250.

Anselm would not have approved of either the railroad or pan story, yet they grow out of the atonement thought of people who have taken his basic idea of satisfaction and adapted it to fit the legal systems of a different era than his. The shift away from feudal obligations to criminal law changed markedly the character of the satisfaction Christ provided. As we noted, Anselm does not present a wrathful God punishing Christ in our place; rather, Christ satisfies, or pays a debt we owe. In a criminal-justice system such as ours, however, "satisfaction" has to do with the apprehension and punishment of the guilty. Therefore, in this context, Christ does not pay a debt humans owe to God but rather bears the punishment of God against human sin. This shift in legal framework signals the main differences between Anselm's satisfaction model and the penal substitution model.

This shift is evident already in Luther and Calvin. For instance, Calvin writes, "God in his capacity as judge is angry toward us. Hence, an expiation must intervene in order that Christ as priest may obtain God's favor for us and appease his wrath" (*Institutes* 2.15.6). Calvin and Luther, however, do not work out a detailed, all-encompassing penal theory. They also use other images of atonement. For instance, Aulén claims that Luther placed more emphasis on a *Christus Victor* model than on a penal model. Penal substitutionary thinking, however, became more and more dominant. Most Protestant theologians developed models of the atonement in which some version of penal substitution was presented as the singular explanation of the saving significance of the cross.[38] We will take a more in-depth look at the model by summarizing Charles Hodge's explanation of it.

Charles Hodge: Penal Substitution Model

Charles Hodge (1797-1878) was perhaps the leading theologian in the United States during the nineteenth century. He taught at Princeton Seminary for fifty years. His three-volume systematic theology, first pub-

---

[38]The dominance of penal substitution continues today among evangelical theologians. Beginning with Schleiermacher, however, there was a renewed interest in an Abelardian-type approach that continued throughout the nineteenth and twentieth centuries among many.

lished in 1872-1873, had great influence and was republished as recently as 1981. Chapter seven of the second volume dedicates over sixty pages to the theme "satisfaction of Christ."

Hodge states that God cannot simply pardon sin "without a satisfaction to justice, and He cannot have fellowship with the unholy" (492).[39] Hodge acknowledges that some might say that God can do anything God wants to do, but he argues that God cannot stop being just. God's justice, his moral excellence, "demands the punishment of sin. If sin be pardoned it can be pardoned in consistency with divine justice only on the ground of a forensic penal satisfaction" (488). God's justice "renders it necessary that the righteous be rewarded and the wicked punished" (490).

The wages of sin is death, and therefore Hodge explains that "every sin of necessity subjects the sinner to the wrath and curse of God" (516). But through the cross, God acts to save sinners from this situation and from our alienation from God. Hodge allows that the sufferings of Christ may "illustrate and enforce truth, and exert a moral influence on others; [but] these are all subordinate and collateral ends" (516). He also states that Jesus' death on the cross was not a natural consequence of "subjecting himself to the common lot of humanity." Rather, Hodge believes God orchestrated Jesus' suffering and death on the cross. In commenting on Galatians 3:13 he writes:

> They were divine inflictions. It pleased the Lord to bruise him. He was smitten of God and afflicted. These sufferings were declared to be on account of sin, not his own, but ours. He bore our sins. The chastisement of our peace was on him. And they were designed as an expiation, or for the satisfaction of justice. They had, therefore, all the elements of punishment, and consequently it was in a strict and proper sense that he was made a curse for us. (517)

In these few paragraphs we have communicated the core of Hodge's

---

[39]All citations in this section are from Charles Hodge, *Systematic Theology*, vol. 2 (Grand Rapids, Mich.: Eerdmans, 1981).

position. He writes much more, however. He responds to possible objections and has lengthy sections that list various passages of Scripture, especially those dealing with the cross in terms of sacrifice, to show how they support his position. He also explains certain aspects of the model in greater detail. For instance, he distinguishes between meeting the demands of justice and meeting the demands of the law and explains how Jesus does both. "To satisfy justice is to satisfy the demand which justice makes for the punishment of sin. But the law demands far more than that punishment of sin." The law also requires the fulfillment of all righteousness. Therefore, Christ, "by his obedience and sufferings, by his whole righteousness, active and passive, he, as our representative and substitute, did and endured all that the law demands"(493-94).

In addition Hodge explains how penal substitution provides deliverance from the power of sin and Satan, something more directly associated with a *Christus Victor* model of the atonement. In relation to liberation from the power of sin, he explains that "deliverance from sin is a true redemption. A deliverance effected by a ransom, or a satisfaction to justice, was the necessary condition of restoration to the favour of God; and restoration to his favour was the necessary condition of holiness" (518). Hodge states emphatically that the cross delivers us from the power of Satan, but he refuses to describe it as a direct confrontation and specifically rejects a *Christus Victor* type of explanation. Instead, he attempts to show how Christ's penal satisfaction of justice and the law also free us from Satan. He makes three points. First, humans "are in a state of bondage through fear of the wrath of God on account of sin." Second, "in this state they are in subjection to Satan who has ... the ability and opportunity of inflicting on them the sufferings due to them as sinners." Third, the death of Christ delivers humans from "the state of bondage and subjection to the power of Satan ... by satisfying the justice of God, [freeing] them from the penalty of the law; and freedom from the curse of the law involves freedom from the power of Satan to inflict its penalty" (519).

Hodge also explains what an individual needs to do to appropriate

Christ's work for his or her life. Again attacking the moral influence approach, he writes, "It is not enough that we should open our hearts to all the influences for good which flow from his person and work." We must give up the idea "that we can satisfy the demands of God's justice and law, by anything we can do, suffer, or experience." Instead, Hodge states that we must trust in Christ, "renounce our righteousness and confide in his for our acceptance with God." Hodge then explains that our justification is not a subjective work. "It is not wrought in us either naturally or supernaturally. . . . But if God, in justifying sinners, declares that with regard to them the claims of justice are satisfied, it confessedly is not on the ground that the sinner himself has made that satisfaction, but that Christ has made it in his behalf"(522).

We could list many other theologians who have written about the penal substitution model of the atonement and discuss the nuances of difference between those theologians. As in the other sections, however, we have chosen to focus on one writer to allow our evaluation to be specific to a particular writer in one time and place. We will, however, briefly summarize a more recent statement of this position, an essay entitled "Why Did Christ Have to Die?"[40]

David Clark spends almost a third of his article describing Jesus' physical suffering on the cross. On one hand, it seems Clark highlights Jesus' suffering in order to demonstrate that his suffering was equal to the punishment demanded. Yet Clark acknowledges that others have suffered similar physical torment, and some, like Jesus, have suffered it unjustly. He asks if this physical suffering would be enough to save us. No, he concludes, then argues that Jesus' spiritual suffering and his experience of God's wrath were even greater than the physical agony, and these were sufficient.

> But when the Lord suffered, the wrath of God was poured out in such measure upon him, that the Father was satisfied. His sufferings were sufficient for all the sins that his elect would ever commit! Who can even begin

---

[40]David Clark, "Why Did Christ Have to Die?" *New England Reformed Journal* 1 (1996): 35-36.

to grasp the "width and length and depth and height" of the true spiritual suffering of our Lord and our God as his Father turned his back upon him. Who can begin to comprehend the love that drove a Father to pour out his unmitigated wrath upon his dearly beloved Son for such rebellious worms and wretches as us? . . . Perhaps now we can begin to understand why God had to die for man. Surely only God the Son could bear the unmitigated wrath of God the Father.[41]

Clark's essay clearly demonstrates that Hodge's position of 130 years ago continues to be championed today.

Hodge's Penal Substitution Model: An Assessment

At the heart of Hodge's explanation of the atonement is a legal metaphor that would have been readily understood by people of his era. That may be less true today with the dissolution of an accepted framework of universal moral law. Hodge also, however, leans heavily on the biblical image of blood sacrifice, something very distant from his students in nineteenth-century New Jersey. His concern does not appear to be to develop a presentation that will connect with people's reality but to articulate a logical, intellectually sound and biblically correct theory of the atonement. He cites many scriptural passages to support his explanations, thus at least giving his position the appearance of being biblical. Upon closer examination, however, we find that Hodge's model actually falls short in this regard.

Because Hodge read the Bible through the lens of the criminal justice system of his era, the Bible appeared to support his explanation. In other words, if readers come to the biblical text with the presuppositions Hodge has about justice, God's wrath and judgment, and the mechanics of biblical sacrifice, then indeed his model seems biblical. If, however, we attempt to allow the Bible itself to shape the way we think about those same terms, his model appears fundamentally flawed because it operates with

---

[41]Clark, "Why Did Christ Have to Die?" p. 36.

an understanding of these terms that is foreign to the Bible.

Although Hodge rejects the penitential system and does not participate in a feudal society, the foundational ideas of his model are borrowed from Anselm who, as we have seen, based his concept of satisfaction not on New Testament teaching but on feudalism and penance. Using this extrabiblical foundation fundamentally shapes the whole building Hodge constructs. It distorts biblical words and phrases to the point that they are no longer recognizable in their biblical contexts. For instance, Hodge ends up with a God who can only operate within certain legal confines as determined by a particular concept of justice—in contrast to a biblical understanding of justice that is covenantal and relational and almost synonymous with faithfulness.[42] Hodge explains the penal substitutionary model in a way that makes it appear self-evident that God must behave according to late-nineteenth-century American notions of justice. This, however, leads him to depict God as having no option but to act in ways that do not match up with the God we see revealed in the Bible and ultimately in Christ. Rather than presenting a Father and Son who are one, Hodge has one member of the Trinity punishing another member of the Trinity. Within a penal substitution model, God's ability to love and relate to humans is circumscribed by something outside of God—that is, an abstract concept of justice instructs God as to how God must behave. It could be said that Hodge presents a God who wants to be in relationship with us but is forced to deal with a problem of legal bookkeeping that blocks that relationship. The solution is having God the Father punish God the Son. However, Hodge's presentation is more likely to lead his readers to picture a God who has a vindictive character, who finds it much easier to punish than to forgive.

Earlier we demonstrated that a mistaken concept of God's wrath as retributive punishment lies behind this picture of God (see chapter two). In a playful but also jarring way Robin Collins has made the same point

---

[42]Cf. Richard B. Hays, "Justification," in *ABD*, 3:1129-33.

by inserting the Father described by penal substitution into the parable of the prodigal son. When the son returns and recognizes the error of his ways, Collins has the Father respond, "I cannot simply forgive you . . . it would be against the moral order of the entire universe. . . . Such is the severity of my justice that reconciliation will not be made unless the penalty is utterly paid. My wrath—my avenging justice—must be placated." Collins also provides a different ending to the parable. The older son offers to do extra work in the fields and pay his brother's penalty. "And finally, when the elder brother died of exhaustion, the father's wrath was placated against his younger son and they lived happily for the remainder of their days."[43]

We could also mention that because of the singular focus on penal satisfaction, Jesus' resurrection is not really necessary according to this model. Penal substitution, however, is unbiblical not just because it distorts or leaves out biblical concepts but also because of its attempt at having one image or model serve as an all-encompassing theory, the only correct and needed explanation of the atonement. As we have seen, the New Testament provides a number of images that in different contexts of the Christian mission were used to proclaim the saving significance of the cross. Hodge, however, presents one model as though it were *the* explanation of the atonement for all times and places. This creates significant missiological problems. It implies both that we have no need to develop a different model, and, indeed, that we would be wrong to try. Yet the reality is that in many societies—at the time Hodge lived, and even more so today—people have different concepts of justice, so that for them penal substitution is simply unintelligible. The weakness of forcing all atonement thinking into the mold of one image became especially apparent when Hodge attempted to explain victory over Satan and the power of sin in terms of penal substitution. In contrast with the tight logical arguments of the other sections, in these it appeared he was

---

[43]Robin Collins, "Understanding Atonement: A New and Orthodox Theory," unpublished manuscript, pp. 1-2.

trying to force a square peg into a round hole.

Hodge's penal substitution model takes sin very seriously in that it presents sin as a huge barrier between God and humans. Yet it is a limited concept of sin that portrays it only in terms of moral failure or transgression of a law. Even within that concept of sin, however, the model does not intersect with the day-to-day reality of actual people. Describing the atonement as a legal transaction within the Godhead removes it from the historical world in which we live and leaves it unconnected to personal or social reconciliation. And in actuality it only addresses our reconciliation with God at an abstract level. That is to say, it is so objective, so outside of us (and in a sense outside of God) that what changes through the cross is a legal ruling. According to the logic of the model, an individual could be saved through penal substitution without experiencing a fundamental reorientation of his or her life.

Ethically this model has little to offer; it can do little more than serve as an example to point to when calling individuals to imitate Christ. Yet the life of Jesus that this model presents is as disengaged from his historical reality as the atonement it provides is from our day-to-day reality. The model needs Jesus to have lived a perfect life, to have met the standard of justice and the law. Jesus' conflict with the powers of his day and their putting him to death is of no significance. There is no sense that Jesus' life led to his death. Instead, Hodge portrays God as having to orchestrate Jesus' death. What is significant about Jesus' life is that he did not sin. In this model the only aspect of Jesus' life that is presented concretely is his physical suffering, which helps to validate that the penalty was sufficient. Unfortunately, then, in calling people to imitate Christ the model too easily has been misused to glorify suffering and encourage passive tolerance of abuse.

In conclusion, we might say that Hodge's approach has repeatedly led him to theological innovations at odds with those suggested in our biblical study. He has turned to the world around him at those points where he should have relied on the Bible and has gone to the Bible when he would have done better to engage his own cultural context. He roots his model in an individualistic, legal framework borrowed from the world of his day rather than from the Bible. His portrait of God is therefore governed more by concepts of justice among his contemporaries and not by God's revelation of himself in Christ. It is not surprising, then, that the Bible does not shape his fundamental conception of the saving work of the cross. Then he borrows metaphors—like sacrifice, ransom and redemption—from the Bible without taking into account that these images were foreign and largely unintelligible to people of his age. The problem, however, is not just one of communication. In the context of his work these metaphors do not function as they do in the Bible; indeed, they are set within a framework that is alien to the world of Scripture, and within that framework they operate with different meanings.

As we observed in the first chapter, a penal substitution model too easily leads to a situation in which we might conclude that Jesus came to save us from God. Of course, Hodge and current proponents of penal substitution would protest that they explicitly state that because God loved us, he sent his son to die for us. They affirm that God is a God of love. Yet in the context of Hodge's model this feels a little like having the owner of a dog who is barking, growling and straining at its leash say, "Don't worry, he doesn't bite." Maybe it is true, but the combination of messages we receive leads us to keep a safe distance from the dog. In the same way, Hodge's presentation makes it much easier for us to conceive of a God who punishes with vindictive retribution—a God from whom we need to be saved!

Conclusion

Today penal substitution is viewed by many as the one correct approach to explaining the saving significance of the cross. Yet, as we stated in the beginning of this chapter, the Christian church has never defined one model or theory of the atonement as being the only orthodox one. In this chapter we have looked at four different models of atonement thinking to make clear that the tradition of the Christian church does not present us with one "correct" view of the atonement. In relation to this issue, the earliest theologians we looked at, Irenaeus and Gregory of Nyssa, offer us a helpful example. Although each highlighted a *Christus Victor* approach to explaining the work of Christ on the cross, they also included other models or images of the atonement in their writings. That is, like the New Testament writers they understood that a single metaphor could never capture all that Christ accomplished on the cross. They also understood that different models can be used in complementary ways.

Irenaeus and Gregory offer us a helpful example of not limiting ourselves to one model, but we are not recommending that today we simply restate what they wrote. Rather, the historical overview in this chapter calls us to pay careful attention to the issue of the relationship between a person's particular sociohistorical environment and the images used to communicate the saving significance of the cross. On one hand, we have seen, through both positive and negative examples, the importance of using metaphors and language that draw on the shared experience and vocabulary of people of that time and place. Otherwise, our explanation of the atonement may remain largely unintelligible. On the other hand, in this chapter we have seen, especially with Anselm and Hodge, the error of uncritically borrowing language and images from an individual's world. We must ask not just whether a model is easily understood but also whether the framework and metaphors used to communicate an explanation of the atonement distort biblical teaching and thus cause the cross to lose its saving character. Communication of information is not, however, our only goal. Like the New Testament writers, we seek to shape people and social systems; hence, to root our explanations of the atonement in the society around us uncritically means that our models will not critically engage society. The cross will lose its scandalous character.

In the chapters that follow we turn to look at some contemporary examples of presentations of the atonement that were developed by people who, like the New Testament writers, have wrestled with how to present the message of the cross within the context of mission to differing audiences. They have attempted to learn from the strengths and weaknesses of the work of theologians presented in this chapter and sought to present models of the atonement that both communicate to and challenge the society around them.

6

REMOVING
ALIENATING SHAME

The Saving Significance
of the Cross in Japan

*I*n 1981 a Japanese church leader in Hokkaido asked a missionary, "Why did Jesus have to die?" The Japanese man immediately clarified that he was quite familiar with the standard explanation missionaries gave, that Jesus had to die to pay the penalty for our sins required by God, but he added, "To be honest, I don't find that explanation satisfactory."[1] Norman Kraus was this missionary. He had just arrived in Japan to serve as a theological resource person for Japanese churches after many years of teaching theology in the United States. He went to Japan with the hope of helping the Japanese to develop a more contextual theology. This leader's question and dissatisfaction with the answer he had heard from other missionaries confirmed to Kraus the need for what he had envisioned.

---

[1]This incident and all other examples of the Japanese context in this chapter, unless otherwise cited, were reported to us in a telephone interview with C. Norman Kraus, May 12, 1999.

Obviously missionaries had "packed" the doctrines they had learned in Bible colleges and seminaries in North America and Europe, brought them to Japan, pulled them out of their boxes and taught them just as they learned them. Unlike the New Testament-era theologian-missionaries we discussed in chapters two through four, these did not struggle to find context-specific ways to communicate the truth of the cross in a new setting. Instead, they used the very images and metaphors they had heard from professors like Charles Hodge—images that, unfortunately, were difficult for the Japanese people, even Japanese believers in Christ, to understand.

A tragic accident provided Kraus with his first clues as to why the common penal substitution explanation of the atonement, so clear and logical to Western missionaries, had not satisfied this Japanese church leader. A young man from Kraus's congregation was driving a company truck and accidently hit and killed two women walking by the side of the road. The police and court demonstrated more concern for relationships and people's responses than to written codes. They handled the case in a way markedly different from American legal processes. The young man immediately confessed that the accident was his fault because he had been going too fast. The judge put him in custody but released him to attend the funerals of the two women who had been killed. The judge attended the funerals also and carefully observed not only how the young man behaved but how the families responded to him. In the meantime the police carefully investigated and exonerated the young man. They said he could not have been going as fast as he reported, and they discovered that the company truck had a steering defect. The young man was let out of jail to do a work of public service for the rest of the year, and then he was fully released and rehabilitated. This case demonstrated to Kraus that the Japanese had a different concept of justice and a different concept of how justice is achieved—different, that is, from Kraus's experience in the United States.

Kraus sought to learn more by discussing the Japanese concept of justice with a small group of Japanese colleagues with university and business experience. When he asked them, What is justice? they discussed among themselves and answered, "Justice is what the judge says it is." Kraus observes that in the West the image of justice is of a blindfolded goddess impartially weighing someone's guilt or innocence based on the evidence and a set standard of law. In contrast, the Japanese image is of a male judge with his eyes wide open, observing the situation so that he can do whatever will best preserve human relationships. Kraus told his group of Japanese colleagues that in the United States we talk of criminals serving time and paying their debt to justice. He then asked if they had used similar phrases or ideas. They reported that these concepts and phrases sounded quite strange. Japanese criminals are imprisoned as a shameful act of exclusion from society. The lengths of the sentences are measured according to the enormity of their social scandal.

As Kraus pondered what he had learned, and as he continued asking questions, he came to realize that Japan was a shame-based culture very much unlike the guilt-based culture in which most North Americans live. The result is a very different concept and practice of justice. Understandably, then, Japanese church leaders would not find a penal substitution theory of the atonement satisfactory, for it was built on a penal approach to justice alien to them. During his years in Japan, Kraus worked to understand better this shame-based culture, then began to think about how he might answer the question "Why did Jesus have to die?" in a way that would make sense and be heard as good news in Japan.

Comparing Shame and Guilt

In order to understand and appreciate Kraus's presentation of the saving work of the cross in a Japanese context, Western readers first must understand the difference between shame and guilt and have a sense of how a shame-based culture differs from ours. Kraus provides the chart and explanations in figure 6.1.[2]

---

[2]C. Norman Kraus, *Jesus Christ Our Lord: Christology from a Disciples' Perspective* (Scottdale, Penn: Herald, 1990), p. 204. The chart is slightly different than the previously published version because it reflects revisions Kraus has made to it since it was published. All further citations from this book in this chapter will be noted with page numbers in the text.

SHAME	GUILT
(Focus on the self)	(Focus on the act)

Nature of Fault

Failure to meet self-expectations	Offense against legal expectations

Internal Reaction

Embarrassment/Disgrace	Condemnation/Remorse
Self-depreciation	Self-accusation
Fear of abandonment	Fear of punishment
Resentment	Anger
Self-isolation ("rage")	Self-justification
Alienation	Hostility

Social Reaction

Ridicule & exclude	Blame & hold responsible
Disgrace & hold in contempt	Accuse & condemn
Disapprove & reproach	Punish & retaliate

Remedy

Identification & communication	Propitiation through restitution or penalty
Love banishes shame	Justification banishes guilt

Figure 6.1. Shame versus guilt

Kraus came to realize that shame is associated with such concepts of sin as defilement or uncleanness, whereas guilt is associated with specific acts and is experienced as a burden of responsibility that a person must bear for his or her acts. Kraus maintains that to relate the significance of the cross to the experience of shame in Japan is not at all to distort the biblical presentation of the cross. Rather, he states that "the cultural expression of shame is much more evident in the Bible than most Western readers are aware" (214). The Old Testament concepts of ritual purity and uncleanness, views of disease and death, exile as a form of punishment—these "point toward a shame rather than guilt orientation. . . . To a greater extent than is often recognized, the problem of sin in Israel was the problem of purifying the nation of its pollution without permanently expelling the unclean person" (214).

Although Kraus is critical of thinking about the cross exclusively in relation to guilt, he does not deny that guilt is a problem addressed by the cross. He contends:

> The role of the cross in reconciling us to God must be seen in broader terms as an answer to both shame and guilt. And further, the resolution of the shame problem—both the problems of social exclusion as a moral sanction and the inner anxiety of failure that shuts us off from others and paralyzes moral response—provides the context and paradigm for understanding the resolution of guilt, not vice versa. (208)

In his writing Kraus explains how he sees the cross addressing both shame and guilt.[3] In our discussion, however, we will focus specifically on the cross and shame in relation to the Japanese context.

Characteristics of Shame

Kraus describes four social-psychological characteristics of shame. First, shame is experienced as exposure to others and to oneself. In fact, some say the deepest shame accompanies failure to meet one's self-expectations.

---

[3]For his discussion of the cross and the guilt of sin see Kraus, *Jesus Christ Our Lord*, pp. 223-27.

External sanctions and group ridicule and exclusion are obvious in a shame-based culture, but shame can also be an internal sanction of disappointment and disapproval of one's own weakness and failure. Shame is both a spiritual and psychological obstacle to personal relationship with God and others.

Second, "shame anxiety" occurs as a result of not living up to individual and group ideals. In contrast to "guilt anxiety," which is focused on punishment of transgressions by superiors, it is God's all-seeing, all-knowing eye that is feared in the condition of shame. Kraus observes, "If this analysis is correct, it suggests that where shame is a major factor in psychological and cultural development, *relationships and ideals will be more important and persuasive than law and punitive threats*" (210).

Third, shame can potentially disrupt relationships more than guilt. Since guilt results from an offense that is measurable and pardonable, the offender remains relatively open to relationship with others. Condemnation or punishment itself is a form of communication. Shame, however, is an isolating alienating experience. Kraus observes that

> this is an especially important insight for understanding the nature of human alienation from God. . . . Our shame of the weakness that led us to betray the trusting, loving Friend causes us to hide. . . . Fear of being discovered in our nakedness or exposed in our uncleanness makes us hide in resentful embarrassment. . . . Our rage against God is the projection of our self-loathing. We must be reconciled to ourselves as well as to God. (210-11)

Fourth, shame cannot be eased by punishment or expiated through substitutionary compensation or retaliation. "No payment can balance accounts and thus restore lost honor. . . . Only forgiveness which covers the past and a genuine restoration of relationship can banish shame. . . . Shame is banished when open communication is established through loving identification and the worth of each can be mutually affirmed" (210).

Forgiveness and Shame

Kraus explains that in relation to shame, forgiveness is different and more complicated than in relation to guilt.

> Where sin is thought of as an act of transgression and the consequences are conceptualized as an objective debt (guilt), forgiveness is viewed as pardon or release from the debt. But where sin is conceived as an uncleanness, weakness, or blemish and its consequences devaluate the worth and self-esteem of the sinner (shame), then how shall we understand the meaning of forgiveness? . . . When guilt is objectified, the offender can be pardoned. When shame is objectified, the offender can only be excluded.
>
> What does it mean to offer forgiveness to one who feels shamed for some moral failure? How can alienation be overcome and communication be restored? How can the impurity or failure be removed? Can it be atoned for without the removal of the offender? If the offender is not removed, must he or she continue to live in shame? The dilemma is no longer keenly felt in modern individualistic societies that have made values relative and made the individual the final arbiter. In the group-oriented cultures of Asia, however, this is still a live issue. (212)

Shame in Japan

In a shame-based culture like Japan, public exposure and exclusion are important means for regulating social behavior. A prison term, commonly quite long, is not viewed as penal equivalency or rehabilitation but as a way of excluding someone from society. These sanctions work effectively because social relationships and interpersonal dependencies are of paramount importance. People place a premium on "saving face." Kraus reports that while he was in Japan a man was released from prison when, after twenty years, his innocence came to light. Upon his release, he first went to his father's grave and told his father that the family shame had been resolved.

Shaming another person is the most effective way of breaking a relationship. Therefore, the sanctions of shame must be used cautiously.

Once someone has been shamed, there is little chance for reconciliation. "A respectful relationship is considered a higher moral value than legalities or ideological truth" (213). In this cultural setting, confession or admission of a fault is a form of self-shaming and thus not common.

North Americans were startled when a Japanese student studying in the United States commented that he would never say, "I forgive you." Kraus, however, observes that is a common sentiment in Japan. "Forgiveness becomes problematic because to say 'I forgive' implies that I affirm the other person's badness, and thus forgiveness reaffirms his or her shame. Thus it is far easier to overlook, excuse, or forget than to confess and forgive. Indeed, *yurusu*, the Japanese word translated 'forgiveness,' means to excuse, indulge, or permit" (212).

It is common for close associates to tolerate and even make excuses for a comrade's serious misdeeds and thus maintain the web of inner-group relationships by *indulging* the indiscretion. Kraus quotes Chie Nakane as she describes this situation in Japan:

> If a man happened to make a mistake in his work his friends in the group would protect him. Even in a very serious case, where no reasonable excuse could justify his actions, they would protect him with the group power and fabricate some irrational and emotional justification. They are at all times firmly on his side, not necessarily because he is right but because he is one of them. His fellows know well enough that he has committed a fault and is in the wrong, but even so, they retain to a striking degree their tolerance and sympathy for him. . . . One could point to many cases in which a man had committed a serious error and had even broken the law (and would have lost his position in another society), but remained comfortably in his post in spite of social accusations on the part of the general public. (213)

When it becomes impossible to hide or ignore misdeeds, exclusion is the only recourse, with virtually no possibility of reconciliation. When it came to light, for example, that a missionary had been involved in serious sexual misconduct, church leaders responded by saying he must leave. If an offender owns responsibility and excludes himself or herself in an act of atonement, there may be a certain moral resolution, but it is the self-exclusion itself that justifies such resolution. "Therefore, it cannot lead to reaffirmation of the former relationship. Indeed, suicide, which is the ultimate act of self-exclusion, epitomizes the dilemma" (213). For instance, when it was reported in Japanese newspapers that a Japanese man was involved in a crime in Holland, his father responded to the shameful situation by committing suicide. In that situation it was interpreted as an of act of atonement, but its consequence was not restored relationships, but the most permanent self-exclusion possible.

Kraus observes that in this situation we can really only speak of the annulment of sin, not its forgiveness. He observes that, so far as the offender is concerned, physical removal to a new place provides the only possibility for a new beginning. "This finding a new place where one can begin again with a new identity is just what the Christian doctrine of forgiveness and reconciliation proclaims" (216).

Salvation from Shame

What are we to make of this situation? Clearly, the message of the cross as this has been honed in nineteenth- and twentieth-century America has little meaning in a context such as the one Kraus describes. One approach would be to attempt to re-enculturate the Japanese people so that they could understand the Christian message in the same way that we do. If we imagine that, say, penal-substitutionary atonement is the one correct way to understand the cross, then this is the avenue that we must take—and indeed, this is the avenue that many of our brothers and sisters in the missionary movement have taken. As a result, communicating the Christian message requires that we first invest a target culture with Western categories of thought and teach them stories and analogies by which to make sense of our message.

As we have repeatedly seen, however, both from biblical and historical-theological perspectives, it is simply not the case that penal substitutionary atonement is the one correct way to make sense of the saving significance of Jesus' death. The problems with this particular model of the atonement aside (see chapter five), we have seen that no one model or metaphor can serve to capture or communicate the totality of the meaning of Jesus' death "for us." Rather than requiring that people such as the Japanese learn that they have deep-seated problems that they did not know they had, in order that we might be able to resolve those problems with the message of the cross, we might inquire into the ways in which the cross addresses the problems that are self-evident in Japanese culture. In fact, recent work in applying what we have learned about cultural anthropology and social psychology to the Scriptures reveals how much more at home the Bible is in the Japanese context than in a Western society. One of the reasons for this is that honor and shame were pivotal values for the worlds of the Old and New Testaments.[4] In other words, far from "compromising the gospel" by inquiring how it might be located on Japanese soil, our questions about the significance of the cross for the Japanese people might actually bring us *closer to the pages of the New Testament!*

This does not mean that Japanese culture must provide all of the terms of discussion for the Christian church in Japan. Japanese churches must also embrace the task of Christian formation by which believers in Christ learn and embody the biblical story of God's dealings with his people—a story deeply rooted in sometimes alien thought forms more at home in ancient Israel and in Roman antiquity, but nonetheless an ongoing story that includes as one of its chapters the saving work of God among the Japanese people. This is true for Japanese churches in the same way that it is true for those in Ireland or the United States or Peru. At the same time, not only in the missionary movement but in the growing indigenous church in Japan, the good news will find modes of articulation that are, in fact, good news in Japan.

---

[4]This perspective was introduced into New Testament study especially by Bruce J. Malina, *The New Testament World: Insights from Cultural Anthropology* (Atlanta: John Knox Press, 1981).

In what ways is the cross of Christ good news in Japan? In his exploration of this question Kraus discovered that the cross provides liberation from shame through revealing God's love, through vicarious identification, through exposing false shame and through removing alienation.

God's Love and the Agony of Shame on the Cross

Although we tend to emphasize the physical pain of death on the cross, in the Roman era crucifixion was dreaded first and foremost because of its shameful character. It was designed to be an instrument of contempt and public ridicule. The victim died naked, in bloody sweat, helpless to control body excretions. The cross "epitomizes human concepts of defilement and exclusion" (216). By Roman law no citizen could be disgraced through this dishonorable means of execution. The cross was reserved for insurrectionists, foreigners and slaves.

In relation to the cross, rather than thinking of a detached, rational, angry God driven by a moral compulsion to be justified in holiness, Kraus agrees with Kazoh Kitamori that "anguish" is more appropriate to describe the tragic moral pain God endures in order to overcome the shamefulness of our evil. "It is the anguish of love for his desecrated creatures that 'never gives up'" (217). God's love is characterized by a commitment to achieve his original purpose of creating creatures in his own image. "The cross is the revelation of this purpose to create by means of the power of love. . . . This love of God expressed itself through solidarity with us in Jesus and especially through his shameful death on the cross" (217).

Kraus argues that the cross is the revelation of God's love, not the propitiation of God's anger. Shame does not respond to punishment; rather, it is love that banishes shame. Therefore, in the Japanese context a presentation of the saving significance of the cross is built on these foundational concepts: the shameful character of crucifixion and God's love. God willingly experienced that shame out of love for us.

Vicarious Identification

The cross was not a unique moment of shame and exclusion in the life of Jesus. The cross was the epitome of Jesus' identification with us in shame, but his whole life displayed this identification.

> Jesus identified with the "poor." He was born and raised among the lower classes, associated with outcasts, and chose artisans, fisher folk, and tax collectors for his disciples. He belonged to the multitudes whom the religious leaders pronounced "accursed because they know not the law" (John 7:49). He identified with the socially excluded and despised and shared the stigma of their inferiority. (217)

Because of this identification Kraus can tell the Japanese, and others debilitated by shame, that Jesus knows fully the shameful exclusion they fear. Yet Kraus does more than that. He proclaims to them that Jesus' identification provides us the possibility of identifying with him and overcoming shame.

> As one who shares our weakness and yet overcomes, he is an enabling communication (word). . . . Only insofar as he was identified fully with those suffering the debilitating stigma of shame could his own "despising the shame" enable them to live above the existential circumstances in which they were trapped. Only as the carpenter's son conceived out of wedlock from the lowly Galilean town of Nazareth could his own sense of worth as God's Son and his total trust in God as loving Father begin to change their perception of themselves as God's children. Only *as one of them* in whom the glory of God's image was personified could he communicate that glory to others. His identification with us in our shameful situation enables us to identify with him in his realization of "the glorious liberty of the children of God" (Rom 8:21). (218)

Kraus calls the Japanese to repent, which includes a radical change in their self-image to conform to Christ as the image of God.

> Christ's vicarious identification with us enables us to identify ourselves

with him and thus gain a new perspective on our true situation and to realize a new self-identity as children of God. His compassionate, personal communication with us as the Son and true image of God sharing our existential shame enables us to emerge from our self-isolation and confess our failure, feelings of unworthiness, and despair. Thus the possibility of accepting him as the true image of God and identifying with him as a member of God's family is opened to us. (220)

Jesus' solidarity with the shamed and excluded of his day led to the ultimate experience of shame—the crucifixion. Jesus did not separate himself from others to protect his own moral purity and reputation. In the eyes of his accusers he was contaminated by his intimate association with tax collectors and sinners. Jesus' identification with the multitudes underscored, in the mind of his accusers, the accuracy of their charges of blasphemy. His identification also made the crowds more vulnerable to his presumed delusions. It seemed appropriate and necessary that he must die rather than have the whole nation perish in delusion (Jn 18:14). In this sense Jesus took the place of the Jewish nation as a representative substitute. Kraus adds that the apostolic witnesses extended this concept. "Jesus took the place of all humankind inasmuch as his revelation is a universal one. As one totally identified with and representing humanity, he faced his destiny of death on the cross" (220).

Jesus truly died for the benefit of the whole nation; what his accusers said was true in ways they did not know. But their accusation of blasphemy was false. In reality, since Jesus was the true revelation of God, it was his accusers who were the blasphemers and worthy of condemnation. Kraus states that in this sense we can say that Jesus

suffered not his own punishment but that which his accusers deserved. And inasmuch as we include all humanity in this generic rejection and dishonoring of God, we must say also "the chastisement of our sins was upon him." But this is not the substitution of a legal penalty which pays our debt to God's justice. It is rather the *substitution of total identification which accepts responsibility for all the group. He took our place including the consequences of this identification.* Thus "he who knew no sin was made sin for us" (2 Cor 5:21). (218-19)

Based on the first part of this subsection, Kraus can proclaim to the Japanese that Jesus' identification with them enables them in turn to repent and realize a new self-identity as children of God. Based on the latter part of this subsection, Kraus can proclaim that the substitutionary nature of Jesus' death on the cross means that he has already experienced the ultimate shameful exclusion for them. Therefore, they can be free of the burden of exclusion they have already experienced and free from the fear of shameful exclusion. They have the opportunity for a new start.

Exposing False Shame

The crucified Christ not only resolves the resolution of shame anxiety; the cross also exposes false shame and breaks its power to instill fear. On the cross Jesus was inappropriately shamed, and the cross and resurrection exposed the lie. The cross exposed, or shamed, the powers that falsely shamed Jesus (Col 2:15). "Many social expressions of shame have been ethically misplaced and perverted. They represent our selfish and often ignorant human attempts to control and dominate others for our own purposes" (221). Shame is defined by a society's taboos, mores and laws that reflect what that society's distorted concept of what is truly human. The cross exposes this false shame and reveals the true nature of human shame. That is, the crucified Jesus reveals God's authentic image for humanity. From Jesus' example and teaching we learn that evil intentions, selfish desires, deceit, dishonoring parents, fornication, theft, adultery, coveting and the like are the truly shameful acts (Mk 7:21-23).

Kraus notes:

Jesus did not shift the categories from defilement and shame to transgression and guilt but gave to shame an authentic moral content and internalized norm, namely, exposure to the eyes of the all-seeing, righteous, loving

God. Indeed, he described the judgment of God as making public the shameful things that we have imagined were hidden from sight (Lk 12:1-3). This transfer from an external social standard to an internalized theological standard is important for Christian formation in societies which continue to depend upon the shame of public exposure as a primary sanction against undesirable conduct. If it is not accomplished, the conscience remains bound to relative authorities such as tradition and local social approval. (221-22)

So on one hand, Jesus and the cross expose the lie of the inappropriate shaming in Japanese society and provide freedom from its tyranny. On the other hand, Jesus turns the attention of the Japanese to things for which they appropriately feel shame.

Removing the Alienation

Jesus willingly suffered this most shameful death and thus exposed the extremity of sin's shameful consequences and the despicable character of our humanly devised shame. He "despised the shame" (Heb 12:2). "Thus we can say that Jesus both shared our shame and has borne the shame for all who through his disclosure of God's holy love find freedom from its dread and power. His identification and suffering with us as the truly pure and honorable one has potentially released all humankind from the authority of false standards of value which cause hostility and dehumanization" (222). Yet Kraus acknowledges that there is appropriate shame, that there are things for which humans should feel shame. The most shameful act in history was crucifying God incarnate. Those who sought to shame Jesus were in fact those who acted shamefully. Shame alienates and destroys relationships, but on the cross Jesus responded with forgiveness. God removes the alienation of shame through love. In exposing the misplaced shame and lovingly revealing the true failure of us all, Jesus, the "friend of sinners," removed the stigma and hostility that alienates us from each other and God (222).

Assessment

Kraus's four-part presentation of the saving significance of the cross for the Japanese presents us with an excellent model for thinking about the cross in the context of mission. His cultural sensitivity allowed him both to recognize the inappropriateness of teaching a Western penal substitution theory of the atonement and to discover an approach to which people could relate. Kraus's thought displays significant understanding of shame and of the Japanese culture. This allows him to describe the work of the cross in terms that will make sense to someone from a shame-based culture. We would hope that Kraus and others will be able to use the framework he has worked out to develop parables and images that would be accessible to the common person on the streets of Tokyo, so to speak—images that would allow them to experience freedom from shame through the cross of Jesus Christ.

In order to emphasize the specific contextual nature of his work, we have referred to Japan and the Japanese people throughout this chapter. In reality, however, Kraus's ideas have potential application throughout Asia and other shame-based cultures. Thus his work has enormous missiological implications. First, Kraus helps us recognize that for a huge percentage of the world's population the penal substitution model of the atonement is a stumbling block to people's experiencing salvation in Jesus Christ, not because it presents the scandal of the cross but because its language and images are foreign to their reality and difficult to understand. Then Kraus removes that obstacle by developing an explanation of the atonement that uses terms and images intelligible in a shame-based society.

We saw in chapter five, however, the importance of not only following the New Testament theologian-missionaries in presenting metaphors of the cross that are easily understood in a given setting but also of using images that are theologically sound and not so enmeshed in the culture that they fail to challenge the culture with the scandal of the cross. Kraus succeeds here in ways that Anselm and Hodge, for example, did not.

Specifically, he talks of the cross in terms of shame, yet he does so in a way that allows for challenging a society's concept of shameful behavior and practice of shaming. In a general way we can say that Kraus develops his shame-based teaching of the atonement in a way that is strongly rooted in the pivotal themes we observed in New Testament writing on the cross: humanity's need for salvation, the necessity of human response, a demonstration of God's love that does not pit Son against Father, and the importance of the work of Christ for all persons (and not for one group over another).

In penal substitutionary approaches to the atonement, there is a certain sense of God's doing something he would rather not do, kill his son, but which he does do because a certain standard of justice demands he do so. The theory of penal substitutionary atonement allows a cultural norm particular to modern Western society, rather than the biblical narrative, to determine God's nature and actions. In contrast, Kraus avoids having a society's legal system and concept of justice or honor determine the nature of God. Rather, Kraus allows the Bible to shape his concept of the nature of God, then he works at developing a model of the atonement that coheres with that concept of God. In a similar way, rather than focusing on Jesus' death in relation to an abstract concept of justice that shifts the focus and significance of the atonement to an imagined heavenly courtroom, Kraus seeks to show how the forces of sin actually operated in history and interprets Jesus' death and the atonement in relation to those concrete forces.

Because of the contrast between Anselm and Abelard, some have thought of subjective and objective approaches to the atonement as mutually exclusive and that a person must choose one or the other. Kraus, however, emphasizes both the subjective and objective aspects of the atonement. He describes how the cross changes realities outside of the human as well as within the human. Kraus also encourages us to think about the substitutionary nature of Jesus death in different ways. Many, including both proponents and opponents of penal substitution, have a narrow definition of substitution that does not allow for any understanding other than a legal/penal one that pictures Jesus standing in the place of humans and suffering God's retributive punishment that was to have been directed at humans. Against such a definition Kraus argues that sub-stitution is a much broader term that can be used with reference to a vari-ety of metaphors. For instance:

> A ransom or hostage is a kind of substitute. A go-between is a kind of sub-stitute. A leader who identifies with his/her people and represents their cause is a substitute as well as one player who takes the place of another. Further if we think in terms of substitute payment there are different types. The payment may be a restitution of what was taken, a payment of a bad debt, the payment of a ransom, or it might be payment of a legally-pre-scribed penalty (a fine) in place of the offender.[5]

With this breadth of possible meaning in mind, Kraus has sought in his work to describe Jesus' dying in our place, as our substitute, in other than a legal/penal way. He thus helpfully opens the way for others to do the same thing in other contexts of mission.

Kraus's work then is useful at a number of levels. It has direct missiologi-cal significance in shame-based cultures. It offers a positive model of how to think about the atonement contextually. Because of strong similarities between Asian shame-based societies and the biblical world of honor and shame, his work can helpfully illuminate our biblical thinking about the atonement. Although many of us do not live and minister in shame-based societies, we still wrestle with issues of shame at some level, and Kraus's work can help us think about the saving significance of the cross in a way that intersects with that experience. Finally, Kraus invites us to step out of the rigid boundaries and definitions of substitution, subjective and objective as we work out the meaning of the cross in our different contexts.

---

[5]C. Norman Kraus, "From Biblical Intentions to Theological Conceptions: Reply to T. Finger," *Conrad Grebel Review* 8 (1990): 213.

7

CONFOUNDING EVIL
THROUGH CUNNING
& COMPASSION

---

*A*tonement theology, we have seen, has many guises, both in Scripture and in the history of Christian theology and mission. How the cross "speaks" to a particular people is in part dependent on how and what they are able to hear. Sometimes this means that those who communicate the gospel must be adept at translating the good news into new conceptual forms. This "translation" is already at work within the pages of the New Testament as we watch the "good news" of Jesus, articulated in a predominately peasant culture, taken up and refashioned by Paul within predominately urban settings. The words "a sower went out to sow" may invite a hearing among folks in ancient Galilee but would not attract an audience among the urban elite in Athens or Corinth. Indeed, the latter would likely need a commentary on Jesus' parabolic teaching.

At other times, of course, the task of communicating the gospel involves instructing persons in "the language of Zion"—persons, that is, for whom this is foreign idiom. Most of the time, though, communication is a two-way street, involving translation and reeducation. How this works out with respect to atonement theology is perhaps best exemplified in a society like the one in which many of us live, one in which Christian faith has a lengthy history. In the Western Hemisphere this lengthy history is spotted with both good and bad stories to tell regarding what has been done in the name of Jesus. Unfortunately the doctrine of the atonement itself is a part of that ambiguity, crucial in evangelism and teaching about salvation but also expounded in ways that actually foster and even legitimate suffering for the marginal in society.

One of the most forceful criticisms of atonement theology has come from women who take offense at a model of the saving significance of Jesus' death that accentuates harsh images of God and speaks of retributive justice. Such a model, it is argued, has a deleterious effect on how we conceive of God-human and human-human relations, not least within families. Has the cross of Christ meaning for persons with these concerns? Can the atonement be faithfully articulated in ways that account for feminist criticism?

In this chapter we present the work of one feminist theologian, Darby Kathleen Ray, whose work must be understood both as a critical assessment of the doctrine of the atonement and as a constructive proposal for one way we might communicate the saving significance of the cross.

Christianity Without the Cross?

Ray evaluates explanations of the atonement "not solely on the basis of their noble intentions or conformity to standards of orthodoxy, but also in light of their experienced effects" (21).[1] Like many other feminist theologians (see chapter four), she concludes that the experienced effects of tra-

---

[1] All page numbers cited in the text of this chapter are from Darby Kathleen Ray, *Deceiving the Devil: Atonement, Abuse, and Ransom* (Cleveland: Pilgrim, 1998).

ditional construals of the atonement include a theological sanctioning of sexual and domestic abuse, and an increased level of passivity in the face of injustice. "Ironically," she observes, "the very doctrine whose job it is to attempt to understand and articulate God's response to evil perpetuates evil in the lives of many women, men, and children" (2).

Ray lists three possible responses to this ironic reality. One possibility is to reject Christianity, a second is to embrace a version of Christianity minus the atonement, and a third possibility is to reconfigure the doctrine of the atonement. She has a growing conviction that the second option is not viable in the way that she once thought.

> When we talk about "atonement," we are talking about the process of reconciliation that is possible between God and world—a process in which evil is confronted in a decisive way, opening up the possibility of right relationship. Furthermore, within *Christian* tradition, this liberative dynamic is understood to be uniquely manifest in the life and death of Jesus of Nazareth. To claim that atonement is ancillary to Christianity is to deny either the centrality of the process of reconciliation to Christianity or the important role that Jesus plays in this process, or both. (4)

To extract the cross from Christianity as if it were an appendix leaves us with a body that is no longer Christianity and leaves "crossless" Christians without the capacity to address evil fully—including the evils caused in part by distorted versions of atonement theology. Ray therefore opts to address directly the problems and perversions of atonement language, and to work at developing alternative images and ideas "to support Christian individuals and communities in their struggle to confront evil and to renew and sustain right relationship" (5). Ray does this in her book *Deceiving the Devil: Atonement, Abuse and Ransom.* She first summarizes and critiques two main streams of atonement thinking—the first being satisfaction/penal substitution approaches, which she labels the Anselmian tradition; the second comprising moral influence approaches, which she labels the Abelardian tradition. Then she offers an alternative: a reworking of the *Christus Victor* model.

Evil Produced by Atonement Language

Although as we observed in chapter five, these two streams of atonement thinking—the Anselmian and the Abelardian—are markedly different, Ray points out that they both affirm suffering, self-sacrifice and obedience as supreme values in ways that have potentially deadly consequences.

> Romantic visions of a martyred Savior function in many cases to keep victims of abuse in their death-dealing situations. The sacralization of death stymies outrage against death and attitudes, actions, and systems that create it. It can also be used as a weapon of control by abusers who play on the religious sensitivities of their victims. When Jesus' death, interpreted as a salvific martyrdom, is combined with social prescriptions of women's sexual purity, the result can be fatal for victims of sexual violence. Even when this combination is not apparent, however, Jesus' death becomes the example of perfect self-sacrifice that believers ought to emulate; and as we have seen, this kind of theological idealization of self-sacrifice can perpetuate cycles of victimization. (57)

Ray thus suggests that upholding Jesus' suffering as a model can be twisted into an oppressive tool in a variety of settings, including but hardly limited to sexual abuse. Victims of slavery, unjust wages, racism, torture and political oppression, to name only a few, can all be led to believe that quiet passivity is the appropriate "Christian" response.

The problems of traditional atonement language and its potential to promote or facilitate evil go beyond a model of self-sacrificial suffering. Ray explores in detail the concepts of sin and of God implicit in these two models of the atonement and describes the potential consequences of these views. For instance, Ray describes recent work by feminist theologians who have challenged traditional configurations of sin and evil that have concentrated exclusively on disobedience, rebellion and willfulness, and viewed pride as the primal sin.[2] These theologians have offered other

---

[2]The seminal essay arguing this point was Valerie Saiving Goldstein, "The Human Situation: A Feminine View," *JR* 40 (1960): 100-112. For more recent developments, see Carol Lakey Hess, *Caretakers of Our Common House* (Nashville: Abingdon, 1997), pp. 55-86.

ways of thinking of sin, including the numbing of the self, betrayal or lack of trust, alienation and sin as distortion of the self's boundaries.

> From a feminist perspective, the implications of the Anselmian view of sin and evil are profoundly problematic. The implied model of relationship based on the unilateral power of one over another not only mirrors situations of systemic violence and personal abuse, but also offers them divine sanction. The sharp dichotomy of love and justice that is implied creates the false impression that these two are mutually exclusive rather than organically related so that the claims of each impact the exercise of the other. In both Anselmian and Abelardian traditions, the focus on disobedience includes a definition of love in terms of obedience, which is problematic for all those who need or want to resist the prevailing order. Although the Abelardian model avoids the love-justice dichotomy, it still exhibits the problems associated with viewing sin in terms of disobedience and willfulness . . . [which] defuses rage, resentment, and other catalytic emotions, entrapping abused women and children in cycles of violence buttressed by cultural and religious assumptions of male authority and prerogative. (31, 35)

Combined with this view of sin, Ray finds Anselm's picturing of God within a hierarchical system as a medieval king or feudal overlord to be dangerously amenable to power politics. This is because it provides "religious examples of and justification for systems and relationships of sustained inequality. . . . The human will to power is seen as inevitable or natural reflection of the divine will, and patterns of victimization become part and parcel of 'the way things are'" (39).

Ray believes that, rather than providing a solution to the pervasive evil in the world, these two strains of atonement thinking have contributed to it. Unlike many feminist theologians, however, her response is not to stop talking about the cross. Rather, this situation underlines for her the complexity and tenacity of human evil, and therefore the necessity of an atonement theology that "empowers concrete acts of resistance to evil and that yields moments of genuine transformation and hope" (7).

Reinterpreting the *Christus Victor* Motif

Ray describes the *Christus Victor* approach, which she calls the *patristic view of the atonement*, much as we did in chapter five. We will not repeat her summary of Irenaeus's and Gregory's words but simply note her concluding comments. She states:

> In Irenaeus we see the main contours of what I am calling the patristic model—the recognition of the reality and profound influence of evil; the definition of evil as unjust or avaricious use of power; and the conviction that in the person of Jesus, God has acted not only to reveal the true nature of evil but also to decenter and delegitimate its authority by luring it into exposing its own moral bankruptcy and thus defeating itself, hence opening up the possibility for human beings to escape enslavement to evil....
>
> Gregory's account indicates that the devil was brought to his demise by two things—first, and most important, his lust for power; and second, and derivatively, the inventiveness of God who, recognizing the devil's insatiable appetite for power, disguised the Divine Self.... In trying to ... consume or control the Other absolutely the absurdity and delusion of the devil's pretension are laid bare, and he is left to choke on his arrogance.... Gregory's account suggests, it seems to me, that God's response to evil is to expose and dramatize the violence and greed at its root, allowing the force of its own avarice to discredit it in the eyes of the moral community and empowering that community to embrace power guided and limited by compassion and justice. (123-24)

Ray acknowledges that this model of the atonement has its drawbacks. For instance, its dualistic framework for understanding evil "bypasses the complexity and subtlety of evil as we know it, feeding illusions of purity and innocence, on the one hand, and permitting the demonization of those people and groups viewed as unclean or damaged, on the other" (126). The *Christus Victor* model also has a "tendency to depict redemption as a purely cosmic affair, an otherworldly fight . . . which undermines human responsibility for evil" (127-28). She is also concerned by the tendency of portraying the atonement as a "done deal" that results in an absolute and universal triumph over evil. Our lived experience points to a different reality.

Ray believes that the patristic, or *Christus Victor,* model nevertheless offers great strengths and that its liabilities can be addressed in part because one of its strengths, its metaphorical character, gives it a pliability conducive to multiple readings. She writes:

> For while its images can whet our theological appetites and energize our imaginations, it does not give us a clear-cut or simple formula into which we can plug the life and death of Jesus and come up with a neat solution to the problem of evil. . . . Its narrative character opens rather than closes discussion. (130)

In Ray's contemporary retrieval of the *Christus Victor* model, Jesus Christ confronts not merely individual or personal sin. Rather, Satan or the devil represents the sum total of evil. The model defines evil as an abuse of power, it does not privilege the already privileged, and it has both individual and systemic relevance. To talk about evil as "cosmic" is not necessarily to render it ahistorical but rather to point to the "countless ways in which human beings are mired in, even bound by, the powers of evil" (131). To say abusive power is demonic is to recognize its power to seduce, captivate and destroy.

Ray describes redemption in similarly expansive terms. Salvation is freedom from enslavement to evil and is not reduced to either the personal or institutional. It includes both.

> Redemption understood in this way does not imply the abolition of evil itself but a transformation in one's relationship *to* evil. To be liberated from bondage to evil means that evil no longer determines one's being and actions, that one is free to resist evil and to try to reduce it. . . . Even as this model highlights the unfinished nature of the struggle against evil and the necessity of locating the struggle within the finite world—that is, within the realm of human activity and responsibility—it also recognizes that human effort alone is insufficient. (132-33)

This in-breaking of saving power and re-creative possibility were fully realized in Jesus when the transformative power of compassion broke into the historical world in a new way, creating a radical alternative to the enslaving idolatry of power as control.

In and through Jesus, God confronted evil in a definitive way. God did not use the tools of evil itself, coercive power or unjust force, "but unconventionally, indirectly, immanently, incarnationally, [God used] 'weakness' to confront and confound 'dominance' " (138). While many others consider the patristic theme of God's deception of the devil bizarre and have not taken it seriously, Ray develops the theme in a thoughtful way in relation to both Jesus' life and contemporary life.

> While the idea of divine deceit may appear immoral to some, it points to the reality that any struggle against oppression and injustice that seeks to avoid violent means or that emerges from a context of relative powerlessness must rely on cunning and ingenuity rather than ascribed authority or power.... When resources are scarce, survival itself requires ingenuity.... Parody, satire, and other mischief-making ploys can unsettle the comfortable and change popular conceptions of the Real, creating a space of alterity in which the grip of unilateral power is loosened and the limits of its strength exposed. (138-39)

Ray notes that people in situations of powerlessness have creatively used cunning and ingenuity to confront those with power over them. "The centrality of the trickster theme in African and African-American narrative traditions reflects this realization. Figures like Brer Rabbit and Signifying Monkey demonstrate that confronting power from the underside requires a gritty resourcefulness, a willingness to take what is at hand and turn it into a tool of subversion" (139). To the examples that Ray offers we would add that the Bible itself offers a number of examples of the trickster theme. Jacob is perhaps the champion trickster. There are, however, also a number of woman who match up well with Ray's definition of trickster, including Tamar (Gen 38), Israelite midwives (Ex 1:15-

21), Moses' mother (Ex 2:1-9) and Jael (Judg 4—5). Movements of non-violent resistance are well-known examples of luring wielders of unjust power into exposing and discrediting themselves.

Another approach is to use the language and presuppositions of the dominant discourse in a way that actually subverts it. Ray points to the medieval mystic Hildegard of Bingen as an example of this strategy. "Using the sexist assumption of women's natural 'airiness' to support her claims to 'receptivity to the wind of the Holy Spirit,' Hildegard laid claim to spiritual and ecclesial authority normally reserved for men" (139).

Ray interprets both Jesus' life and death through this lens of strategic cunning. She does not simply focus on the cross and the deception of the devil but also the way Jesus practiced this strategy in relation to the religious and political rulers of the day—that is, the guardians of the status quo.

> Through a public praxis of healing, compassion, and denunciation of the status quo, [Jesus] calls into question the legitimacy of reigning conceptions of power, of ruling classes and dominant moralities, he creates a crisis; he threatens the moral authority of those in power and hence provokes their wrath, forcing them to exert the only power they know—power-as-domination, violence. (140)

Just as the devil is exposed in his overextension and grasping, so these leaders are exposed and discredited in the public eye when they can no longer tolerate Jesus and respond with violence.

> The patristic model illuminates the fatal flaw of power-as-control—its Achilles' heel. Its symbolics demonstrate that the collapse occurs at the point of overextension; in this moment, this space, the truth about human evil is revealed. But it is also here that an alternative, a salvific possibility is manifest. . . . Jesus' encounter with human evil is seen as a groundbreaking response. His use of courage, creativity, and the power of truth to uncover and disrupt the hegemony of power-as-control becomes a prototype for further strategies and action. He actively opposes violence with the nonvi-

olent power of truth, exposing evil for what it is and challenging those around him, and all those who hear his story, to recognize the victim-producing effects of unilateral power to risk embodying a different kind of power—relational power . . . power-as-compassion. (141, 144)

Responding to evil is a constant and ongoing challenge. On the one hand, the profundity of evil demonstrates the necessity of God's in-breaking salvific action. At the same time, Ray states that the salvific possibility of the amazing grace and redemptive power of Jesus' life and death depends on people living it out in concrete acts.

Assessment

Darby Kathleen Ray's work on the atonement is an admirable attempt to take seriously the criticisms of atonement theology that have surfaced especially among feminist theologians in the West in recent years. It is particularly stimulating to look over her shoulder, so to speak, as she seeks to gain a hearing from other feminist theologians who have dismissed the atonement as hopelessly enmeshed in language and approaches that promote violence and abusive practices while encouraging passivity in the face of such injustices. For that reason, an important part of her book is the critique of the two main streams of atonement thinking. She demonstrates that she understands and shares these concerns with the problematic nature of both the satisfaction/penal substitution model and the moral influence model.

She desires, however, to move beyond critique and rejection in order to promote and participate in constructive reflection and retrieval. In this respect, she joins a small cadre of others for whom the tradition of theological discourse on the atonement is neither univocal (i.e., speaking singularly in penal categories) nor hopelessly implicated in destructive and dehumanizing images and practices. Margo Houts, for example, is "grateful for the alarm which feminist theologians have sounded with regard to abusive aspects of atonement theology," but is clear that the doctrine of the atonement ought not to be aborted as a result. Instead, she urges Christian leaders to "(1) guard against using atonement images which carry abusive and tritheistic overtones, (2) be ready to explain the historical and cultural influences which have shaped each atonement theory, and (3) offer a response which is contextualized."[3] Gayle Gerber Koontz, Leanne Van Dyk and Deanna Thompson are other welcome voices in this regard, calling for theological resources that enlarge our perspective on the saving significance of Jesus' death—both historically and in the present.[4] In today's theological world, Ray may still be a voice crying in the wilderness, but hers is not the only voice!

Her study aims to convince those who have excised the atonement from their theology that the atonement is not an optional emphasis in Christian theology and that it is possible to develop a model of the atonement that not only avoids the pitfalls but also provides help in addressing the very evils associated with what some feminists have called a divine child-abuse model of the atonement. So, her aim is not simply that feminist theologians and others who share this galaxy of criticisms of traditional atonement theology will find her work as acceptable or nonproblematic; she also hopes to carve out a place for atonement theology as an integral part of Christian faith, one that does not promote but actually confronts evil.

The great strength of her work is her careful reworking of the *Christus Victor* model in a way that avoids the liabilities that feminist theologians have associated with penal substitution models, and which also addresses the limitations she finds in patristic versions of *Christus Victor*. It is at the intersection of these two aims that we want to raise some questions.

We would appreciate hearing more from Ray regarding how atone-

---

[3]Margo G. Houts, "Classical Atonement Imagery: Feminist and Evangelical Challenges," *Catalyst* 19, no. 3 (1993): 5-6.

[4]Gayle Gerber Koontz, "The Liberation of Atonement," *The Mennonite Quarterly Review* 63 (1989): 171-92; Leanne Van Dyk, "The Three Offices of Christ: The *Munus Triplex* as Expansive Resources in Atonement," *Catalyst* 25, no. 2 (1999): 6-8; Deanna Thompson, "Theological Proximity to the Cross: A Conversation between Martin Luther and Feminist Theologians" (Ph.D. diss., Vanderbilt University, 1998).

ment theology is integral to the Christian narrative about God and God's dealings with humanity and the cosmos. Ray's discussion draws a clear line from the ministry of Jesus to the nature of his death and thus may well point to how the centrality of the cross might be more fully developed. At the same time, in Ray's presentation we are yet some distance from a robust account of the triune God in which Jesus' death is to be understood.

In fact, to push this issue further, the question of the relationship between the person of Christ and his work might have been more fully examined in Ray's work. It would have been interesting to see her pursue the nexus between incarnation and atonement, or atonement and exaltation, but this is not our primary concern here. Rather, having worked through her theology of the atonement, we are unsure as to how Ray might present the singularity of Jesus' work on the cross. Jesus' redemptive ministry is an example to be followed—this is obvious from Ray's study, but in her work the cross of Christ appears not to have actually won redemption for humanity. Admittedly, Ray does write of the necessity of God's in-breaking salvific action. However, she does little to demonstrate how Jesus' action against evil was unique or qualitatively different than what humans can and should do today. Jesus' uniqueness appears to lie primarily in his blazing the trail or pioneering the way. He was a prototype; is he more?

Clearly, Ray wants to develop a model of interpretation that presents the atoning work of Jesus Christ with both objective and subjective elements. At the same time, she is apparently so concerned to avoid communicating that Jesus' crucifixion signaled the complete victory over evil that she ends up placing much greater emphasis on the subjective action of Jesus' life and death—how they move people to live differently. Again, this emphasis is understandable, since Ray is concerned to undermine the potential of talk about the atonement to promote passivity or confusion in the face of the reality of evil today. But this accent on how Jesus provides us a model for confronting evil leaves little room for differentiating the role of Jesus' life, death and resurrection from our own actions in addressing evil.

Of course, it is helpful and needful to talk of the atonement in subjective terms that are concretely rooted in Jesus' life and our own. Even so, might she have done more on the objective side? Our sense is that Ray's model, in contrast to Abelard's, *is* capable of addressing more fully the objective aspects of the atonement—that is, concrete ways that Jesus' life, death and resurrection have dethroned and exposed powers of evil.

Although she takes a more subjective approach, it cannot be said that Ray takes evil lightly. Her reworking of the *Christus Victor* model does, however, seem narrowly focused on moving and enabling humans to confront forces of violence and evil outside of themselves. She does not explore how Jesus' atoning work addresses alienation rooted within one's own being, nor does she significantly develop how the cross provides for the possibility of restored relationship with God and others. We are not making this critique because we expect any single model of the atonement to capture all that was accomplished at the cross. Rather, we make this observation because it appears the *Christus Victor* model provides the means for addressing these issues but has not yet done so in Ray's presentation.

In sum, we find here a theologian who helpfully takes the presence and power of evil seriously and who, on this basis, undertakes the challenge of communicating both the necessity and the promise of atonement thinking to people that are resistant to that message. As our questions demonstrate, we see significant limitations in Ray's work as it stands. Yet we are heartened to see a feminist theologian addressing the atonement in a constructive way. We have much to learn from Darby Kathleen Ray's capacity to learn from early Christian writings and to adapt their metaphors so as to make them intelligible to her target audience.

8

HEARING
OTHER VOICES

Exploring the Ongoing
Significance of Jesus' Death

*C**hrist died for our sins.*" This is one of the central affirmations that runs through much of the New Testament. We have seen how this simple, straightforward affirmation might be expressed in dozens of different ways, both in the New Testament and in the history of Christian mission and thought. In fact, there are even more ways of communicating the message of the atonement.

Thus, although the preceding chapters have presented in-depth summaries of the saving significance of the cross in particular church and mission contexts, we might have explored others as well. What we have attempted thus far is not only to display what has been said about the cross in those contexts but also to reveal something of the shape of the theological reflection lying in the background of those interpretations. We believe that others, living and serving faithfully in other contexts, will be able to learn from these instances of coming to terms with the particular meaning of the gospel. The previous two chapters provided exemplars, therefore, designed to help us as we think carefully about how to talk about the atonement in our own settings.

Of course, we do not mean to imply that every time we preach, witness or write about the cross we must go into such detail or try to explain the variety of ways the cross intersects with our realities. In addition to attempts to account as fully with the significance of the atonement as these chapters have done, we want to encourage the exploration and articulation of images that capture some aspect of the meaning of the cross in particular situations. In that spirit, in this chapter we offer brief examples of people talking about some facet of the saving significance of the cross in ways that attend to the importance of the story of the cross as this is developed in the New Testament, as well as to the centrality of the atonement in Christian tradition.

Christus Victor and the Devil in Modern-Day Great Britain

The so-called modern scientific mind is resistant to notions of the devil or resurrection, not to mention the idea that Jesus' death and resurrection conquered the devil. This is true in Great Britain, where Rowan Williams preaches, as well as in many other parts of the world, especially in the West. Williams nevertheless addresses precisely these issues in a sermon entitled "An Enemy Hath Done This," and he does so in a way that not only can earn a hearing but can lead listeners to experience an important aspect of the salvific nature of the cross today.[1]

We appreciate not only the way Williams has taken ancient terms and a patristic explanation of the cross and made them intelligible and meaningful for his contemporaries but also that he has done so in a way that is faithful to the message of the New Testament. He demonstrates that wooden, literal language is not required to communicate the meaning of

---

[1] Rowan Williams, "An Enemy Hath Done This," in *A Ray of Darkness* (Boston: Cowley, 1995), pp. 75-79.

the cross in a way consonant with the Bible. We also appreciate that Williams does not present this as the singular model for explaining the atonement. Without contradicting anything he says here, he could easily give a sermon the following week that uses a different metaphor to extract the meaning of the cross for our lives today.

The beginning of Williams's sermon emphasizes that we live with a certain illusion of being in control—both as individuals and civilizations. We have the illusion that we can construct the patterns of our lives. Yet "there are moments for all of us when the liberal, rational, humane categories we normally operate with suddenly collapse." We see this in extermination camps or ethnic cleansing but also in day-to-day interactions with others. We recognize "that benevolence and rationality are not at the heart of people's actions" (75). Indeed,

> human activity is misunderstood if it is seen as a sequence of "responsible" decisions taken by conscious and self-aware persons in control of their lives. More often it is a confused, partly conscious, partly instinctive response to the givenness of a world we do not dominate, a world of histories and ideas, languages and societies, structures we have not built. More perhaps than we ever realize or accept with our minds, we are being acted upon as much as acting. . . . Reality, even human and personal reality, resists the mind's desperate attempt to organize it reasonably. (76)

After helping his listeners sense and feel the inadequacy of rational categories and ideas to explain the incomprehensible forces that are at work in and through us, Williams mentions the devil, the creator of discord. He rejects thinking of the devil as merely a symbol but also warns against conceiving of the devil as a totally independent superhuman power or as something merely human inside each of us. "The intolerable fact is that we meet the really alien in what is really human: if that is not so, the scriptural 'mystery of iniquity' ceases to be mysterious" (77).

Williams asks, How can we be preserved from disintegration and senselessness? How can we be saved from this situation? He turns to the language of the *Christus Victor* tradition, stating that in many ways it is

> a better model for us than any theory that sees the atonement as bringing
> order and control into the world. It takes with full seriousness the uncontrolled
> and uncontrollable, the alien and the menacing in the world, and says not that
> Christ has obliterated them, but that Christ has overcome them. They are
> there still, but their horror is seen in a new perspective: the wounds they inflict
> are the prints of the nails in the body of the Lord. He has battled with the unin-
> telligible dark, the *surd* of evil, and still lives. He contains evil, he has shown
> that evil cannot contain him: the darkness comprehended it not. He has
> looked into the "heart of darkness": he has held the burning world to himself,
> and holds it always, at the cost of a pain we cannot begin to conceive. (78)

Returning again to the issue of the devil, Williams affirms, "The questions, 'Inside or outside?'; 'I or not I?' begin to seem insignificant because
the glorious victory of our Lord teaches us at once both the enormity, violence, and reality of Satan's power, and the truth that it is not final. Satan
is the prince of this world; chaos and menace are the texture of our lives—
yet the compassion of God encircles the whole" (78).

The final part of the sermon includes reflections on our response to
Jesus' victory. Williams asks, "Can we now understand that our unity,
integrity, wholeness, *salus, shalom* is not in us but in God-in-Christ, who is
our peace?" The unpredictable, uncontrollable power of the devil cannot
block us from God's love.

> Only we—the conscious and rational and self-determining we—can do
> that, because we alone can say "no" to God's acceptance. . . . [Yet] the one
> freedom that is assured to us, the only freedom that finally matters, is the
> capacity to say "yes" to God's great "yes" to us in Christ, and . . . no powers
> of darkness and chaos and evil can rob us of that without our consent. (79)

Jesus' Sacrifice: Cleansing from Sin and Creating New Community in Tanzania

In his autobiography Bishop Kisare of the Mennonite Church in Tanza-

187

nia recounts a time in 1942 when, after a period of significant tension in the church, the Spirit moved and reconciliation occurred.[2] The tension had been present at different levels—between missionaries and Africans, between church members from different tribes, and between church members from different villages. During a time of prayer at a district conference meeting, the men and women attending all burst out crying, and after an hour of weeping over the state of their lives and the church, individuals began confessing what was keeping them from being in good relationship with others in the church. The person leading the prayer time pronounced forgiveness and proclaimed the possibility of reconciliation because the blood of Jesus' sacrifice on the cross had cleansed them of the sin and jealousy and pride that had created the barriers between them.

The concept of the cleansing and reconciling power of Jesus' death on the cross was easily understood by the people because of the role blood sacrifice had played in the traditional religion and culture of the predominant tribe—the Luo.

Kisare explains that the strong bond of loyalty within a village leads people to overlook small wrongs committed by others. Yet some actions are too grievous to ignore—such as killing someone else or a man sleeping with one of his father's wives. A person caught in an action like this will usually run away; if not, he or she is thrown out of the village. The person is then outside of the village covenant, has no village and cannot return. Kisare gives an example of what might happen in the case of a son who offended his father and the village with some extreme action.

> He may stay out for 40 or 50 years. But the time will come when he will become old and he will not want to die outside without a family. So he will send word to his father's village asking to be accepted by them.
>
> No matter how good a man he may have been or how much the people of the village may have admired him, it is never possible for him to return unless a sacrifice is made which is powerful enough to undo the evil thing

---

[2]Joseph C. Shenk, ed., *Kisare: A Mennonite of Kiseru* (Salunga, Penn.: Eastern Mennonite Missions, 1984).

which he did. We know in our society that only the blood of a sheep killed in ritual sacrifice has the power to break the curse which the man brought upon himself when he sinned against his father and his village.

The date is set for the return of the sinner. A low opening is made for him in the village wall, at the far end, opposite the village entrance. Before the lost son may enter the village, a sheep is killed. The sheep's blood, along with juices from the small intestine, and certain herbs are mixed together. The lost person then confesses fully the evil things which he did against his father and the village.

After he has confessed, he is symbolically cleansed. This is done by sprinkling him with the prepared liquid. He drinks some of it. He then stoops down in humility and enters the village through the low entrance that was made for him. After he is on the inside of the village enclosure, more cleansing ceremonies are performed. Then he is taken to a small hut, prepared for the occasion where he eats with members of his father's village. (80)

Kisare recalls that on that evening in 1942 he and others came to understand and experience the reality that

both the missionaries and the Africans were all lost from the one true village, the new village of God our Father. It was sin which kept us concerned only with our own earthly families, our ethnic villages. The Holy Spirit showed us that Jesus' sacrifice made it possible for all of us to be brothers and sisters in the same village. . . . We saw the crucified Lamb of God whose blood removes the walls that separate people from each other and from God their Father. . . .

We now saw each other in a different way. Earlier such things as theft, adultery, lying, malicious gossip, and jealousies were not so bad if they were directed against people of another village. But if we were all members of the same new village, then we needed to hold the character of each other person as sacred. We needed to ask forgiveness and make things right even with those of a different ethnic background. . . .

It was wonderful to go to a place where you had never been before and to be welcomed as dear, honored relatives. An example of this new unity was that if a brother wished to marry but was so poor he didn't have the bride dowry, other brethren across ethnic and church boundaries would get the dowry together for him, just as they would were he their own blood brother. (81-82)

This beautiful story challenges all of us and also illustrates some of the main points we are trying to make in this book. Since many of us read biblical sacrificial imagery through the lens of an Anselmian satisfaction or penal substitutionary model, we understand Jesus' sacrificial death as a payment made to God. Yet in the Luo culture blood sacrifice was understood not as a payment to God or the gods but as a way of removing a barrier or curse—a cleansing of the consequences of an evil action. Of course, other cultures have used sacrifices in different ways. Our point is not that the Luo tribe's traditional sacrifice matches up with the *one* correct biblical view of sacrifice. Rather it is a concrete reminder to us of a point we made earlier in the book. In the Old Testament the Jewish people themselves had different types of sacrifices, and we would do much better to allow their understanding of sacrifice to inform the way we think of Jesus as sacrifice rather than viewing sacrificial imagery through the lens of the penal substitutionary model.

Someone might borrow Kisare's story to explain Jesus' death as a sacrifice because it avoids the theological problems encountered in common explanations of Jesus death as a sacrificial payment to satisfy God the Father's demand for justice. Yet we all recognize that talking to a North American audience about Jesus' death in terms of Luo sacrificial ritual will not have the same impact as it would for a Luo audience. Although we can perhaps imagine how it is liberative for them, we will be left asking questions: How does it cleanse from sin? How does it break the curse of evil? Such questions apparently do not arise for the Luo, for whom such imagery is integral to their lived reality.

The Luo example helps us to understand better how sacrifice is an image of tremendous salvific import for some people, yet for most of us it does not connect with our immediate reality. It remains an intellectual curiosity or abstraction—important, but not necessarily for us life giving. Therefore, this story offers us a double illustration of the importance of searching for metaphors that connect with people's reality. On the positive side we witness the powerful moving of the Spirit through the use of an image that allowed the Luo people to understand and experience the saving power of the cross. On the negative side we can see that the same image used in a different setting would be foreign and would likely have little impact. Thus Kisare's story challenges us to find images and models as effective in our setting of mission as this sacrificial imagery was in his.

Kisare's description of Jesus' atoning work impresses us not only because of its contextual nature but also because it presents Jesus' salvific work in a way that is corporate—community-forming and personal—restoring an individual's relationship to God, and because of its ethical impact—it changes the way people live out their lives.

An Embrace of Love: Dramatizing the Cross for College Students in the United States

The setting is a weekend conference for university students. Curtis Chang, an area director with InterVarsity Christian Fellowship in Boston, begins the weekend by describing to students how he had spent the days before his first year at college collecting the right mix of posters and photos to decorate his dorm room. He calculated what kind of posters would lead people to want to be his friend. He then lists other things college students collect in an effort to feel good about themselves and hope others will be impressed as well—grades, friends, money, drinking performances at parties, and so on. Yet no one can collect enough, and all fear they will be exposed as not measuring up. This fear promotes further collecting—cheating to collect even more.

Then, through drama and narrative, Chang leads the students through some of the events of Jesus' last days and weaves in contemporary scenes as well. The central theme is betrayal. Chang tells how someone who was

191

trying to "collect" more money betrayed him. He also, however, leads the students to feel how each of us, through our efforts to collect and present a certain persona to the world, betray God, others and ourselves. He shows how Jesus sought to expose this "collecting" and betraying activity in the lives of people he encountered but also how he embraced those same people. Chang makes this most concrete through vignettes of Jesus' interaction with Peter and Judas.

Chang states, "Jesus embraces us even while he knows we will betray him. And he does so in order that we may come clean, be made clean. But how? How exactly will he make us clean? How does he heal an entire society that has betrayed God and his poor?"[3] With these questions Chang moves the drama into issues related to the atonement and the cross. He first presents the possibility that Jesus could have responded to Judas' betrayal with punishment, with a sword—or even the flaming swords of a thousand angels, but punishment, even deserved punishment, is not the plan for healing. Rather, healing comes from Jesus' entering totally into our experience. Jesus both experiences betrayal and is treated as a betrayer. Chang describes it with these words:

> Hanging on the cross . . . his body is covered with the same bruises and bloodied lashes that traitors suffer. He has taken on all the marks of betrayal because he embraces all of us, every aspect of our lives—even our falsely collecting, secretly betraying selves. Some of us do not really know this Jesus . . . we think Jesus only really embraces you when we are nice and clean and good. In some of our hearts, we imagine Jesus would recoil in disgust if he found out just how much we have collected, hidden, betrayed. But . . . Jesus hangs on the cross and embraces us at our very worst, our most treacherous selves. And he embraces not just with a distant pat, but he actually takes on to himself our very condition. He shares with us the very marks of betrayal.[4]

---

[3] Curtis Chang, third message, "Last Days of Jesus" conference (fall 1998), p. 1.
[4] Ibid., p. 7.

Through further narrative and drama, which includes participants from the audience, Chang portrays Jesus' final hours on the cross. We will pick up the story at its climax:

"Father, into *your* hands, I give my spirit." The voice rings out, echoing further and further out. The voice cuts through and silences all other voices in its wake. The sound builds in resonance and beauty as it rings through the universe. It swells into the universe's greatest love song, a declaration of love, hope, and faith in the Other that has never been remotely matched by human music. And Jesus' voice builds to a powerful crescendo, so powerful that when it reaches Hell itself, its gates crumble instantly and the Great Betrayer flees instantly. . . . But the beautiful music will not end. Because from heaven itself, another voice answers Jesus' voice. . . . If you could translate the sound of this utterly transcendent voice into mere human words, it would sound something like the words that Jesus heard all through his life: "This is my Son, the Beloved, with him I am well pleased." . . . Just as the Son has given himself into his Father's hands, the Father is holding on to the Son, even to death. . . .

This is their plan for our healing. Jesus has opened his arms wide enough to embrace all humanity. He embraces all who we are, even our traitorous hearts. . . . The forces of betrayal first squirm, then pound, then beat on Jesus. They do everything to break the Son's grip on to the Father. . . . But Jesus bears the full weight of betrayal, he endures its full brunt, and he outlasts its power. Straining with his every effort and breath, he hangs on to His Father in love. . . . Only a love that is greater, more enduring, more powerful than betrayal can heal betrayal.

The cross then stands as the victory of God. . . . The weight of our sin sought to suffocate God himself, but the Son and the Father have together suffocated sin in their embrace. . . . [Jesus] has won for you a victory over betrayal and you are embraced and welcomed in the very love that is shared by the Father and the Son. This is the objective reality. You don't change whether Jesus has done it by whether you believe it or not. . . . However, you can choose whether to enter this objective reality or not. You can choose to cling to what is false and unreal or live in truth and reality. This process of turning from our falsehood to God's truth is what the Bible calls repentance.[5]

In the final session Chang addresses concretely the reality of present suffering in terms of the "already but not yet" nature of Jesus' victory. The above material, however, is enough to give us a sense of how he is talking about the saving significance of the cross to college students today. Like the other people in this chapter Chang's references to the cross in a mission setting do not communicate all there is to say about what Jesus accomplished on the cross. Yet in contrast to some that do try to say more, what he does say does not conflict with the theological teaching about the cross we observed in the New Testament. For instance, he does a wonderful job of presenting the Father and Son united in the atoning work of the cross. And his central images of "collecting," betrayal and loving embrace, which he illustrates with both contemporary and biblical examples, connect with the world of his listeners.

Looking at the Cross Through the Lens of Christ as Prophet, Priest and King

This section, unlike the others in this chapter, is not based on a particular moment of ministry. Rather it summarizes an essay by Leanne Van Dyk. We have included it, however, because it meshes well with the spirit of this chapter. Her essay provides a framework that encourages and facilitates presenting the atoning work of the cross in ways that avoid the reductionism that labels atonement theology as being only a reflection of an authoritarian, punitive God and a source of victimization. Van Dyk recognizes that some models of the atonement have legitimated suffering and abuse and have led people to develop distorted images of God. Yet like Darby K. Ray in the previous chapter, Van Dyk states that discarding the doctrine is not the solution. Rather "what is needed are theological resources that expand, enlarge, give room, and

---

[5]Ibid., pp. 11-12.

offer vision and scope and perspective."[6]

Van Dyk notes that one way of expanding and enlarging atonement theology and giving new practical implications for the life of the church is to bring it into closer relationship with other major Christian doctrines. As an example she proposes reflecting on the cross through the lens of the threefold office of Christ—prophet, priest and king.

> The prophetic perspective on the cross is that the cross proclaims the true nature of God.... This proclamation of God does not reveal a God of vengeance but a God of love and compassion.... The cross is not the scene of divine child abuse, but the vivid, paradoxical display of the love of God as it takes up and overcomes the brokenness of the world.... Christ's sufferings were not the result of God's punitive and vindictive wrath; neither were they an expression of Christ's passivity. They are, rather, a revelation of the heart of God. (6)

Van Dyk acknowledges the highly paradoxical quality of a violent execution being the revelation of the loving heart of God, yet she states this is precisely the content of the Christian gospel. "The priestly perspective on the cross is where the classic themes of sacrifice, propitiation, substitution, representation, and satisfaction all find voice" (7). It is also here that the most difficult issues of relating divine love and divine wrath occur. In response, Van Dyk writes:

> The potential of the priestly perspective for an enlarged view of the cross in contemporary theology lies in several directions. First, it may be helpful simply to point out that the difficult themes of sacrifice and satisfaction and other corresponding motifs are not the complete package in atonement theology. The cross is not merely the place of sacrifice and substitution. These themes are profoundly important, they are deeply biblical, but they do not in themselves carry the full richness and scope of atonement. The prophetic and kingly are also required. (7-8)

---

[6]Leanne Van Dyk, "The Three Offices of Christ: The *Munus Triplex* as Expansive Resources in Atonement," *Catalyst* 25, no. 2 (1999): 6. In-text citations used throughout this section refer to pages in this work.

Second, Van Dyk calls for a reexamination of some of the most awkward or problematic themes such as satisfaction and sacrifice. Satisfaction, she points out, has a flexible and varied use throughout the history of the church. Athanasius, for example, in *On the Incarnation of the Word*, says that Christ satisfied God's integrity in the cross, not God's honor. It was God's truthfulness at stake—God's own fidelity and character. Here is a view of satisfaction that enlarges the Anselmian treatment (8).

In discussing sacrifice Van Dyk points to the reality we have just observed in the Luo tribe. Sacrifice is a concept that continues to have significance in a wide spectrum of cultures, and it appears frequently in Scripture and continues to be used in liturgy and hymns. It should not be so quickly dismissed and ignored. At the same time, in relation to this theme, she calls us to "avoid the pitfall of assigning certain parts of the body of Christ the role of self-sacrifice" (8).

Finally, Van Dyk insists, "The kingly role of Christ is also a resource for an expansion or enrichment of the doctrine of the atonement."

> A few brief examples can be mentioned. First, the nature of Christ's kingly reign from the cross must be explored as a highly paradoxical and dialectical victory. Second, the kingly perspective must affirm recent restatements of the power of God such as those found in D. Migliore's *The Power of God* (Westminster, 1983). Third, ecclesiology and christology must be integrated. How is the church fulfilling the kingship of Christ in community, in social action for justice, in mission? (8)

Van Dyk offers a helpful model of taking seriously contemporary concerns about atonement theology without jettisoning the tradition of the church or doing violence to the biblical witness. She realizes that the history of Christian reflection on the atonement, including Christian reflection in the last two centuries, must be open to criticism. Indeed, for her, contemporary concerns about the message of the atonement do spotlight certain deficiencies in modern thinking about the saving significance of Jesus' death.

Van Dyk thus wisely recommends expanding and broadening our portrayals of the atonement and helpfully suggests that one of the ways forward is to link our presentation of the atonement to other major doctrines such as the incarnation, Trinity and resurrection. Through briefly working this out in relation to the three offices of Christ, she helps us to see how relating presentations of the atonement to other doctrines protects from reductionism and theological error. She presents a helpful model that others can apply in their particular settings of mission.

Conclusion

As twenty-first-century Christians we face a gargantuan but vital task. This is true for the variety of situations in which we find ourselves socially and geographically. For many of us who make our homes in the West, we face the challenge of working out the significance of the sacrificial death of Jesus for people who have very little concept of sacrifice. We face the challenge of working out the importance of Jesus' death as a victory over powerful forces in a world where "powerful forces" are often not recognized or admitted as a part of reality. We face the challenge of exploring the saving effect of Jesus' death among people who do not want to be "saved"— indeed, who have no perceived need for "salvation." For those of us who find ourselves outside of the West, or who live in the West but participate in a subculture that has not embraced values and behaviors associated with the West, the challenge is no less pressing and no less important. "Sacrifice" may be a well-known idea to the people among whom we live; how can the death of Jesus be understood as a sacrifice without being subsumed by popular ideas? Spirits may pervade the world of the people around us; how can we use familiar terms relating to this spirit world in sometimes unfamiliar ways so as to explain the saving effects of Jesus' death?

Irrespective of the particulars of our contexts, we hope the examples in this chapter have been exciting and stimulating as we reflect on their potential impact in helping our communities and us to understand and experience the saving power of the cross. We also hope that hearing others talk about the cross using new images and different terms and phrases fosters new levels of appreciation for the variety of ways in which the cross has saving significance in our lives.

One image or model is simply inadequate to communicate all that God has done and continues to do through the cross. What other images might faithfully represent the work of Christ? What other models might prove effective in bringing others into a more full awareness of the saving significance of Jesus' death?

9

COMMUNICATING THE ATONEMENT TODAY

E *arly on in the life of the church,* reflection on the nature of Jesus coalesced around affirmations of the preexistence and deity of Jesus. Short summaries of Christian belief, known as "rules of faith" or "rules of truth," typically affirmed the incarnation of Jesus, and the great ecumenical councils of the church in the fourth and fifth centuries struggled to commit to precise language the nature of the *person* of Jesus Christ. Classical faith thus affirms the doctrine of the incarnation even as it grapples with how best to represent the central confession that Jesus is fully human and fully divine.

If this is true of Jesus' "person," what of his "work"? In fact, no such orthodoxy has ever existed with regard to the atonement. The primary creedal statement of the Western church, the Apostles' Creed, has it that Jesus Christ "suffered under Pontius Pilate, was crucified, dead, and buried"; the Creed affirms the importance of these historical moments, but it does so without sketching the theological ramifications of the death of Jesus. The same may be said of many early creedal statements—some of which do not mention the crucifixion at all, most of which have little to say beyond a historical reference to the cross.

Instead, not only in Scripture but throughout the history of the church's faith and mission, the significance of Jesus' death has been articulated in different ways at different times in different places. *That* God took on human form in Christ Jesus is secure. To paraphrase Anselm, *why* God became a human, even to the point of ignominious death, is a question that begs (present tense!) for interpretation. We have come to the conclusion that this question is incapable of being addressed fully or decisively for all times and places. This is because of the limitations of human language, and of even our most impressive metaphors, to account fully for this mystery, the cross of Christ.

Why the church has never been content with a single interpretation of Jesus' death is clear on another front as well. If we think of communicating the good news by employing the model of journalism, then we can appreciate the need to address a particular audience mindful of what that audience can and will take for granted. Seen in this light, theological discourse (whether in a seminar at church, at an inner-city mission or on the streets of Bangladesh) must take seriously the social and cultural presuppositions that determine whether or not the message will gain a hearing.[1] The question whether it is accurate to refer to the West as ever having been marked as authentically Christian aside, the hard reality is that our view of Christendom in the United States must be superseded by the images of new missionary outposts. Whether inside the walls of the church or outside, we cannot assume "the language of Zion"—that is, the idiom of Christian faith. Nor can we assume the sort of general intimacy with the history of

---

[1] This image is borrowed from David Lowes Watson, "The Church as Journalist," *International Review of Mission* 72 (1983): 57-74.

God's dealings with Israel that would provide the basis for understanding our metaphors of atonement as shorthand ways of referring to the biblical drama.

What is the saving significance of the death of Jesus? One coordinate for answering this question is the nature of the human situation to which the cross must address itself.

"Sin" and Popular Atonement Images

Our most popular images of atonement theology are oriented toward a definition of sin as "disobedience," "an infraction of the laws of God." According to the human story thus conceived, "salvation" is forgiveness. Thus far, the mural we are painting is consistent with the biblical drama; this is not to say, however, that it *is* the biblical drama. In fact, the painting that typically results from these beginning strokes of the brush lacks the texture and complexity necessary to account for the biblical witness. This is true for at least four reasons.

1. The biblical concept of sin includes the notion of disobedience, but this does not make acts of disobedience the foundation of our understanding of sin. What is more, other categories of thought are included in biblical discussions of sin as well, and we will turn to some of these shortly.

2. This identification of sin with acts of disobedience has too easily been coupled in the United States with the widespread cultural norms of autonomous individualism, with the result that Christian notions of "disobedience" and "forgiveness" are typically understood as applying to "my relationship with God." That forgiveness, for example, is essentially a relational term, that it involves incorporation (or reincorporation) into the family of God's people—such considerations are often not central to the "plan of salvation" grounded in a disobedience-forgiveness understanding of sin and salvation.

3. If sin is explained in terms of disobedience and salvation is understood according to individual-oriented notions of forgiveness, then it is

possible to conceive of salvation apart from any notion of human transformation. The divine words "I forgive you" are comforting, to be sure, but according to the drama we are discussing, these words do nothing to address the practices of disobedience with which our experience, individually and collectively, teaches us we were born. Sharply put, salvation according to this scenario takes the form of an accounting transfer that takes place "on the books" but does not address our lived realities. In this case, the death of Jesus is necessary so that the books will balance at the end of the day—enough punishment meted out to cover the full complement of disobedient acts committed. In this case, sins might be forgiven, but are we any less likely not to engage in disobedience tomorrow?

4. Finally, according to our most popular notions of the atonement, sin as disobedience is tied to a particular image of God, whose sense of justice requires that he respond with retribution. As a result, disobedience invites punishment, but humanity need not suffer punishment on account of the willingness of God to transfer our just desserts onto his son, Jesus. Is this the only way of conceiving the gracious gift of forgiveness? Hardly! Note, for example, how Jesus pronounces the forgiveness of sins in the case of a paralytic, without reference to the sacrifice of any animal and without reference to his own, still-future death (Mk 2:1-12).

Understanding sin narrowly as an infraction of the laws of God falls short of the biblical account of sin. This is perhaps troublesome enough, but linking this view of sin with a Western penal view of justice also proposes, and for some even requires, a concept of God that is incongruent with the biblical witness. This is the enraged or infuriated God, bent on retribution. Of course, many proponents of penal substitution recognize that God is not foremost an angry God who desires to punish humans, and they attempt to explain that God is foremost a merciful God, a God of love, even though the penal substitutionary model of the atonement would lead one to think otherwise.[2] Unfortunately, trying to nuance the

---

[2]Cf., for example, John R. W. Stott, *The Cross of Christ* (Downers Grove, Ill.: InterVarsity Press, 1986), pp. 150-51.

meaning of this model in the pages of a theology book has not proven sufficient to protect people in the pew from the damaging effects of the image of God this model communicates and seems to demand. Tragically, many Christians (and former believers) still live in fear of a God who seems so intent on punishing, and much less willing to forgive, than folks we encounter in day-to-day life.

Again, disobedience must be included in any discussion of sin, just as forgiveness is integral to salvation as this is developed in Scripture. We are simply insisting that sin and salvation are larger categories, that they involve more than our most popular atonement images allow.

What is the human condition to which the cross addresses itself? Even to raise the question is to be confronted with the limitations of any answer. We can speak in broad and basic terms about the human situation. At the same time, we must realize that the fundamental, nonnegotiable human need for God is experienced in different ways by different people in different places and at different times. Indeed, in our own lives as Christians, we have come to God with arms open wide with different needs: hope in the midst of despair, direction in the midst of lostness, love in the midst of rejection and so on. If this accurately reflects our autobiographies as Christians, can we not see how different peoples might understand and articulate their life questions in ways that are both like and unlike our own?

The "Domain" of Sin

One way to underscore the importance of the question we are raising is to look briefly at the various ways in which "sin" is understood and represented in the pages of the New Testament. Unfortunately, this is not simply a matter of looking up the word *sin* in the concordance and cataloging the range of uses to which this term is put. This is because the concept of sin is sometimes present even when the term itself is absent. A relatively straightforward approach would be to focus on terms belonging to the "semantic domain" of sin.

One of the basic insights of modern language study is that we understand words in relation to other words. The semantic domain of "sin" comprises all of those terms used within the New Testament by which the concept of "sin" might be signaled. According to the standard reference tool for engaging in this sort of study,[3] the following terms would be included:

☐ *hamartia* (ἁμαρτία)—"a state of sinfulness as an integral element of someone's nature"

☐ *hamartanō* (ἁμαρτάνω)—"to act contrary to the will and law of God"

☐ *hamartēma* (ἁμάρτημα)—"that which someone has done in violating the will and law of God"

☐ *ptaiō* (πταίω)—"to fail to keep the law (of God)"

☐ *proamartanō* (προαμαρτάνω)—"to sin previously or in the past"

☐ *hamartōlos* (ἁμαρτωλός)—"pertaining to sinful behavior" or "a person who customarily sins"

☐ *hyperbainō* (ὑπερβαίνω)—"to transgress the will and law of God by going beyond prescribed limits"

☐ *paraptōma* (παράπτωμα)—"what a person has done in transgressing the will and law of God by some false step or failure"

☐ *opheilō* (ὀφείλω)—"to commit a sin against someone and thus to incur moral debt"

☐ *opheilēma* (ὀφείλημα)—"the moral debt incurred as a result of sin"

☐ *opheiletēs* (ὀφειλέτης)—"one who commits sin and thus incurs a moral debt"

☐ *rhadiourgia* (ῥᾳδιουργία)—"to violate moral principles by acting in an unscrupulous manner"

☐ *agnoēma* (ἀγνόημα)—"sin which is committed as a result of ignorance"

---

[3]Johannes P. Louw and Eugene A. Nida, eds., *Greek-English Lexicon of the New Testament Based on Semantic Domains*, 2 vols. (New York: United Bible Societies, 1988). Louw and Nida are not foolproof, and readers discover from time to time (1) terms that have been overlooked in their domain lists and (2) ways in which theological presuppositions lead to conclusions about the nature and ingredients of particular semantic domains. This tool is nonetheless indispensable as a front-line instrument for beginning this sort of work and will be more than adequate for the point we hope to make.

☐ *deleazō* (δελεάζω)—"to lure or entice someone to sin"

☐ *skandalizō* (σκανδαλίζω)—"to cause to stumble" or "to cause to sin"

☐ *skandalizomai* (σκανδαλίζομαι)—"to fall into sin"

☐ *skandalon* (σκάνδαλον)—"that which or one who causes someone to sin"

☐ *proskomma* (πρόσκομμα)—"that which provides an opportunity or occasion for causing someone to sin"

☐ *peirazō* (πειράζω)—"to endeavor or attempt to cause someone to sin"

☐ *enochos* (ἔνοχος)—"guilty" or "liable"

☐ *ponēros* (πονηρός)—"guilty"

☐ *aition* (αἴτιον)—"guilt as a basis or reason for condemnation"

This list is helpful in terms of demonstrating something of the vocabulary related to "sin" in the New Testament and even points to how easy it would be to oversimplify reflection on the human condition in the New Testament.

Even though, as we mentioned, it is borrowed from the standard language tool for semantic domains in the Greek New Testament,[4] this catalog of terms is itself grossly oversimple. The descriptive term so important to the Gospel of Luke—*apolōlōs* (ἀπολωλώς), "something or someone that is lost"—is not included, for example. Nor do we find here any reference to hard-heartedness, so important to the Gospel of Mark. Other images, important to Paul, are also missing—for example, ungodliness, wickedness, unrighteousness, living according to the sinful nature, the reprobate mind, the darkened heart, lacking worship, enemies of God, dead in one's trespasses and sins, children of (the first) Adam, lacking the glory of God and overstepping. Also missing are those dispositions that are both the effects of sin and the fuel for further sin—including misdirected worship, self-indulgence and the many sinful acts in which people engage (cf. Rom 1:29-31; 1 Cor 5:10-11; 6:9-10; Gal 5:19-21).[5]

---

[4]Ibid., §§88.118, 289-318.

[5]Joseph A. Fitzmyer, *Paul and His Theology: A Brief Sketch*, 2d ed. (Englewood Cliffs, N.J.: Prentice Hall, 1989) §§81-88; James D. G. Dunn, *The Theology of Paul the Apostle* (Grand Rapids, Mich.: Eerdmans, 1998), chap. 3.

This data suggests, first, the many ways in which the human situation apart from Christ might be understood. "Sin" has many guises and can be developed along quite different lines. What might not be so clear but what must be underscored is that, as a whole, the New Testament often takes an approach to sin that differs dramatically from our own. Our tendency is often to focus on particular, sinful acts. New Testament writers, by contrast, tend to focus on particular, sinful acts *as manifestations of a deeper problem*. The letter of James, for example, is centrally concerned with the question of *friendship*—friendship with the world versus friendship with God. How do we know whether a person is a friend? We know through the person's actions whether he or she has befriended the world or is a friend of God. For Mark, on the other hand, responses of fear versus responses of faith are grounded in the condition of an individual's "heart": "Are your hearts still hardened?" (Mk 8:17; cf., e.g., 3:5).

The point then is that the human condition can be variously assessed. This is true not only because the theological vocabulary of sin is capable of diverse expression. It is also true because people at different times of social and psychological development manifest and experience sin in different ways. This is also true for people in different social environments, as we indicated from chapter five on.

Coming to Terms with Sin

If it is true that our understanding of the significance of the cross depends on how we evaluate the human problem, then it is crucial that our engagement with the social worlds in which we find ourselves include serious conversation regarding the human situation as this is experienced "here" and "now." If Jesus is the answer, what is the question?

Sin comes in many forms. In his exploration, theologian Ted Peters discusses seven of these.[6] The first is *anxiety*, the fear of loss, and especially

---

[6]Ted Peters, *Sin: Radical Evil in Soul and Society* (Grand Rapids, Mich.: Eerdmans, 1994). On what follows, see also David Atkinson, "What Difference Does the Cross Make to Life?" in *Atonement Today: A Symposium at St. John's College, Nottingham*, ed. John Goldingay (London: SPCK, 1995), pp. 253-71.

the fear of losing ourselves, ultimately in death. We experience anxiety as the "sting of death" in our lives and combat it with illusions of immortality. We want to deny death—that is, to deny that we have limitations, that our abilities and even our existence has boundaries. The temptation to "be like God" is rooted here, in our unwillingness simply to be human, to be creatures whose lives are finite and dependent on God.

The second is *unfaith*, the failure to trust. Failing to trust God, we refuse to live in his care and assume we must care for ourselves. Nor are we able to trust our neighbors, whose own existence is troublesome to us, not least when their lives interrupt our own or when their success or failures threaten us. We are the gods in control of our own lives, and we replicate in our lives the whims of the mythical gods of old who manipulate people and events to our own ends.

The third is *pride*, where our tendencies toward the divine come to the surface, when our "me," "my" and "mine" occupy center stage. This might be manifested in heightened self-control, in machismo, in prejudice, but also in refusing the social spotlight and in playing the role of the victim. Peters observes that characteristic of the proud is the capacity to ignore the suffering and needs of others—whether those others are simply outside of myself or even belong to another group or nation. National or ethnic or even religious pride are possible embodiments of this third stage.

The fourth is the *desire to possess*, and includes desire, lust, envy, greed and coveting. The desire to possess is also a group or national phenomenon as well as an individual one and is the pseudoanswer to the sinful need to shore up a person's own resources and to pretend that he or she is self-sufficient. Sin parades in the form of self-promotion, self-provision, self-determination and self-perpetuation.

Fifth, pride and the desire to possess lead to *self-justification*, which is nothing less than the desire to possess what only God possesses—namely, goodness. We turn to the mirror to define what is right and what is good. The benchmark is my life. Those who do not measure up must be cut down (say, in gossip) for there is nothing that makes us look so good as to point out the faults in others. Even God becomes susceptible to the out-workings of our self-justification: Having established the benchmark for what is good, we castigate God for not measuring up. Having established the correct definition of loving, we wonder why God can be so unloving. Having established the correct definition of justice, we assume God and his work must conform to this standard. Self-justification is self-delusion-ment, a lie about ourselves that we embrace and that gives us license to speak violent words and do violent acts against those who are not "us" and who therefore do not measure up.

Sixth, then, is genuine *cruelty*, where those who could not connect with those in pain (i.e., the prideful) actually inflict pain—whether physical or social or emotional or spiritual, whether on humans on to other creatures. Is this not the work of a god, wielding the power of life and death over others?

Finally, sin is *blasphemy*, the use of God and the things of God in self-justification. The Scriptures support our position and our actions, we say. God has commanded us to kill, we allege. Who are you to question a ser-vant of God? we ask. The word of the cross, which calls into question all pretensions to power and status, is replaced with our own words. Noth-ing, not the Scriptures, not the church, not the Holy Spirit, nothing can call us into question, just as nothing can give hope to those who suffer under our behavior, since we have drafted God to our own ends.

This catalog is helpful for its focus on human motivations, commit-ments, allegiances and dispositions, even if we might want to explore the relation of these images to others, such as sin as idolatry. It also has its limitations, since it construes sin primarily in terms of self-promotion or self-assertion. In recent decades a number of theologians have observed that sin can just as easily be manifest in marginalized persons and commu-nities as the opposite of what we normally associated with pride. Sin might take the form of a numbing of the self rather than as self-assertion, or as a failure to embrace one's personhood rather than as a predisposition to extend it at the expense of others. Manipulation of others and other coercive behavior, moreover, can be performed by those who seem to be powerless as well as those whose power is more visible and muscular. Seen in this way, "pride," for example, is more pervasive among humans than its popular identification with machismo or conceit might suggest. Although sin might be expressed as machismo, it also has its shadowy sides, as persons at all points of the continuum of power and privilege refuse to embrace either *only* or *fully* their places as members within the human family.

We see more clearly from this way of putting the matter that "acts of disobedience" are deeply rooted in the sick soil of our lives, in deep-seated convictions about the nature of our humanity that run counter to those of God. If "sin" can be articulated in these ways, what difference does the cross of Christ make? If the human family is mired in sin, what is the meaning of the atonement? Does the cross address our anxiety? Does the cross resolve our pride? Does the cross remedy our mistrust? What images of the atonement help us to see that the death of Jesus reaches so deeply into the human situation as to bring transformation, repentance, liberation and hope?

Of course, our task in this chapter, and in this book, is not to provide definitive answers to these pressing questions. Our perspective is that these questions must be addressed truly but can never be addressed fully and that a central task of Christian communities wherever they are gathered is to participate in a biblically and theologically informed cultural criticism that brings to the surface dominant images of the human situation and that learns to articulate the gospel as, indeed, good news in these contexts.

The Craft of Articulation

The question that presses against us then is how best to articulate the significance of the cross in the many worlds in which we seek faithfully to serve today. If the word of the cross to first-century Corinth can scarcely be heard if the same words were used today in downtown Memphis, what words are adequate?

The Problem of Articulation

As we suggested earlier, sociologist Robert Wuthnow provides us with a helpful orientation to the task before us. In his study of *Communities of Discourse,* he concerns himself with the relationship of discourse to its social environment. The problem is two edged. On the one hand, discourse must make itself relevant to its environment if it is to speak to it, and in order to make itself relevant to its environment, it must reflect that environment. On the other hand, if that discourse reflects that environment too closely, if it becomes too intimate with its environment, then it has nothing of significance to say to it. "The process of articulation," Wuthnow observes, "is thus characterized by a delicate balance between the products of culture and the social environment in which they are produced."[7]

One of the illustrations Wuthnow uses has to do with the early decades of the Protestant Reformation. How did people like John Calvin win the support of large segments of late medieval society at the same time that they undermined the very basis of that society? How might the Reformers draw on the financial resources of their patrons in sixteenth-century towns and villages without their succumbing to the acceptable norms and desires of those patrons? The same question confronts (or ought to confront!) every preacher every week: How can I communicate this message in terms that make sense in this world in which we live while at the same time calling this world into question?

The nature of the church is to be characterized by such a delicate balance. Sometimes our position is cast in terms that depend heavily on prepositions: *in,* not *of,* the world. Whatever language is employed, the issue is central to our identity and mission as God's people, but it is often not taken with the necessary seriousness. Standing within our own cultural horizons, we have difficulty seeing those places where our under-

---

[7]Robert Wuthnow, *Communities of Discourse: Ideology and Social Structure in the Reformation, the Enlightenment, and European Socialism* (Cambridge, Mass.: Harvard University Press, 1989), p. 3.

standing of the gospel has become too enculturated. Self-criticism, not least when it involves critical reflection on the shape of the gospel as we have learned it, does not come easy. Conversely, when departing our world and entering another, we may have difficulty understanding why people around us do not see and experience life as we do. Our attempts to frame the gospel are easily tied to *our* categories of life and thought—and thus not sufficiently rooted *in* this new "world."

With regard to atonement theology, the challenge before us is how to articulate the message of the cross in ways that are culturally relevant *and* that remain faithful to the biblical witness. The poles between which we move are sometimes friendly, sometimes quite hostile. That is, in some settings, the biblical witness speaks with some immediacy into the world of our contemporaries. Earlier we suggested that this was the case with Norman Kraus's attempt to work with the saving significance of the cross in a culture whose pivotal values were honor and shame. Because the world within which Kraus was seeking to articulate the atonement significantly overlapped on this set of values the ancient Mediterranean world in which the New Testament books were written, the word of the cross could be spoken clearly with relatively little conceptual translation. We saw this was the case too with the Luo people, for whom sacrifice was integral to the community's memory and experience. In both instances, the problem of communication might have centered elsewhere. Failing to see the points of significant contact between the pages of the New Testament and the categories of cultural values and experience around them, people like us might have (and indeed have) presumed that the gospel of the New Testament must be reconceived in American terms for distribution to other peoples. The truth, of course, is that those of us who have lived alongside people of the Pacific Rim, for example, have been brought closer to a near experience of the world Jesus and Paul addressed. This does not mean that Japanese or Luo culture might simply be embraced as biblical or baptized as though it were Christian. Indeed, we observed in chapter six that Kraus found in his reflection on the significance of the cross in the New Testament reason to challenge Japanese definitions and experiences of shame. People concerned with faithful witness in such contexts must develop their own sensitivities lest the word of the cross be made to serve categories more at home in Tokyo than in 1 Corinthians or the book of Revelation.

If this is true in the case of social environments in which solidarity with the world of Scripture is more self-evident, it is all the more true in cultures where the distance between "our world" and "theirs" is the rule. Of course, our own ethnocentrisms—that is, our propensities toward thinking that all people in all times and all places experience the world as we do—have the capacity to camouflage this distance. We easily make Jesus over into our own image. We easily export our categories of justice into Scripture. We easily define God's love in ways that make the most sense to us. If we have learned from Wuthnow's perspective, however, we would see the need to engage in a cultural criticism that (1) refuses to collapse the "new heaven and new earth" of God's purpose into the present, disallowing our ability to see where our present is challenged and judged by the kingdom of God, and (2) nevertheless struggles to represent God's purpose in terms that can be heard in the present.

The sad but often true reality is that the church is worst at engagement in this brand of cultural criticism when it is most at home in the world that has helped to create it. In many sectors of the Christian church today, especially outside of evangelical circles, for example, eschatology is a four-letter word. Institutions whose existence is predicated on their self-representations as full expressions of God's work in the world are unlikely to proclaim the coming of the end, with its promised catastrophic reordering of reality around the gracious throne of God. Those most happy with the status quo are not likely to express hope in the coming revolutionary work of God.

It may seem perverse to suggest that the same could be said about the church's message on the atonement. After all, does the church, especially the evangelical church, not affirm and proclaim the importance of justification by faith on account of the death of Christ? We wonder if this is not too comfortable a position. Given the diversity of witnesses to the saving significance of the cross in the New Testament, should we not look with caution, even dismay, when we see the atonement articulated in terms of one model only, and especially when that model coheres so fully with the emphasis on autonomous individualism characteristic of so much of the modern middle class in the West.[8] Given the witness of the New Testament—whether we are thinking of the correlation of the cross with the effect of the gospel on practices of care within the community of God's people (e.g., 1 Cor 11:17-34) or the implications of the cross for Jew-Gentile relations (e.g., Eph 2), or some other—should we not have questions about making as the centerpiece of the gospel those models of the atonement that have failed to address social relations within the church, that need not raise a finger against the blight and sin of racism, and that seem not at all concerned with the general rise of materialism within the church? Can it really be true that the salvation available to us by means of the cross of Christ could fail to address these crucial issues with judgment and transformation? Can the messianic community so pervasively fail to embody the concerns that led historically to the crucifixion of the Messiah?

Our point then is that, in the United States, we have tended too easily to assume that our models of the atonement are not the product of an integration of biblical and historic concepts with pervasive cultural symbols and values. What is more, we believe that our primary models of thinking about the atonement have articulated far too closely with dominant cultural values. A gospel that is focused on salvation for persons whose sin, or need for salvation, is understood solely or primarily in autobiographical terms can hardly be said to subvert the individualism and self-centeredness so characteristic of our social environment. A gospel

---

[8]On "autonomous individualism" as characteristic of the American middle class, see Robert N. Bellah et al., *Habits of the Heart: Individualism and Commitment in American Life* (San Francisco: Harper & Row, 1985).

that allows me to think of my relationship with God apart from the larger human family and the whole cosmos created by God—can it be said that this gospel is any gospel at all?

How best to articulate the saving significance of the cross? Our first answer is that we must take seriously the social environments in which we seek faithfully to live and communicate. Our first answer is that we would take seriously the delicate balance to be maintained between articulating with and over against that environment, so that our forms of communication would be shaped within but not wholly determined by that environment.

Learning a Craft

A dominant feature of the perspective on the atonement we have taken is that the tradition of atonement theology is and must be a living tradition. We believe that the saving significance of Jesus' death is central to Christian faith and life, and must never be relegated to a display case in a theological museum. Nor in our view may the atonement be regarded as a frozen tradition, as though our taking the tradition seriously requires that the patterns of atonement thought hammered out in the thirteenth or sixteenth or twentieth century simply be overlaid onto our witness in the twenty-first. Indeed, *that* we can even speak of models of atonement theology is already a key indicator of the reality that we are dealing with a living tradition that must continue to account for the historical and contextual nature of its particular embodiments in the history of the Christian mission.

A potentially helpful way of thinking of the task before us is suggested by Alasdair MacIntyre, who contrasts two ways of engaging in the sort of inquiry that concerns us.[9] The first is the way of "technique." "Technique"

---

[9]Alasdair MacIntyre, *Three Rival Versions of Moral Enquiry: Encyclopaedia, Genealogy, and Tradition,* 1988 Gifford Lectures (South Bend, Ind.: University of Notre Dame Press, 1990). The model that follows is simplified from MacIntyre's third chapter. We were directed to this approach to the issue by P. Mark Achtemeier, "Living Tradition," *Catalyst* 25, no. 4 (1999): 7.

refers to proceduralized activity that follows well-defined steps that can be routinized, learned and transported from one place to another. "Technique" is involved in cooking, at least at basic levels, where recipes might be followed: Step 1, Step 2, Step 3 . . . The rudiments of mathematics are similarly subject to this approach. Techniques are learned for multiplying fractions or doing long division. Adding and subtracting can be practiced, following the same routines, whether one lives in 350 B.C. or A.D. 2001, whether on the North Pole or in Lima, Peru.

The second is the "craft," which might involve procedures and steps, which might build on a history of performance, but which is ultimately defined by complexity and innovation that break out of those procedures and help to constitute its own rules. MacIntyre writes,

> The authority of a master within a craft is both more and other than a matter of exemplifying the best standards so far. It is also and most importantly a matter of knowing how to go further and especially how to direct others towards going further, using what can be learned from the tradition afforded by the past to move towards the *telos* [aim or end] of fully perfected work. It is thus knowing how to link past and future that those with authority are able to draw upon tradition, to interpret and reinterpret it, so that its directedness towards the *telos* of that particular craft becomes apparent in new and characteristically unexpected ways.[10]

Mastering a craft thus entails standing in a tradition and engagement with the present, but it is especially about developing particular intuitions, forming particular dispositions, becoming a particular kind of person whose commitments and predilections have been shaped in relation to activity in question. Practicing a craft and education into a craft are thus less about fixed procedures and more about apprenticeship to a master in relationship to a community defined by that craft.

What is the task of "doing theology"—a technique or a craft? To be

---

[10]MacIntyre, *Three Rival Versions*, pp. 65-66.

more specific, as we work toward an articulation of the saving significance of Jesus, are we engaged in a technique or in a craft? The truth, of course, is that different people define the task differently. Some do in fact see the task of communicating the atonement as essentially technique driven. Evangelism and discipleship are thus understood as a series of discrete steps, and the "plan of salvation," always and everywhere, has a well-defined set of particular emphases. Those who want to communicate the gospel must do so in such-and-such a way. Here is the tradition. Accept it. Memorize it. Repeat it.

The shape of discipleship in the Gospels subverts this understanding, and so does the theological content of the New Testament taken as a whole. Together these suggest that (1) following Jesus is focused on transformation of faith and life—becoming a new kind of person, and (2) faithfulness is a process or journey of working out the significance and implications of the gospel in the face of new challenges. Doing theology, then, is not a matter of repeating the tradition or committing to memory a ten-step manual. It has to do with formation as practitioners of the gospel.

To whom shall we apprentice ourselves? The most obvious and first answer must be the biblical writers themselves. But to answer in this way is immediately to raise the issue of how they must serve in this way. If our tendency has been to read the Scriptures only to learn their content, then we have yet to submit as apprentices to these masters. This is because it is not enough to know the words they use, the concepts they explicate; we also want to know why they used these words (and not those), how they worked in this social context and that social context to bring the ways of God to bear on the challenges faced in these instances. We want to learn how to be theologians like they were theologians. Why did Paul use justification language here but not there? Why did Peter draw so explicitly on the words of Isaiah but Hebrews did not? What had they learned, from the people to whom they wrote, from the advent of Christ and from the ancient story of God's involvement with his people, that shaped their messages in these different ways? Other masters are available too, though their "mastery" must always be measured in relation to those of Scripture—Origen, for example, and Irenaeus, Luther and Wesley, and other women and men in the Christian community, historically and globally, who have worked faithfully to enunciate the redemptive meaning of the death of Jesus for the lives of people around them.

Imagining the work of articulating a theology of the atonement in this way places a priority on hearing and observing and reflection. Some may feel overwhelmed by the task as we have portrayed it; is it not much easier to parrot the tradition as we have learned it? If it was good enough for us, should it not be good enough for them? For others, it will raise questions about theological faithfulness; how can we certify that conceiving the theological task as a craft will not lead to innovations that can no longer be called "Christian"?

The Church and the Atonement

If we think of communicating the good news by employing the model of journalism, then we can appreciate the need to address a particular audience mindful of what that audience can and will take for granted. Seen in this light, theological discourse must take seriously the social and cultural presuppositions that determine whether or not the message will gain a hearing. This is what it means for theology to take the mission of the church seriously.

How can we be sure that the results of our integrative and contextual work will be authentically Christian? We believe that this question cuts two ways at once. Most obviously, perhaps, the question is, If we do not use the language of the tradition we have learned, if we do not use images that have been handed to us by the tradition, are we not in fact departing the tradition? Are we not stepping outside the boundaries of what can genuinely be labeled as "Christian"? The concern here is one of control, and it is a legitimate one. On other hand, the fundamentally *historical* character of our faith demands that a theology that is authentically Christian be shaped in particular historical exigencies. The scandal of the incarnation is that the Word became flesh some two thousand years ago, as a male reared in Galilee, who spoke Aramaic, wore sandals and attracted a ragtag band of followers. Born in another time and place, the Word of God would have spoken another language, worn different attire, constructed the revelatory message in different ways. And if the Word of God is to come alive as good news in the world today, it must do so by drawing on the local environment, relating itself integrally to the patterns of life and values resident in particular contexts.

In the short term there are no guarantees that the end result will be authentically Christian. This is the hard reality of the task set before us. We cannot go to the bookstore or log on to the Web in order to purchase or otherwise access tried-and-true answers for the questions that confront us. The frontiers of Christian mission are just that, frontiers, and the theological manuals written for other times and places, while important and suggestive, can never be determinative on the frontier. Communities of believers everywhere are charged with the task of grappling with the biblical witness and the theological tradition, and with the thought forms and deeply held values of the people next door, so as to address their world with the good news—that is, with a message that is and can be heard and embraced as good news.

Although we cannot guarantee short-term fidelity, we can proceed with confidence concerning the longer term. Our confidence for the long haul is rooted in three points of orientation.

First, we see in Scripture and have come to believe that God and his ways cannot be understood fully nor in any way circumscribed by the models, images and words we have chosen. God is not limited to this or that way of speaking to people of his gracious and salvific act in the cross. The reservoir of significance has not run and will not run dry, with the consequence that we have the license (indeed, the mandate) to continue to return to Golgotha with the questions, What took place here and why?

Second, our commitment to the Scriptures of the Old and New Testaments as the Scriptures of the church provide us with room to maneuver as well as with a limit to our maneuvering. Though behind the various books of the Bible we believe there stands the one voice and purpose of God, as we hear these individual books, we also hear a diversity of voices. They do not speak with the same idiom. They do not communicate the purpose of God in lockstep fashion. They do not enunciate the good news in the same way. In fact, in many cases the words of Scripture stand in dynamic tension.

Those who are committed to this Bible find themselves on the same path, to be sure, but at a number of points and on many issues this path is especially wide, not only allowing for diversity of thought and life but actually embracing that diversity as integral to what it means to be Christian. As we have seen, this is certainly the case with regard to the atonement, and it would be unthinkable for Christians today or in any age to declare that those who do not hold to such-and-such a view of the atonement reside outside the boundaries of authentic Christian faith. The diversity of the canonical witness on the death of Jesus thus cuts both ways, for it engenders context-specific reflection on the saving significance of the death of Jesus at the same time that it insists that the death of Jesus has saving significance. The canon authorizes diversity at the same time that it sets perimeters around the diversity that might develop. Thus our ongoing commitment to the canonizing role of the Scriptures will, in time, push us to fresh ways of elucidating the word of the cross as well as pull us back when our attempts at mission-minded theology have pushed us beyond the frontiers of biblical theology.

Finally, we believe that the Holy Spirit works through the community of God's people in a way that is both creative and cautionary. Even a surface reading of the book of Acts will indicate the degree to which the Holy Spirit was active both to push the early Christian community beyond its structures and commitments so as to engage in a sometimes surprising and serendipitous work of God *and* to close the door to certain innovations in the mission. As a whole, the New Testament witnesses show one part of the Christian movement was capable of reminding another of its roots in the revelation of God and God's ways in Jesus Christ—either to spur further innovation or to urge more critical reflection on its concepts and practices.

The centuries-old debate on the nature of the atonement is undoubtedly a manifestation of this same activity, as the church in new times and locales places to the side or ignores, or embraces anew or develops further, an earlier portrayal of the saving significance of the cross of Christ.

At the opening of the third millennium, we find ourselves with unprecedented opportunities to learn from the Christian community in other parts of the globe, as well as the witness of the church in previous generations. Although the momentum of Enlightenment thinking caused many Christians to disregard the witness of Christians in earlier centuries, in the late-twentieth century we in the West began to develop a new appreciation for and new forms of access to early Christian writings. Similarly, the embarrassment and travesty of some nineteenth- and twentieth-century missionary movements, in which it was not always clear that the good news had as much to do with Jesus of Nazareth as with modernity and Western sensibilities, have suggested the need for greater contextual sensitivity. What is more, missionaries from other hemispheres have turned to the United States, which today comprises one of the Earth's largest mission fields.

As a result, not only do we have much to learn from the witness of the others, we live in a place where we can genuinely hear the voices of the historical and global people of God. If we have ears to ear, we can receive correction from other, local Christian communities when our theological reflection has been too anemic or too aggressive.

Conclusion

The reality we face is that we live in a fresh missionary moment, in which hand-wringing anxiety over theological homogeneity is not only impossible to justify biblically and historically but also practically detrimental to the church's identity and mission. We believe that the popular fascination with and commitment to penal substitutionary atonement has had ill effects in the life of the church in the United States and has little to offer the global church and mission by way of understanding or embodying the message of Jesus Christ. Whether or not others share our belief in this regard, we nonetheless hope that we have been successful in helping to broaden the discussion on the saving significance of Jesus' death. We hope that we have been able to show that missionaries and theologians within the New Testament were determined not to limit theological reflection on the atonement but to find context-specific ways of making the word of the cross accessible and challenging to varied audiences. And we hope that we have been able to indicate that the images of the atonement that have surfaced in the history of the church have often taken shape through similar commitments to articulating the significance of the cross in particular settings.

This encourages us to believe that no one model of the atonement will fit all sizes and shapes, all needs and contexts where the church is growing and active in mission. This means, ultimately, that the next chapter of this book is being written in hundreds of places throughout the world, where communities of Jesus' disciples are practicing the craft of theologian-communicator and struggling with fresh and faithful images for broadcasting the mystery of Jesus' salvific death.

Bibliography

Abelard, Peter. "Exposition of the Epistle to the Romans." In *Readings in the History of Christian Thought*, edited by Robert L. Ferm, pp. 239-43. New York: Holt, Rinehart & Winston, 1964.

Achtemeier, P. Mark. "Living Tradition." *Catalyst* 25, no. 4 (1999): 7.

Aulén, Gustaf. *Christus Victor: An Historical Study of the Three Main Types of the Idea of the Atonement*. London: SPCK, 1953.

Allison Dale C., Jr., *The End of the Ages Has Come: An Early Interpretation of the Passion and Resurrection of Jesus*. Philadelphia: Fortress, 1985.

Atkinson, David. "What Difference Does the Cross Make to Life?" In *Atonement Today: A Symposium at St. John's College, Nottingham*, edited by John Goldingay, pp. 253-71. London: SPCK, 1995.

Barrett, C. K. "*Theologia crucis*—in Acts?" In *Theologia Crucis–Signum Crucis: Festschrift für Erich Dinkler zum 70. Geburtstag*, edited by C. Anderson and G. Klein, pp. 73-84. Tübingen: J. C. B. Mohr (Paul Siebeck), 1979.

Barth, Karl. *Church Dogmatics*. Vol. 4.1. Edinburgh: T & T Clark, 1956.

Barth, Markus. *Das Mahl des Herrn: Gemeinschaft mit Israel, mit Christus und unter den Gasten*. Neukirchen-Vluyn: Neukirchener, 1987.

Batstone, David. *From Conquest to Struggle: Jesus of Nazareth in Latin America*. Albany: State University of New York, 1991.

Behm, Johannes. "θύω κτλ." In *TDNT*, 3:180-90.

Bellah, Robert N., et al. *Habits of the Heart: Individualism and Commitment in American Life*. San Francisco: Harper & Row, 1985.

Bergman, Jan, and Elsie Johnson. "אָנַף." In *TDOT*, 1:348-60.

Bliss, Philip P. "I Will Sing of My Redeemer." n.d.

Boff, Leonardo. *Passion of Christ, Passion of the World: The Facts, Their Interpretation, and Their Meaning Yesterday and Today*. Maryknoll, N.Y.: Orbis, 1987.

Brock, Rita Nakashima. "And a Little Child Will Lead Us: Christology and Child Abuse." In *Christianity, Patriarchy, and Abuse: A Feminist Critique*, edited by Joanne Carlson Brown and Carole R. Bohn, pp. 42-61. New York: Pilgrim, 1989.

———. *Journeys by Heart: A Christology of Erotic Power*. New York: Crossroad, 1988.

Brown, Joanne Carlson, and Rebecca Parker. "For God So Loved the World?" In *Christianity, Patriarchy, and Abuse: A Feminist Critique,* edited by Joanne Carlson Brown and Carole R. Bohn, pp. 1-30. New York: Pilgrim, 1989.

Burkert, Walter. *Greek Religion.* Cambridge, Mass.: Harvard University Press, 1985.

Carey, George L. "The Lamb of God and Atonement Theories." *TynB* 32 (1981): 97-122.

Carroll, John T., and Joel B. Green. *The Death of Jesus in Early Christianity.* Peabody, Mass.: Hendrickson, 1995.

Chang, Curtis. Unpublished manuscript for the "Last Days of Jesus" conference. Fall 1998.

Chilton, Bruce D. *A Feast of Meanings: Eucharistic Theologies from Jesus Through Johannine Circles.* NovTSup 72. Leiden: E. J. Brill, 1994.

Clark, David. "Why Did Christ Have to Die?" *New England Reformed Journal* 1 (1996): 35-36.

Collins, Robin. "Understanding Atonement: A New and Orthodox Theory." Unpublished manuscript.

Cousar, Charles B. *A Theology of the Cross: The Death of Jesus in the Pauline Letters.* OBT. Minneapolis: Fortress, 1990.

Crossan, John Dominic. *The Cross That Spoke: The Origins of the Passion Narrative.* San Francisco: Harper & Row, 1988.

Cunningham, Scott. *'Through Many Tribulations': The Theology of Persecution in Luke-Acts.* JSNTSup 142. Sheffield: Sheffield Academic Press, 1997.

Dillistone, F. W. *The Christian Understanding of Atonement.* Philadelphia: Westminster, 1968.

Driver, John. *Understanding the Atonement for the Mission of the Church.* Scottdale, Penn.: Herald, 1986.

Dunn, James D. G. "Paul's Understanding of the Death of Jesus as Sacrifice." In *Sacrifice and Redemption: Durham Essays in Theology,* edited by S. W. Sykes, pp. 35-56. Cambridge: Cambridge University Press, 1991.

————. *The Theology of Paul the Apostle.* Grand Rapids, Mich.: Eerdmans, 1998.

————. *Romans.* Vol. 1. WBC 38a. Dallas: Word, 1988.

Eco, Umberto. *Semiotics and the Philosophy of Language.* AS. Bloomington: Indiana University Press, 1984.

Fiddes, Paul S. *Past Event and Present Salvation: The Christian Idea of Atonement.* Louisville: Westminster John Knox, 1989.

Fitzmyer, Joseph A. "Crucifixion in Ancient Palestine, Qumran Literature, and the New Testament." In *To Advance the Gospel,* pp. 125-46. New York: Crossroad, 1981.

————. *Paul and His Theology: A Brief Sketch,* 2d ed. Englewood Cliffs, N. J.: Prentice Hall, 1989.

————. "Reconciliation in Pauline Theology." In *No Famine in the Land: Studies in Honor of John L. McKenzie,* edited by James W. Flanagan and Anita Weisbrod Robinson, pp. 155-77. Missoula, Mont.: Scholars, 1975.

Furnish, Victor Paul. "The Ministry of Reconciliation." *CurTM* 14 (1977): 204-18.

Green, Joel B. *The Acts of the Apostles.* NICNT. Grand Rapids, Mich.: Eerdmans, forthcoming.

————. "Death of Christ." In *DPL*, pp. 201-9.

————. "Death of Jesus." In *DJG*, pp. 146-63.

————. "The Death of Jesus and the Ways of God: Jesus and the Gospels on Messianic Status and Shameful Suffering." *Int* 52 (1998): 24-37.

————. *The Death of Jesus: Tradition and Interpretation in the Passion Narrative.* WUNT 2:33. Tübingen: J. C. B. Mohr (Paul Siebeck), 1988.

————. "The Demise of the Temple as Culture Center in Luke-Acts: An Exploration of the Rending of the Temple Veil (Luke 23.44-49)." *RB* 101 (1994): 495-515.

————. "Good News to Whom? Jesus and the 'Poor' in the Gospel of Luke." In *Jesus of Nazareth: Lord and Christ. Essays on the Historical Jesus and New Testament Christology,* edited by Joel B. Green and Max Turner, pp. 59-74. Grand Rapids, Mich.: Eerdmans, 1994.

————. *The Gospel of Luke.* NICNT. Grand Rapids, Mich.: Eerdmans, 1997.

————. "The *Gospel of Peter*: Source for a Pre-Canonical Passion Narrative?" *ZNW* 78 (1987): 293-301.

————. "'Salvation to the End of the Earth': God as the Saviour in the Acts of the Apostles." In *Witness to the Gospel: The Theology of Acts,* edited by I. Howard Marshall and David Peterson, pp. 83-106. Grand Rapids, Mich.: Eerdmans, 1998.

Gregory of Nyssa. "The Great Catechism." In *Readings in the History of Christian Thought,* edited by Robert L. Ferm, pp. 197-204. New York: Holt, Rinehart & Winston, 1964.

Grigsby, Bruce H. "The Cross as an Expiatory Sacrifice in the Fourth Gospel." *JSNT* 15 (1982): 51-80.

Gundry-Volf, Judith M. "Expiation, Propitiation, Mercy Seat." In *DPL*, pp. 279-84.

Gunton, Colin. *The Actuality of the Atonement: A Study of Metaphor, Rationality and the Christian Tradition.* Edinburgh: T & T Clark; Grand Rapids, Mich.: Eerdmans, 1989.

Guthrie, Shirley. *Christian Doctrine.* Rev. ed. Louisville: Westminster John Knox: 1994.

Harrison, Beverly W., and Carter Heyward. "Pain and Pleasure: Avoiding the Confusions of Christian Tradition in Feminist Theory." In *Christianity, Patriarchy, and Abuse: A Feminist Critique,* edited by Joanne Carlson Brown and Carole R. Bohn, pp. 148-73. New York: Pilgrim, 1989.

Hays, Richard B. "Justification." In *ABD*, 3:1129-33.

Hengel, Martin. *The Atonement: The Origins of the Doctrine in the New Testament.* Philadelphia: Fortress, 1981.

————. *Crucifixion in the Ancient World and the Folly of the Message of the Cross.* Philadelphia: Fortress, 1977.

Heron, Gary A. "Wrath of God (OT)." In *ABD*, 6:989-96.

Hess, Carol Lakey. *Caretakers of Our Common House.* Nashville: Abingdon, 1997.

Hodge, Charles. *Systematic Theology.* Vol. 2. Grand Rapids, Mich.: Eerdmans, 1981.

Hooker, Morna D. "Interchange and Atonement." *BJRL* 60 (1978): 462-81.

————. "Interchange in Christ." *JTS* 22 (1974): 349-61.

————. *Not Ashamed of the Gospel: New Testament Interpretations of the Death of Christ.* Grand Rapids, Mich.: Eerdmans, 1994.

Houts, Margaret G. "Classical Atonement Imagery: Feminist and Evangelical Challenges." *Catalyst* 19, no. 3 (1993): 1, 5-6.

Irenaeus. *Against Heresies.*

————. *Proof of the Apostolic Preaching.*

Kähler, Martin. *The So-Called Historical Jesus and the Historic, Biblical Christ.* Philadelphia: Fortress, 1964.

Koontz, Gayle Gerber. "The Liberation of Atonement." *The Mennonite Quarterly Review* 63 (1989): 171-92.

Korn, Manfred. *Die Geschichte Jesu in veränderter Zeit: Studien zur bleibenden Bedeutung Jesu im lukanischen Doppelwerk.* WUNT 2:51. Tübingen: J. C. B. Mohr (Paul Siebeck), 1993.

Kraus, C. Norman. "From Biblical Intentions to Theological Conceptions: Reply to T. Finger." *Conrad Grebel Review* 8 (1990): 205-15.

————. *Jesus Christ Our Lord: Christology from a Disciples' Perspective.* Scottdale, Penn.: Herald, 1990.

Lakoff, George, and Mark Johnson. *Metaphors We Live By.* Chicago: University of Chicago Press, 1980.

Léon-Dufour, Xavier. *Sharing the Eucharistic Bread: The Witness of the New Testament.* New York: Paulist, 1987.

Levenson, Jon D. *The Death and Resurrection of the Beloved Son: The Transformation of Child Sacrifice in Judaism and Christianity.* New Haven, Conn.: Yale University Press, 1993.

Longenecker, Richard N. "The Foundational Conviction of New Testament Christology: The Obedience/Faithfulness/Sonship of Christ." In *Jesus of Nazareth: Lord and Christ: Essays on the Historical Jesus and New Testament Christology,* edited by Joel B. Green and Max Turner, pp. 473-88. Grand Rapids, Mich.: Eerdmans, 1994.

Louw, Johannes P., and Eugene A. Nida, eds. *Greek-English Lexicon of the New Testament Based on Semantic Domains.* 2 vols. New York: United Bible Societies, 1988.

McDonald, H. D. *The Atonement of the Death of Christ: In Faith, Revelation, and History.* Grand Rapids, Mich.: Baker, 1985.

McGrath, Alister E. *The Genesis of Doctrine: A Study in the Formation of Doctrinal Criticism.* Grand Rapids, Mich.: Eerdmans/Vancouver, B.C.: Regent College, 1990.

————. *Iustia Dei: A History of the Christian Doctrine of Justification.* 2 vols. Cambridge: Cambridge University Press, 1986.

MacIntyre, Alisdair. *Three Rival Versions of Moral Enquiry: Encyclopaedia, Geneaology, and Tradition.* 1988 Gifford Lectures. South Bend, Ind.: University of Notre Dame Press, 1990.

Marshall, I. Howard. "The Development of the Concept of Redemption in the New Testament." In *Jesus the Saviour: Studies in New Testament Theology,* pp. 239-57. London: SPCK; Downers Grove, Ill.: InterVarsity Press, 1990.

————. "Lamb of God." In *DJG,* pp. 432-34.

————. *Last Supper and Lord's Supper.* Grand Rapids, Mich.: Eerdmans, 1980.

————. "The Meaning of 'Reconciliation'." In *Jesus the Saviour: Studies in New Testament Theology,* pp. 258-74. London: SPCK; Downers Grove, Ill.: InterVarsity Press, 1990.

Martin, Ralph P. *Reconciliation: A Study of Paul's Theology.* Rev. ed. Grand Rapids, Mich.: Zondervan, 1990.

Meier, John P. *A Marginal Jew: Rethinking the Historical Jesus.* Vol. 1: *The Roots of the Problem and the Person.* ABRL. New York: Doubleday, 1991.

Mertens, Herman-Emiel. *Not the Cross, but the Crucified: An Essay in Soteriology.* LTPM 11. Louvain: Peeters; Grand Rapids, Mich.: Eerdmans, 1992.

Meyer, Ben F. *The Aims of Jesus.* London: SCM, 1979.

Morris, Leon. *The Apostolic Preaching of the Cross.* 3d ed. Leicester, U.K.: Inter-Varsity Press, 1965.

————. *The Atonement: Its Meaning and Significance.* Leicester, U.K.: Inter-Varsity Press; Downers Grove, Ill.: InterVarsity Press, 1983.

————. *The Cross in the New Testament.* Grand Rapids, Mich.: Eerdmans, 1965.

Nickelsburg Jr., George W. E. *Resurrection, Immortality, and Eternal Life in Intertestamental Judaism.* HTS 26. Cambridge, Mass.: Harvard University Press, 1972.

Oden, Thomas C. *Systematic Theology.* Vol. 2: *The Word of Life.* San Francisco: Harper & Row, 1989.

Page, Sydney T. "The Authenticity of the Ransom Logion (Mark 10:45b)." In *Studies of History and Tradition in the Four Gospels,* edited by R.T. France and David Wenham, pp. 137-61. GP 1. Sheffield: JSOT, 1980.

Peters, Ted. *Sin: Radical Evil in Soul and Society.* Grand Rapids, Mich.: Eerdmans, 1994.

Pinnock, Clark H. *Tracking the Maze: Finding Our Way through Modern Theology from an Evangelical Perspective.* San Francisco: Harper, 1990.

Pobee, John S. *Persecution and Martyrdom in the Theology of Paul.* JSNTSup 6. Sheffield: JSOT, 1985.

Ray, Darby Kathleen. *Deceiving the Devil: Atonement, Abuse, and Ransom.* Cleveland: Pilgrim, 1998.

Roloff, Jürgen. "ἱλαστήριον." In *EDNT,* 2:185-86.

Saiving Goldstein, Valerie. "The Human Situation: A Feminine View." *JR* 40 (1960): 100-12.

Schnackenburg, Rudolf. *The Gospel According to St. John.* Vol. 1. New York: Crossroad, 1990.

Schweizer, Eduard. *Luke: A Challenge to Present Theology.* London: SPCK, 1982.

Shenk, Joseph C., ed. *Kisare: A Mennonite of Kiseru.* Salunga, Penn.: Eastern Mennonite Missions, 1984.

Sölle, Dorothee. *Thinking about God: An Introduction to Theology.* London: SCM, 1990.

Spicq, Ceslas. *Theological Lexicon of the New Testament.* 3 vols. Peabody, Mass.: Hendrickson, 1994.

Strauss, Mark L. *The Davidic Messiah in Luke-Acts: The Promise and Its Fulfillment in Lukan Christology.* JSNTSup 110. Sheffield: Sheffield Academic Press, 1995.

Stott, John R. W. *The Cross of Christ.* Downers Grove, Ill.: InterVarsity Press, 1986.

Stuhlmacher, Peter. "Vicariously Giving His Life for Many, Mark 10:45 (Matt 20:28)." In *Reconciliation, Law, and Righteousness: Essays in Biblical Theology,* pp. 116-29. Philadelphia: Fortress, 1986.

Swinburne, Richard. *Responsibility and Atonement.* Oxford: Clarendon, 1989.

Sykes, S. W. "Outline of a Theology of Sacrifice." In *Sacrifice and Redemption: Durham Essays in Theology,* edited by S. W. Sykes, pp. 282-98. Cambridge: Cambridge University Press, 1991.

———. "Sacrifice in the New Testament and Christian Theology." In *Sacrifice,* edited by M. F. C. Bourdillon and Meyer Fortes, pp. 61-83. London: Academic, 1980.

Thompson, Deanna. "Theological Proximity to the Cross: A Conversation Between Martin Luther and Feminist Theologians." Ph.D. diss., Vanderbilt University, 1998.

Travis, Stephen H. *Christ and the Judgment of God.* Basingstoke, U. K.: Marshall, Morgan and Scott, 1986.

———. "Christ as Bearer of Divine Judgment in Paul's Thought about the Atonement." In *Jesus of Nazareth: Lord and Christ. Essays on the Historical Jesus and New Testament Christology,* edited by Joel B. Green and Max Turner, pp. 332-45. Grand Rapids, Mich.: Eerdmans, 1994.

———. "The Doctrine of the Atonement: Popular Evangelicalism and the Bible." *Catalyst* 22, no. 1 (1995): 1-3.

———. "Wrath of God (NT)." In *ABD,* 6:996-98.

Tuckett, C.M. "Atonement in the NT." In *ABD,* 1:518-22.

Turner, Max. "Atonement and the Death of Jesus in John: Some Questions to Bultmann and Forestell." *EvQ* 62 (1990): 99-122.

———. *Power from on High: The Spirit in Israel's Restoration and Witness in Luke-Acts.* JPSSup 9. Sheffield: Sheffield Academic Press, 1996.

Van Dyk, Leanne. "The Three Offices of Christ: The *Munus Triplex* as Expansive Resources in Atonement." *Catalyst* 25, no. 2 (1999): 6-8.

Watson, David Lowes. "The Church as Journalist." *International Review of Mission* 72 (1983): 57-74.

Wilcox, Max. "'Upon the Tree: Deuteronomy 21:22-23 in the New Testament." *JBL* 96 (1977): 85-99.

Weaver, J. Denny. *Keeping Salvation Ethical: Mennonite and Amish Atonement Theology in the Late Nineteenth Century.* Scottdale, Penn.: Herald, 1997.

Williams, Rowan. *A Ray of Darkness.* Boston: Cowley, 1995.

Wright, N. T. *Christian Origins and the Question of God.* Vol. 2: *Jesus and the Victory of God.* Minneapolis: Fortress, 1996.

———. *The Climax of the Covenant: Christ and the Law in Pauline Theology.* Minneapolis: Fortress, 1991.

Wuthnow, Robert. *Communities of Discourse: Ideology and Social Structure in the Reformation, the Enlightenment, and European Socialism.* Cambridge, Mass.: Harvard University Press, 1989.

Author & Subject Index

Scripture Index